002

D1061781

DISCAR~~DED~~

Nashville
Public Library
Foundation

*This book
made possible
through generous gifts
to the
Nashville Public Library
Foundation Book Fund*

Property of
Nashville Public Library
615 Church St., Nashville, Tn. 37219

GENERAL
WILLIAM DORSEY PENDER

GENERAL
WILLIAM DORSEY PENDER

A Military Biography

Edward G. Longacre

COMBINED PUBLISHING

Pennsylvania

Published by Combined Publishing
For information, address:
Combined Publishing
P.O. Box 307
Conshohocken, PA 19428
E-mail: combined@combinedpublishing.com
Web: www.combinedpublishing.com
Orders: 1-800-418-6065

Copyright© 2001 Edward G. Longacre

Maps by Paul Dangel.

First edition, first printing

All rights reserved. No part of this publication may be reproduced, stored in a retrieval system or transmitted in any form or by any means, electrical, mechanical or otherwise without first seeking the written permission of the publisher.

Library of Congress Cataloging-in-Publication Data

Longacre, Edward G., 1946–
    General William Dorsey Pender: a military biography / Edward G. Longacre.
        p. cm.
    Includes bibliographical references (p.) and index.
    ISBN 1-58097-034-6
    1. Pender, William Dorsey, 1834–1863. 2. Generals—Confederate States of America—Biography. 3. Confederate States of America. Army—Biography. 4. United States—History—Civil War, 1861–1865—Campaigns. I. Title.
    E467.1.P367 L66 2001
    973.7'3—dc21   2001032329

Printed in the United States of America.

To my best friend
MELODY ANN LONGACRE
who also happens to be my wife

CONTENTS

Photos on pages 97 to 104, and 208

Maps

ACKNOWLEDGMENTS

I am indebted to many individuals and institutions, without whose help this book could not have been written. Mrs. Elizabeth "Boo" Pender of Virginia Beach, Virginia, widow of General Pender's grandson, William, provided family information on, and photographs of, the general. My long-time research assistant, Bryce Suderow of Washington, D. C., helped me plumb the depths of the National Archives. Suzanne Christoff, Alicia Mauldin, and Judith A. Sibley of the United States Military Academy Archives went beyond the call of duty to provide information on General Pender's academic and delinquency records at West Point.

Others who provided assistance and support include: Betty A. Ancona, Special Collections, Alderman Library, University of Virginia, Charlottesville; Steven Case, State Library of North Carolina, Raleigh; Dr. John Coski, Eleanor S. Brockenbrough Library, Museum of the Confederacy, Richmond, Va.; Captain Leland Heath, USAFR, Washington, N. C.; Janie C. Morris, Special Collections Library, Duke University, Durham, N. C.; Will Nathanson, Historical Society of Pennsylvania, Philadelphia; Bev Powers of the Ralph Brown Draughton Library, Auburn University, Auburn, Ala.; Andy Phrydas, Georgia Department of Archives and History, Atlanta; Linda H. Selby, Portsmouth, Va.; Bob and Lois Smith, Tarboro, N. C.; and the reference staffs of the North Carolina State Department of Archives and History, Raleigh, and the Southern Historical Collection, Wilson Library, University of North Carolina, Chapel Hill.

My publisher, Bob Pigeon; my editor, Ken Gallagher; and my cartographer, Paul Dangel, treated me with patience and understanding throughout the project. So did my wife, Ann, who has both commodities in abundance.

PREFACE

Historians offer many explanations for the combat success of the Army of Northern Virginia, including the army's abundance of young, savvy, and aggressive mid-level commanders. Perhaps the most talented member of this group was Major General William Dorsey Pender of North Carolina. From mid-1862 to mid-1863 Pender commanded a brigade of Tarheels in Lieutenant General Ambrose P. Hill's division, and for five weeks before his mortal wounding on the second day at Gettysburg he led the "Light Division" itself, one of the most celebrated commands in the Army of Northern Virginia. In both positions, Pender revealed himself to be courageous and tactically astute. Despite a reserved and sometimes stern demeanor and a fondness for strict discipline, he gained the confidence of superiors and subordinates alike, and the esteem of most.

One of his greatest admirers was the man at the top. By late 1862, Robert E. Lee had come to regard the North Carolinian as one of his most essential lieutenants. On one occasion, hearing that another subordinate had been disabled in battle, Lee lamented that "I am gradually losing my best men," among whom he listed Pender as well as the legendary Stonewall Jackson. According to at least one source, Lee believed that only Pender could have successfully filled the shoes of "Old Blue Light" following Jackson's death after Chancellorsville, an appointment that only Pender's lack of seniority prevented Lee from making. Perhaps an even greater indication of Lee's regard for his young subordinate was a comment attributed to him in postwar life: "I ought not to have fought the battle of Gettysburg. It was a mistake. But the stakes were so great, I was compelled to... and we should have succeeded had Pender lived."

This was heady praise for any Confederate field commander, and especially for one so young. When he died two weeks after his wounding at Gettysburg, Pender was still shy of his 30th birthday. His youth had played a role in his slow rise to divisional command, a position he attained only after conspicuous performances at Seven Pines, Gaines's Mill, Cedar Mountain, Second Manassas, Harpers Ferry, Fredericksburg, and Chancellorsville. On four of those fields Pender had exposed himself so readily to enemy fire that he received a wound—a fact not lost on his commander, who appreciated subordinates who could be found in the thick of battle.

Perhaps, then, it is not surprising that the loss of Pender coincided with the slow, painful decline the Army of Northern Virginia experienced in the aftermath of that bloody summer of 1863. Pender may not have been a perfect human being—he was, after all, a martinet; he could be curt to officers and men; at times he appeared egotistical and vain; and he was slow to appreciate the healing comforts of religion. But on the battlefield, where such limitations counted little, he was without peer. As Robert E. Lee came to understand, men of Pender's caliber were simply irreplaceable.

Chapter One

SOLDIER MATERIAL

T HE WAGONS HAD BEGUN TO ASSEMBLE before dawn, but not till 4:00 P.M. did the several-mile-long column of ambulances and supply vehicles begin to head south from Gettysburg. The task of forming and manning the train that would convey the Army of Northern Virginia's wounded, baggage, and spoils back to Virginia had been arduous enough without interference from the weather. Then a cloudburst struck and the situation deteriorated rapidly. "The rain fell in blinding sheets," recalled Brigadier General John Imboden, whom the army's commander, Robert E. Lee, had appointed to guide the train to and across the Potomac River. Not only did dusty roads quickly become seas of mud, "the meadows were soon overflowed, and fences gave way before the raging streams.... Canvas was no protection against its fury, and the wounded men lying upon the naked boards of the wagon-bodies were drenched. Horses and mules were blinded and maddened by the wind and water, and became almost unmanageable...."

Those confined to the ambulances suffered the most. Men suffering from gunshot wounds, broken bones, and severed limbs screamed in agony with every jounce of the springless wagons, which swerved precariously across the flooded roads. Riding the length of the column, Imboden was assailed by a cacophony of moans and shrieks. In a pain-filled voice one man beseeched the teamsters to stop "just for one minute; take me out and leave me to die on the roadside!" Others begged able-bodied comrades to put them out of their agony with a pistol shot.[1]

Not every occupant gave way to anguished cries, as some slept under the merciful spell of opiates and others fought off the pain and endured the journey in silence. Some suffered less from their wounds than from the realization that their army was retreating from the state it had invaded three weeks before in the hope of winning a climactic victory on enemy soil. Two days of battle had seen the Confederates on the verge of decisive success time and again, only to suffer a frustrating repulse on the third afternoon. The reverse, and the obvious fact that his army had been fought out, had convinced Lee that he must withdraw to his base of operations and supply in Virginia. There Lee had racked up a year's worth of victories against the Army of the Potomac; there he might regain his winning hand.

One of those more concerned with the recent defeat than with his injuries was William Dorsey Pender of Edgecombe County, North Carolina. At 29 the youngest major general in Lee's army, Pender owed his promotion to inspired leadership and dramatic performances on several fields—performances that had given him a reputation as one of Lee's most valuable subordinates. Thus, the wound that had prevented him from seeing the fighting at Gettysburg to its conclusion—unhappy though that conclusion had been—frustrated and depressed him as much as it filled him with pain. Surgeons had bandaged the two-inch-square gash that a piece of Yankee shell had cut in his left thigh, and already it appeared to be healing. Quoting Pender's surgeons, a Richmond newspaperman reported that the general had been wounded "severely, but not dangerously."[2]

Here was further confirmation that the young North Carolinian led a charmed life. His July 2 wound was the fifth he had received during fourteen months of combat. None of the earlier injuries had kept him out of action for more than a few hours, and although this one was more serious, once again it appeared he had been spared to fight another day. A brief stay in a hospital near the railhead at Staunton, Virginia, followed by a more leisurely recuperation at home—where his loving wife, Fanny, would minister to him, with their two young sons looking on—and Pender would be back in action, helping Lee make amends for his unfortunate sojourn in the North.

But first he had to survive the trip home. Although Pender "suffered intensely" throughout the journey, he strove to raise the spirits of his ranking subordinate, Brigadier General Alfred Moore Scales, who had been disabled by a leg wound during the first day at Gettysburg, and with whom he shared an ambulance. After the two reached Staunton, they planned to travel home together.[3]

But on July 10, two days after they arrived in Staunton, trouble began. Before he could be hospitalized, Pender's wound began hemorrhaging. He escaped death by fashioning a tourniquet from a towel twisted around the leg with a hairbrush. When surgeons finally treated him, they repaired the torn artery, but with some difficulty, and Pender quickly decided that his condition was grave. A medical attendant confirmed the diagnosis—the wound had become severely infected and another hemorrhage was likely.

The attendant asked if his patient—who had become a practicing Christian two years before, largely through his wife's influence—would like to speak to a chaplain. Pender confirmed that he would, but before a minister was summoned, he asked the attendant to write Fanny, explaining his situation: "Tell my wife that I do not fear to die. I can confidently resign my soul to God, trusting in the atonement of Jesus Christ. My only regret is to leave her and our two children." He also wished her to know that "I have always tried ... to do my duty in every sphere in which providence has placed me."[4]

If his words sounded like an epitaph, they were. Pender lay on his sweat-stained cot, growing weaker and more feverish as the infection spread. Confined to his bed, increasingly unable or unwilling to move about, he had little to do but think and remember. Ever given to introspection, he would have allowed his mind to wander through the past, conjuring up memories happy and sad, reliving hopes and strivings, recalling the many achievements he had gained in his brief life and the few setbacks he had experienced. An overall evaluation would not have been difficult to arrive at. A little over a year before, he had rendered a verdict on the life and career of Major General William Dorsey Pender, C. S. A.: "What a fortunate fellow I have been anyhow. I have never had a wish unfulfilled. My heart, as a boy, was determined on going to West Point. At my own request, I was transferred to the [First United States] Dragoons [in 1855]. I married the woman I loved best. My promotion in the Confederate Army has been as rapid as any reasonable man could expect. And even those little fellows … [three-year-old Samuel Turner Pender and one-year-old William Dorsey Pender Jr.] are all I could wish.…"[5]

Even on his deathbed, he would have found no reason to alter this pronouncement.

*   *   *

William Dorsey Pender had been born in the tobacco and cotton country of eastern North Carolina, on Town Creek, a few miles south of the Edgecombe County Seat of Tarboro, on February 6, 1834. His parents were hardworking farmers, solid members of the middle class, and staunch Democrats in opposition to the Whiggish politics that ruled the Old North State in this seventh decade of American independence. The work ethic that Pender's father, James, had inherited from his English forebears (the first Pender to come to the New World had settled near Norfolk, Virginia, in the latter part of the seventeenth century) had enabled the family to acquire a 400-acre estate which it worked with the assistance of several slaves. From early youth Dorsey Pender, as he was known to his parents and siblings, shouldered his share of farm work alongside his older brothers, Robert and David. While the boys worked outdoors, their sister Patience, six years Dorsey's senior, labored in the kitchen and the knitting-room under the tutelage of their mother, Sarah, a native of the Virginia tidewater.[6]

In later life Dorsey Pender described his parents in somewhat contradictory terms. He often referred to his "good and affectionate mother" and described his father as an indulgent parent. At other times, however, he spoke of his father's tendency to be cross and disagreeable and characterized both parents as immature and flighty. He also considered them great sinners, "particularly my father who I fear is not much better than an infidel for he has never taken any interest in these matters [of religion], never had any charity for God's ministers and has lived a wicked life." In one wartime letter, he suggested that his boyhood was not all it should have been. "I know it is lonely at my house," he informed his wife, "so much so that I never have been able to stay there long.…"[7]

Pender may have had a similar relationship with his siblings. He got along well enough with his brothers and sister and took an active interest in their welfare. In later life he worried about their physical and financial health, and once he attained high rank he worked hard to help Robert and David (also

Fanny's brothers) attain desirable positions in the army. Still, his few comments about his siblings suggest a coolness, rather than a closeness, toward them; certainly they convey little in the way of familial warmth.[8]

Perhaps the fault—if there was one—lay with the youngest son himself. A good judge of his own strengths and weaknesses, from his early years Dorsey Pender realized that he gave an impression of aloofness, of reticence, in his relationships with others. This trait was the product of a native reserve, but more than a few acquaintances would ascribe it to what he himself called "my cold and unfeeling nature." In later life, he was apt to give this same impression even to his wife, the only person to whom he could truly open his heart. He sometimes feared he was not lavish enough in his expressions of love and devotion toward her. On one occasion when he waxed unusually romantic, he informed Fanny that "you will be astonished at this outpouring of sentiment." He added, pointedly, "I am not always devoid of it [even] when I fail to express it."[9]

However he felt toward them, Pender's parents took an early interest in his education. Along with his siblings, he was tutored first at home and then in the common schools of Edgecombe County, which benefited from the institutional patronage of the state's Whig Party, then in the last years of its power. His education was strictly secular; the family's lack of religious interest ensured that Pender did not attend church services or gain an early acquaintance with the Scriptures. In later years a biographer recalled that, when not in school, young Pender spent much time "in the labors of the farm and the usual sports of country life, riding, hunting, fishing.…"[10]

Like many young Southerners, while still in his teens Pender became an accomplished horseman and developed a working knowledge of firearms. Early on, he also became imbued with the martial spirit, perhaps a product of his family's military heritage. Penders had fought in the Revolution and the War of 1812, and had helped suppress Indian uprisings. His military interest may have been strengthened by America's war with Mexico, which for two years beginning in 1846 was a major topic of news and conversation in his community. Edgecombe County sent into the army several companies of volunteers. As he watched the enthusiastic recruits depart for foreign shores, Dorsey Pender probably had wished he were accompanying them.[11]

While the youngest Pender fantasized about life in the military, the oldest was dreaming of commercial success and personal wealth. By 1849, Robert Pender had established, in partnership with one of his cousins, a mercantile store in Tarboro. He soon had his younger brothers working for him. Although a soldier in his mind's eye, 15-year-old Dorsey had little interest in the schooling that underlay that profession. Therefore he leapt at the opportunity to flee the classroom, as well as his less-than-cheery home, in order to clerk for the firm of Pender & Bridgers.

In time the store became a prosperous enterprise and by 1860 Robert Pender's wealth would exceed sixty thousand dollars. But Dorsey did not prosper with the business, for as bored as he had been with schooling he found store work infinitely more monotonous. It was said that in discharging his everyday chores he displayed "none of the energy and ability" that would characterize his later career.[12]

As he progressed through his teen years, his mind focused increasingly on things military. His earliest biographer noted that by this time "the martial spirit was already strongly developed in him." He envisioned himself on the parade ground, in camp, and in battle where through daring feats of arms he won fame and glory. The broom he wielded when cleaning floors became a rifle to be shouldered, swung into action, and fired at a phantom enemy. He assumed a soldierly dignity that was real and not imagined. At first an affectation, this effort became a lifelong habit. He prized nothing so much as the ability to maintain composure and decorum in any situation.[13]

By 16, he was casting about for an opportunity to make his images of soldier life a reality—preferably by entrance to the United States Military Academy. A West Point education was a prized commodity; it ensured a graduate not only of a military career but, through its heavy emphasis on civil engineering, a lucrative civilian career as well. Moreover, a cadet's schooling came free of charge, a fact of interest to a middle-class family such as his.

Pender's family was not wholly without the political connections that facilitated nomination to the academy. Pender's cousin, Robert R. Bridgers, brother of Robert Pender's business associate, was an up-and-coming lawyer and a prominent member of the local Democratic organization. When he learned of Dorsey's interest in West Point, the future state and Confederate official put discreet pressure on the congressman who represented their home district, John R. J. Daniel, to consider the youngster for the coveted appointment. Bridgers proved persuasive enough that on April 26, 1850, Daniel placed Pender's name before Secretary of War George W. Crawford. The appointment was duly confirmed, Pender accepted it, and his father inked his approval. The deed was done by May 6, less than two months before the commencement of the plebe year of the West Point Class of 1854.[14]

*   *   *

Accompanied by family members and friends, Dorsey Pender made the long, arduous trip to West Point, via stagecoach, train, and Hudson River steamer, in the third week of June. He reported to the august institution, at age 48 one of the most prestigious schools of its type in the world, on June 24. At once he was subjected to a physical and academic examination. He passed the first without difficulty, for by his 16th year he had grown tall—only two inches short of six feet—and hardy, the result not only of an active life but of months of loading merchandise on store shelves. He was neither stocky nor lanky; his compact physique carried no excess weight.[15]

But Pender's academic qualifications were a different matter. Having curtailed his formal studies in his mid-teens, he would have been considerably less prepared to meet West Point's stringent academic standards than many other plebes. In all probability he had crammed for months with the examination in mind, probably with the aid of a tutor. Whatever its form, his preparation proved sufficient, at least for the entrance exam. On the 24th it was announced that he and 70 other candidates had "been found qualified for admission to the Military Academy according to the requirements of para[graph] 23 of the Regulations and will be admitted conditionally as Cadets" to rank from July 1.[16]

On that date, Pender commenced his first summer encampment, the period of field exercise that predated each class year. His traveling companions having returned home, he was now on his own among strangers. The knowledge must have been unsettling, if only for the pangs of homesickness and rootlessness it stirred. The severity of these pains lessened, however, as soon as he became acquainted with classmates who hailed from his region. After the encampment, when assigned a dormitory room, he became fast friends with the fellow North Carolinian who bunked beside him, Samuel Turner Shepperd, son of eight-term U. S. Congressman Augustine H. Shepperd. The youngster's good nature and egalitarian bent bridged the differences of class and pedigree that might otherwise have kept the dormmates apart. The camaraderie that grew between them endured until Sam Shepperd's untimely death five years later.[17]

In time Pender made a number of other friends among the fourth-class cadets, including the honest and likable Stephen D. Lee of Mississippi and the dour but forthright New Englander, Oliver Otis Howard. Another plebe with whom Pender developed close ties, only to fall out with him later in life, was destined to become more famous than any other member of the Class of 1854: James Ewell Brown Stuart. While at the academy, Pender admired Stuart's lively, hale-fellow demeanor; later he came to consider the Virginian (not without foundation) as an egocentric and military politician of the boldest stripe.[18]

In his relationships with others, Pender was more like a Howard than a Stuart. Like the coldwater man from Maine and unlike the Virginia cavalier, he remained quiet and soft-spoken throughout his academy career. Whenever he opened his mouth, whether in the dormitory or in the classroom, he spoke in a low voice, rich with the Southern dialect, whose understated intensity commanded attention. Rarely did he raise the volume—not even on those few occasions when he spoke on the major topics of the day, including the sectional crisis that was dominating discussion in homes throughout the nation as well as in the halls of Congress.

While less reticent cadets made loud and heated pronouncements on slavery and states' rights, Pender kept his own counsel and held his tongue. For this reason he acquired the cadet nickname "Poll." While his biographers appear at a loss to explain its origin, its meaning is not difficult to discern. Most of the appellations given plebes by their classmates rang with irony, and Pender's closed-mouth behavior made him seem anything but a chattering parrot.[19]

Why Pender did not enter more energetically into the national debate is a matter of conjecture. Some who have analyzed him attribute his reticence strictly to those habits of reserve and decorum that had already characterized him for years. Others point to his status as a lightly educated youth surrounded by learned classmates more familiar than he with the issues of the day. Yet another possibility is that Pender lacked a passionate commitment to either side of the sectional divide.

Like thousands of young Southerners, he had grown up with an awareness that the labor of slaves was integral to his family's prosperity. And yet, even as a youth, he appears not to have regarded slavery as a social good. When he read Harriet Beecher Stowe's antislavery book, *Uncle Tom's Cabin*, his was not the heated response of most Southern-born readers. Indeed, he informed

Fanny that "you have no idea how nearly we [the authoress and he] agree on the subject of slavery."[20]

This is not to contend that Pender, either as a callow student or a mature soldier, viewed whites and blacks as equal in any accepted sense of the term. He regarded the great majority of African-Americans—including his wartime body-servants—as childlike innocents who could mature only by assuming the manners and mores of their masters. Even so, at an early age Pender appears to have doubted the moral underpinnings of the "peculiar institution." He was never comfortable with slave sales, especially when they resulted in broken families. That "most cruel practice" was "almost enough to make one an abolitionist." These views enabled him to maintain the friendship of staunch antislaveryites in the Cadet Corps such as O. O. Howard. During the war years that lay ahead, in contrast to the norm for Confederate officers, he would employ free blacks, not slaves, as his body-servants. To these he would pay a monthly salary arrived at by negotiation—an unheard-of practice for any Southerner, soldier or civilian.[21]

On the concomitant issue of state sovereignty, which within a decade would prove too contentious to be settled short of war, Pender was a true believer. From early youth, he had regarded statehood, rather than nationhood, as the cornerstone of the American political system. He owed his fealty, above all else, to North Carolina; he could not envision any situation in which he would take up arms against his family, his friends and neighbors, his county. Yet he would not grant blind devotion to any block of states that bolted the union. At West Point, whenever a Virginia- or Georgia-born classmate promoted Southern nationhood, Pender shook his head in dismay—if only when no one could see. Despite his views on slavery, he would fight, if necessary, to defend the political and social institutions of his state. He would not fight to defend those of Virginia or Georgia.

While political debate demanded a certain amount of attention and thought, Cadet Pender spent the majority of his time on the Hudson reading, reciting, and absorbing lectures. In spite of his limited educational experience, he proved a more than adequate student. His level of academic achievement remained consistent throughout his four years at the academy, although as the size of his class fell prey to a traditionally heavy dropout rate his standing in it dropped. He completed his fourth-class year ranking 17th out of 71 cadets academically. He ranked 19th of 60 students by the end of his second year at

West Point, 20th of 54 at the close of his third year, and, upon graduation, June 1, 1846, 19th in a class of 46.[22]

He gained his highest grades in mathematics and engineering, the core disciplines of the institution, and received lower marks in the study of French, the language of the profession of arms. He never showed much improvement in that discipline, although his originally shaky grasp of engineer-based drawing improved enough to raise his standing in that subject from 24th at the end of his second-class year to 12th one year later.

While Pender struggled with some of the classroom subjects, he excelled in the tactical courses that opened to him during his last year at the Point. He placed 5th, class-wide, in his chosen specialty, cavalry tactics, while ranking 21st in artillery and ordnance instruction. While an above-average student, he appeared to be more of a doer than a thinker—a distinction that posed no obstacle to a successful military career.[23]

Class ranking was not entirely dependent on academic achievement. Then, as now, a cadet's career was influenced by a complex and strictly applied code of behavior whose most visible feature was the awarding of demerits for a variety of infractions—everything from studying after lights-out to physical assault of a fellow cadet. As a cadet progressed in his education, the same offenses drew a greater number of demerits and thus class standing was more easily affected.

To most outsiders, as well as to many cadets, Pender apparently among them, the conduct code was applied in arbitrary and capricious fashion, preventing it from being an accurate gauge of student deportment. Although he did not fall afoul of the code to the degree that many of his predecessors had (more than a few had been dismissed for acquiring the maximum number of 200 demerits per year), Cadet Pender chalked up his share of infractions. He accumulated 28 black marks in his first year at the academy, 81 in his second year, 88 the following year, and, from July 1853 to July 1854, no fewer than 111. On graduation day, out of 203 cadets at the academy he stood 80th on the conduct roll.[24]

Most of his infractions were the typical ones—running late for class or for meals, wearing an unbuttoned jacket during inspection, allowing rust to form on the barrel of his musket. In spite of his quiet demeanor, he was gigged unusually often for talking or laughing in the ranks and on the practice field. Rather frequently he fell victim to nervous energy, being gigged for "swinging arms" while marching between the parade ground and the dormitory.[25]

Only one infraction was serious enough to have a lasting effect on his academy career. Determined to prove himself officer material, he strove hard to win promotion within the corps. His efforts paid off when, during his second-class year, he attained the rank of cadet corporal. The following year he was promoted to sergeant, and shortly before his first-class year began, to lieutenant. Two months later, however, he lost his stripes for neglect of duty. He had failed to make a written report to the commandant of cadets as was required when serving as officer of the day. It may have seemed a minor lapse, but the incident taught him that any breach of military regulations had its consequences.[26]

The loss of the lieutenancy was a severe blow, especially coming as it did during his last, critical year at West Point. Yet he bore up well under his punishment, earning good grades in the tactics of all three combat arms of the service. His strong suit continued to be mounted tactics, a course offered each year at the academy but on which the cadets were graded only during their first-class year. Only four members of Pender's class got a higher grade in cavalry instruction, the highest going to George Washington Custis Lee, eldest son of the academy's superintendent, Colonel Robert E. Lee of Virginia.

When the class of 1854 graduated, Custis Lee stood at its head, Oliver Howard, long the top man, having fallen to fourth place. Both men would become general officers in the Civil War armies, along with nine other of their classmates, including Pender. Future Confederate commanders included Stuart, S. D. Lee, John Pegram of Virginia, John B. Villepogue of South Carolina, James Deshler of Alabama, and Archibald Gracie Jr. (curiously enough, a native of New Jersey). In addition to Howard, Thomas H. Ruger of Wisconsin and Stephen H. Weed of New York would win their stars in the Union ranks. Several less illustrious classmen would also serve in the war that was coming on too fast for anyone's peace of mind.[27]

*   *   *

Pender would consider the fellowship of his classmates, Northerners and Southerners alike, as one of the greatest rewards of his educational experience. And he had West Point to thank for another lasting relationship. A few days after commencement, Pender and two classmates, Shepperd and Stuart, united to make use of the two-month furlough granted every graduate prior to entering upon active duty. Pender must have been especially happy for the opportunity to travel; the records indicate that during his four years on the

Hudson he had been granted a single 11-day leave to visit Albany and New York City. This time he went home to North Carolina, but stopped only briefly at Town Creek. The bulk of the furlough was spent on the Shepperd family estate, "Good Spring," a few miles from the village of Salem.[28]

Congressman Shepperd, his wife, his four other sons, and his two daughters—gracious hosts all—made their young visitors feel at home throughout their stay. Pender would always recall the trip with fondness, not only for the hospitality of his social betters but for the memory of his first meeting with his future wife. Petite and pretty, with pale eyes and a milky complexion that contrasted nicely with her dark hair, 14-year-old Mary Frances Shepperd caught her guest's attention the moment they met and held it throughout his visit. Pender was smitten; when the family entertained their visitors with a musicale, his heart rose and fell with Fanny's charming voice.

Fanny's beauty, her family pedigree, and her finished education made her a desirable catch, but at first Pender must have wondered if the class differences between them, and the uncertain prospects he faced as a junior officer, placed her beyond his reach. He vowed, however, to pursue her, and by the time he and his companions left Good Spring for divergent points, he had reason to believe he had awakened some emotion in this well-bred and accomplished young woman. Fanny had granted his request that he open a correspondence as soon as he had settled in at his first duty station.[29]

From Good Spring, Shepperd and Stuart headed north and west to join their regiments, the 2nd Infantry and the Regiment of Mounted Riflemen, respectively. Pender, who traveled in a different direction, regretted parting with his classmates—one of whom he envied. While he had no interest in the infantry, Pender dearly wished he might have accompanied Stuart into the mounted ranks—if not the Riflemen, then the 1st or 2nd Dragoons. The hitch was that assignments to the support and combat arms were governed by the cadets' class standing. Stuart had finished six places above Pender, high enough to guarantee the posting both cadets desired. The fun-loving Shepperd, who had graduated only ten places from the bottom of the class, had no recourse but a career as a foot soldier.[30]

Pender had avoided Shepperd's fate, but his ranking consigned him to an only slightly more prestigious branch of the service, the artillery. The assignment meant a tour of garrison duty, a fate he probably accepted rather than embraced. He was also resigned to serving as a brevet second lieutenant until a vacancy opened up in the commissioned ranks of his unit. (A full-rank commission would not come until February 1855, although for purposes of seniority it would rank from the previous August.) About the only thought that sustained Pender as he departed North Carolina on that warm September day was the memory of Fanny Shepperd's doe-like eyes and porcelain skin. That memory followed him down Florida's Gulf Coast, via Tampa Bay, to Fort Myers, home to a detachment of the 2nd United States Artillery. Immediately upon reporting, he immersed himself in a sea of assignments and duties.[31]

Pender had not embarked on an easy profession. The life of a junior officer of coast artillery in the mid-1850s was neither glamorous nor luxurious—it was not even comfortable. Garrison duty was multifaceted, onerous, and ubiquitous, especially because the small units that garrisoned each fort lacked a full complement of officers due to illness, detached service, and staff duty. Those subalterns who remained had to take on more than the normal complement of responsibilities. Life inside a casemated fort was spartan and unhealthy, and low pay throughout the lower ranks resulted in a standard of living poor enough to cripple morale.

When Pender reported to Fort Myers, for the first six months of his active-duty career he helped wage war—albeit at some distance—against bands of Seminole Indians who for two decades had been resisting removal to far-off reservation lands. It was hot, dirty, risky, and thankless duty, made more so by ill-defined objectives; by an alligator-infested, malaria-ridden, and quicksand-dotted area of operations; by an enemy who avoided being drawn into an open fight; and by the army's woeful unpreparedness to fight a guerrilla war.

Serving as he did at a fixed base, Pender avoided some of the hardships that foot soldiers and dragoons faced as the confused fighting dragged on. But although he never experienced defeat in combat, his morale suffered along with that of his more actively engaged comrades. There seemed no point, no certainty, and no end to the fighting. It was a miserable way to begin a career in arms.[32]

*   *   *

By the spring of 1855, Pender was seeking escape. Yearning to serve aboard horseback in open country, he applied for a transfer to the 2nd Dragoons, a regiment that served mainly on the western frontier. That was a barren, arid place in which to serve, but on any given day Pender would have preferred a desert to a swamp.[33]

In a manner of speaking, by applying to a dragoon outfit, he was seeking only half of what he longed for. Dragoons were hybrid warriors, a cross between cavalrymen and foot soldiers. At the behest of an economy-minded Congress, they had been armed, equipped, and trained to fight in the saddle and on foot with equal proficiency. Although dragoons rode mainly to reach the scene of action, there to fight dismounted, their tactics, and the wide-open environment they inhabited, had a certain appeal to one who had spent months confined to a garrison.

Another lure was the good reputation the dragoons had gained even in the eyes of infantrymen accustomed to treating horsemen with scorn. The dragoons had performed with distinction during the fighting in Mexico, especially in the actions of Pueblo de Taos and Vera Cruz and outside Mexico City. At Mexico City the 2nd Dragoons had made the most dramatic saber charge of the war, overrunning artillery units and taking many prisoners, including a Mexican general. After an armistice ended the fighting, the hybrid regiments returned to the task they had interrupted in mid-1846, pacifying hostile Indians on the western plains. Their primary opponents were the Apaches and the Utahs who roamed the New Mexico Territory, and the Comanches who terrorized white settlers in outlying sections of Texas.[34]

Although he secured a berth in the 1st, not the 2nd, Dragoons, Pender considered his decision to transfer to the mounted branch one of the smartest moves he ever made. For one thing, his request was granted with unusual speed. Instead of the several months it took most such applications to receive consideration at army headquarters, his was approved barely six weeks after he set things in motion. On May 25, Secretary of War Jefferson Davis of Mississippi wrote to inform him that by appointment of the president he was now the junior officer of the 1st Dragoon Regiment. For unknown reasons, Pender did not formally receive his commission for more than a year. When he studied it, however, he found that it had been dated to rank from March 3, 1855.[35]

Soon after he got the happy news, he was presented with orders to report to Camp Thorn, New Mexico, on the right bank of the Rio Grande near the settlement of Santa Barbara. He lost no time bidding farewell to fellow officers he had barely become acquainted with and boarding a northbound train. Days later he accompanied a wagon train carrying army personnel to Fort Leavenworth, Kansas Territory, portal to the ends of the earth—the farthest reaches of the West. He laid over at that communications center until recruiting parties bound for New Mexico could be assembled in force sufficient to prevent interference by hostile tribes.

His stay at Leavenworth reunited him with Sam Shepperd, who had been stationed there for the previous several months. But the pleasure of renewed friendship was painfully brief. It is likely that Pender was still at Leavenworth, awaiting transportation, when Shepperd took ill, lingered briefly, and then, on June 27, succumbed to a malarial disease. His passing stunned his classmate and friend. For months Lieutenant Pender had carried on an active correspondence with Shepperd's sister, a correspondence that, by dwelling on mutual interests, had helped bring the couple together emotionally. Hereafter, his letters overflowed with grief and sorrow, as did hers in reply. The shared bond of mourning drew the couple closer still.[36]

Pender was still reeling from his friend's death when he resumed his journey west. Without serious difficulty, he made his way to Fort Thorn, where he found himself assigned to Company I of his new regiment and assimilated the duties, tactics, and traditions of mounted service. Almost at once, he found himself at home in the 1st Dragoons. He developed close ties with several colleagues, including two West Pointers, Lieutenants Henry B. Davidson of Tennessee (Class of 1848) and David McMurtrie Gregg of Pennsylvania (Class of 1851). Despite their sectional differences, Pender came to regard Gregg as the closest friend he had in the service.

After acquainting himself with his peers and superiors, Pender took on a raft of duties, including staff work. For the most part his initial service consisted of accompanying scouting missions to and from Fort Craig. Only after several weeks had passed and he had acquired a certain confidence in his ability to master not only the basics but the nuances of his new arm, did he go on campaign with Company I. His maiden outing, during which he exercised temporary command of another company of his outfit, took him as far as the Sierra Almagre Mountains, west of the Gila River. During that March 1856 expedition, the dragoons attacked and dispersed a roving band of Apaches. Apparently, Pender's company was only lightly engaged, for it suffered but one casualty, a relatively benign baptism of fire for Lieutenant Pender.[37]

Only a few months after reaching New Mexico, he left it, along with several squadrons of the 1st Dragoons, for California. For months thereafter he traded the excitement of patrol and battle for the tedium of garrison life at Fort Tejon, northeast of the little port town of Los Angeles. The dragoons had been sent to this former Mexican province to take the place of troops recently transferred to the northwest, where several tribes were on the warpath. With the so-called Rogue River War raging in the Department of Oregon, Pender suspected that his stay at Tejon would be brief.

He was proven correct early in 1857, when most of the horsemen who had marched from New Mexico headed north to Fort Walla Walla, Washington Territory. At that garrison, which one of Pender's colleagues described as situated "in a beautiful spot of the Walla Walla valley, well wooded and with plenty of water," Company I joined other detachments of the 1st Dragoons and other Regular foot and horse units, and bands of half-trained, revenge-driven volunteers, in fighting a running war with a loose alliance of northwestern tribes including the Rogues, Shastas, Scotans, Klamaths, Grave and Cow Creeks, and Umpquas.[38]

Pender probably expected to see action at an early date; if so, this time his prediction missed the mark. Late in the year his company moved closer to the scene of action by marching to Fort Dalles, Oregon Territory, but the unit remained on the fringes of the action while other horse and foot units carried the burden of campaigning.

Although not committed to combat, Pender suffered from the effects of hard campaigning. When in the field he was exposed on a daily basis to barren wastes and baking heat, as well as to plunging temperatures, raw winds, and snow. He found garrison life scarcely more comfortable. On the other hand, he had escaped the stultifying inertia of service in a coastal fort, a fate he could not have tolerated half as well.

In the spring of 1857 he secured an extended furlough, during which he traveled overland to San Francisco, and from there by ship down the coast to Mexico. A long, body-wracking train trip across the Isthmus of Panama eventually deposited him on the Atlantic seaboard.[39]

Once back on American soil, he made straight for North Carolina. In Edgecombe County he had a joyous reunion with family and friends. His stay at Town Creek and Tarboro, however, was brief in comparison to the trip he made to Good Spring. There he renewed his acquaintance with his dead friend's sister, the woman to whom he had been writing long, earnest letters from many out-of-the-way places—letters that had begun to overflow with sentimental allusions and unusually personal expressions.

Chapter Two

LOVE AND WAR

It is not known how long Pender was able to spend with Mary Frances Shepperd—his stay in North Carolina consumed less than three weeks—but his feelings toward her appear to have deepened as a result of his mid-1857 furlough. The occasion marks the last time he was in Fanny's company until, in late 1858, he returned to Good Spring to claim her as his bride. During that year-and-a-half interval their correspondence intensified, in terms of both letters sent and emotions expressed, until Pender was sufficiently hopeful to propose marriage and Fanny was sufficiently confident to accept.[1]

When he left North Carolina at leave's end for the enervating trip west, he returned not to Walla Walla but to Fort Dalles. At that newly rebuilt garrison on the left bank of the Columbia River, he was closer than ever to the scene of Indian troubles. Yet he spent only a few weeks in the area before returning to Washington, via Fort Vancouver, at the head of a party of recruits.

The assignment was not to his liking, and he was not hesitant to make his feelings known. In early December he wrote from Fort Walla Walla to the Headquarters of the Department of the Pacific. He begged leave "to complain of this [escort] detail as an unjust one.... I was on duty at Fort Dalles in charge of & responsible for a Detachment of twenty-seven Dragoons, and one hundred & eight horses pertaining to Cos 'I' and 'C' 1st Dragoons, and a quantity of horse equipage. This order necessarily withdrew me from my Command, and responsibilities, when at that very time, there were two sub-alterns of the 9th Infantry, present at Fort Dalles... and subject to detail for detached service." Furthermore, he complained that since one of those officers accompanied the detachment as far as Fort Vancouver he could have gone on to Walla Walla in charge of the recruits.[2]

In framing his complaint Pender may have won some debating points, but his rather sharp tone and his presumptuousness in composing it could not have sat well with the department commander, Major General John Ellis Wool. It is possible that Wool's adjutant, Major W. W. Mackall, pigeonholed the letter without showing it to his boss. More likely, Wool read the letter but his reaction was forestalled by his relief from command in May and his replacement by Brevet Brigadier General Newman S. Clarke.[3]

Whatever its denouement, the incident is instructive for what it reveals of the complainant's attitude. Lieutenant Pender's pride was as sensitive as that of any officer in the army. If he considered himself slighted or ill-used by his superiors, he would not let the incident pass without putting his displeasure on record.

Pender returned to the scene of Indian fighting early in 1858. By early February he was back at Fort Vancouver, where he took on ordnance duties as well as platoon command. His peripatetic service continued when, in mid-year, he was again assigned to Fort Walla Walla. It was at that garrison, soon afterward, that an expeditionary force was formed to chastise the warrior tribes, a force that furnished Pender, temporarily in command of Company I, with his first taste of combat.

The expedition was raised in the wake of what was known throughout the Department of the Pacific as the Steptoe Disaster. For several months "Indian troubles" had swept many corners of the Northwest. The tribes wrought violence on settlers, Indian agents, and gold-seekers mining the riverbed of the Columbia. Reportedly, the unrest was either orchestrated or exacerbated by Mormons in the Utah Territory, foes of the federal government who hoped the Indians would mount a full-scale rebellion against the United States.[4]

The reported involvement of the Mormons prompted Major Edward J. Steptoe of the 9th Infantry to lead an expedition in the spring of 1858 from Walla Walla along the Oregon Trail to the scenes of Indian depredations, where he might secure evidence of whites' complicity in them. At the beginning of its journey, however, Steptoe's command—159 strong including some infantrymen, a couple of howitzers, and three companies of the 1st Dragoons including David Gregg's company—found its path barred by several thousand Spokanes, Palouses, Coeur d'Alenes, and members of other northern tribes.

When parlays with the warriors failed to clear his path, Steptoe turned back to Walla Walla. Closely pursued by the Indians, he recrossed the Snake River and on the other side was attacked several times. Six soldiers, including two dragoon officers, were killed, and twelve others were wounded. Only good fortune and the power of Steptoe's artillery prevented a massacre. At last locating a route free of Indians, the expeditionary leader led his battered survivors to safety after a long, hard march.[5]

Steptoe and subordinates including Gregg had performed creditably during the mission, but its unhappy conclusion gave the army a black eye and called for retaliation. At 9:00 A.M. on August 7, a larger expeditionary force, under Steptoe's regimental commander, Colonel George Wright, headed north from Walla Walla. Pender accompanied the column, as did Gregg, Davidson, and several other future general officers including Captains Edward O. C. Ord, Erasmus D. Keyes, Charles S. Winder, James A. Hardie, Frederick T. Dent, and Lieutenants Robert O. Tyler and Hylan B. Lyon. As one of Pender's biographers has pointed out, this column was supported not only by an extensive supply train, something Steptoe had lacked, but by hundreds of rifles and carbines that fired the new, long-range, and highly accurate minie ball.[6]

After a several-day march that proceeded without incident, Wright's column penetrated a vast expanse framed by the Snake River on the south and the Columbia on the west. Hostiles could be expected to show themselves anywhere in the region, and every day Pender anticipated a fight. But not until August 30 did the column encounter bands of Spokanes in warpaint. These, however, galloped off before a clash could occur. The following day, other braves showed themselves at long distance, only to retreat when the soldiers drew near.

Pender may have suspected that Wright's column was being drawn into a trap. If so, the consequent feeling of unease lasted only one day. As one of

Pender's colleagues noted in his diary, at sunrise on September 1, "we found the Indians, increased in number [to about 500], still posted on the hills over-looking us. Their manner was defiant and insolent, and they seemed to be inviting an attack."

Just after 8:00 A.M., Wright moved to take the initiative, forming an attack column of dragoons including Pender's company and a second, under Major William N. Grier, composed of infantry and artillery. Together, the wings totaled about 200 men. At Wright's order the dragoons, on the left flank, led off, angling toward the crowded hills.

Pender left no account of his experiences in this, the first battle of his mil-itary career—perhaps because it was so brief and casualties were so light in his unit. As soon as the horsemen topped the bluffs, they dismounted, drew their carbines, and, in the manner of infantry, scattered the nearest hostiles with a deadly fusillade. Once the hills were cleared, Wright's second column advanced. Thanks largely to its long-range ammunition, it forced the Spokanes into the middle of the farther plain. The dragoons then remounted and charged a second time, shooting and sabering the Indians into full-fledged retreat. Not even a grass fire set by the enemy deterred Pender and his comrades, who inflicted numerous casualties but took none in return.

When the tribesmen had been driven almost four miles from the battle-field, Colonel Wright judged them incapable of further resistance. He recalled his horsemen, thus ending the so-called battle of Four Lakes. An artillery offi-cer, Second Lieutenant Lawrence Kip, studied the dragoons as they returned to the main body. He might have been speaking of Pender when he observed that "a number of our men had never before been under fire, but begrimed and weary as they were, we could see in their faces how much they enjoyed the excitement of the fight. Certainly none could evince finer discipline or behave more coolly." The victors camped on the hard-won field and remained there for the next four days.[7]

The success at Four Lakes strengthened Wright's belief that he could bring his enemy to bay and smash them in open battle. His confidence was validat-ed soon after he resumed his northward march on September 5. Throughout that day, Indian bands were seen moving along the right flank of the column, again seeking an opportunity to attack. At midday the enemy ceased follow-ing the column and advanced toward it behind the shield of another deliber-ately set grass fire. As at Four Lakes, however, fire and smoke did not prevent the soldiers from advancing, this time in a counterattack.

The result was not long in coming. Even before the horsemen could strike, Wright's artillery and sharpshooters broke the Indians' formation and propelled them into headlong flight. As the demoralized braves turned about, two companies of dragoons, including Company I of the 1st under Pender, galloped across Spokane Plains and ran down the enemy. The action covered fourteen miles and resulted in the killing of several braves and the capture of many others.

Lieutenant Pender added at least three to the casualty total. As his company closed in on the retreating warriors, he singled out one and drew his saber, only to have it stick in its scabbard. Evidently, his pistol was out of cartridges and thus useless as well. Knowing nothing else to do, Pender resorted to physical strength. To prevent his antagonist from landing the first blow, the lieutenant grabbed for him, yanked him from his horse, and threw him to the ground. A soldier riding farther to the rear immediately "dispatched" the unhorsed brave. Pender continued his charge, using his sword to kill a second foe and wound a third.[8]

Once the Indians' strength had been irretrievably broken, Wright recalled his horse soldiers, tended to the single casualty his command had suffered, and rounded up his captives. Some of the prisoners were later executed for their role in the murder of the Columbia River miners. After a brief respite, the expeditionary force resumed its journey to the scene of Colonel Steptoe's ambush, where it recovered the remains of several soldiers. En route, they skirmished with diehard tribesmen on the Spokane River, overran and destroyed enemy lodges and storehouses, took additional prisoners, and confiscated several hundred Indian ponies. By the first week in October, their mission accomplished, Wright and his men were back at Fort Walla Walla.[9]

Pender's conspicuous role in the fighting, especially in the pursuit from the river bluffs, meant career rewards. In his after-action reports, Colonel Wright commended Pender's conduct at both Four Lakes and Spokane Plains, as did Major Grier; the latter wrote "in the highest terms of the gallantry" of the North Carolinian. Lieutenants Gregg and Davidson of Pender's regiment were also singled out for commendation, the former for his inspired use of the saber, the latter for his expertise with the pistol. Several other officers also received the praise of their superiors, but none so much as Pender. Through his highly visible participation in the fighting, he emerged as one of the true heroes of Wright's punitive expedition.[10]

Undoubtedly as a result, three weeks after Spokane Plains, Pender was promoted to first lieutenant, to date from May 17. The increase in rank was especially opportune. Not only did it solidify his place in his outfit and his army, the pay increase it set in motion gave the young subaltern the incentive he needed to ask Fanny Shepperd to marry him.[11]

*   *   *

The *Raleigh Sandard*, in its Christmas Day 1858 issue, reported that Lieutenant Pender of the 1st United States Dragoons, that "gallant son of Edgecombe," was back in North Carolina. Why this was so, the paper's correspondent could not say, but he predicted for the young officer "high position in the service in some future day."[12]

Pender considered his present position a lofty one as well, fully worthy of the leave for which he had applied while still on Wright's expedition. The extended furlough, he had informed departmental officials, was necessary "that I may visit my friends in the East, and attend to important private business." One friend in particular had prompted his long journey home via ship to New York City. On February 3, 1859, a circuitous and mostly long-distance courtship reached a happy conclusion when the lieutenant married his beloved Fanny at her parents' home in Good Spring.

Following the ceremony, which was conducted according to the Episcopal rite by the Shepperds' pastor, the Reverend A. H. Houghton, the bride's family hosted a grand reception, at which one guest, future Confederate General William Gaston Lewis of Rocky Mount, took note of the groom's "very pleasant manners and his fine military bearing." The festivities over, the couple began a "down home" honeymoon, spent mostly in Edgecombe County among the groom's family and friends.[13]

When the approaching end of Pender's furlough brought the wedding trip to a close, the newlyweds traveled north. They spent their last days in the east at Washington, where he introduced her to army friends and perhaps also lobbied his superiors for a new posting. If he did, his efforts went unrewarded.

The thought of making such a long, uncertain trip through sometimes-hostile country in company with his bride must have bothered him. So too did the climate of affairs he found in the nation's capital. By now, if not long before, sectional tensions had begun to pull the city's temporary and permanent residents in different directions. Pender sensed the effects of this political tug-of-war on his academy classmates, some of them Northerners, some Southerners, whom he met en route to and while in the city. As before, he refused to be drawn into a loud, undignified debate on issues that produced much heat and little light. Assuredly, his bride felt the same way.

Some officers, especially those assigned to territory that harbored angry warriors, chose to serve hundreds of miles from their wives, who lived with their families or in hotel rooms while awaiting their husbands' reassignment. The Penders, however, appear never to have considered living apart. From the first, they intended to travel side-by-side to Fort Walla Walla in the second week in March. They would be accompanied by one of the Pender family slaves, probably the girl named Laura Smith, who would attend Fanny. Pender had planned to head south to New Orleans and from there by steamboat to Fort Leavenworth. At the last minute, however, he learned that the New Orleans packet would sail two days sooner than he had supposed. As a result, the couple and their servant did not leave Washington until April 5.[14]

Following the customarily roundabout and much-delayed voyage, the couple reached the post at Leavenworth at about mid-month. There Pender leased a covered wagon to carry the three of them and his wife's possessions, including her trusty sewing machine and their wedding presents, to the Washington Territory. By the time they made their weary, dusty way, under escort, across the plains, Pender must have felt that he had been gone from Fort Walla Walla for a millennium or two. Fanny, who was three months pregnant, was even worse for wear when she arrived at her husband's station in the wilderness.

After reporting to his commanding officer, Pender moved Fanny's and his belongings into the married officers' quarters, where they set up housekeeping. Despite the spare furnishings, the couple found happiness. From the first, Pender enjoyed married life. He disliked the scouting duties and the detached assignments that took him away from Fanny, and he took great pleasure in returning to his little home after a day's duty. Fanny and he would sit and talk while he read the newspaper, often several days out of date, and she sewed, knitted, or cooked. Now and then they visited other couples in their quarters or in the officers' club at the fort. Some evenings were filled with gaiety and song; on those occasions, Fanny Pender would shine. To the accompaniment of an old melodeon, Fanny would sing in the voice that her husband adored.[15]

Wedded bliss increased on November 28 with the birth of the couple's first son, whom they named after Fanny's deceased brother. Apparently the mother went into labor prematurely, or the post infirmary lacked a bed for her, for family tradition has it that Samuel Turner Pender entered the world atop a billiard table borrowed from the officer's club. Although at times sickly, the child was a delight to his parents and their lives quickly began to revolve around him. As Pender noted, on those few occasions when Fanny and he left Turner's side, they knew the "pleasant anticipation of seeing the baby when we got back."[16]

Pender felt a special closeness to the son he called "that incomparable boy, Turner; the greatest boy in the world." Turner was "his" child, while their second son, Dorsey, would be known as Fanny's boy. In so saying, he was being whimsical; whenever Fanny protested that he favored their eldest too conspicuously, he would assure her that his love was divided, in equal measure, between Turner and Dorsey. Even so, the bond between father and first-born can be unusually close, and it appears to have been so in this case.[17]

Not long after Turner's birth—as soon as Fanny could travel, it seems—the little family left Walla Walla for the western reaches of the Washington Territory. By year's end they had settled in at Fort Vancouver, a larger garrison, with more amenities than Walla Walla. Although Pender, now second-in-command of his company, was kept as busy as ever with staff and line duties, he would come to regard the months spent with Fanny and Turner at Vancouver as the happiest in his military career.[18]

He drew increasing pleasure from a hitherto-untapped source. Whenever possible, he accompanied his wife to the services conducted at the post chapel. At first he did not follow her inside, but later he attended as a favor to Fanny. Over a period of several months, however, he changed from a curious outsider to an interested observer of the Episcopalian rite. He found himself touched by the piety his wife displayed not only in church but in her daily life and he came to be impressed by her interest in, and knowledge of, the Bible. At her urging, he delved into the Scriptures. He expected to find their teachings esoteric and irrelevant; instead, he was intrigued by what he took to be their fundamental message, that by making himself worthy of God's grace, and by accepting Jesus Christ as his savior, man could rise above weakness and sin to enjoy life everlasting.

Although the thought of spending eternity in the presence of the Creator did not immediately captivate him, another vision did. He knew he wished to live the rest of his life with Fanny Shepperd Pender. The prospect that they might continue their union after death exerted a growing influence on him.

At first, he doubted he could make the major commitment that Christianity demanded. A year and a half into their marriage, he informed

Fanny, "I wish I could be good enough to become a member of your church." While he saw no such goodness in himself, he said, "I will try to take more interest in these things than formerly." He began to hope that some of his wife's piety would rub off on him, for he realized that she set a good example for him to follow. In time he came to believe that "a Christian woman is the most Heavenly of earthly creatures."[19]

To Pender's dismay, Fanny and he were often apart. Assignments of one kind or another took him to many corners of the territory while his wife and son remained at Fort Vancouver. On some of these missions, especially when scouting Indian-infested country, he risked the possibility that he would not return to his family, never to see them again on earth. The prospect increased his desire that, if unable to be with Fanny in this life, he might meet her in another, better world.

Indian campaigning was not the only threat to Pender's peace of mind. As the decade of the 1860s began, sectional troubles were intensifying as the result of past events and future possibilities. In mid-October, the nation's composure had been shaken and its passions ignited by an assault launched by a fanatical abolitionist, John Brown, against the United States armory and arsenal at Harpers Ferry, Virginia. At the head of a small but devoted body of followers, black and white, Brown hoped to seize weapons with which to support a slave insurrection throughout the South. But soon after occupying Harpers Ferry, his little army had been surrounded, shot up, and captured by a detachment of Marines under Robert E. Lee with the assistance of Pender's classmate Lieutenant J. E. B. Stuart. Four days after the birth of Pender's son, Brown was hanged at Charles Town, Virginia. The old man had gone calmly to his death but only after a sensational trial. Both in court and just before he ascended the gallows, Brown had predicted that the crimes of his slave-ridden country "will never be purged *away*, but with Blood." To Northerners and Southerners alike, it sounded like a premonition.[20]

Brown's aborted assault raised flags that not even a man such as Dorsey Pender, who spoke calmly and kept his own counsel, could ignore. He regarded as another portent the increasing likelihood that the 1860 presidential campaign would end in victory for an abolitionist-leaning candidate from the North or Northwest, something the South would not abide. Talk of secession and of forming a Southern nation had been part of the public debate for more than a decade, but recently that debate had acquired a tone of dread and foreboding, as if cataclysmic decisions were in the offing.

Pender tried to drown out the clamor by concentrating on his military responsibilities. These included a four-month campaign in the summer of 1860 against braves who had fled reservation lands in the Oregon Territory. Conducted by Major Enoch Steen of Pender's regiment, the expedition was not only prolonged and taxing, but largely barren of result. The hunted tribes habitually dispersed upon the soldiers' approach, to hide in inaccessible mountains, thickets, and woods.[21]

Pender kept Fanny apprised of the results of the mission, or the lack of same. He came to the conclusion that "we are strong, too strong I fear to meet the Indians for they will never meet soldiers unless they think they are superior" in numbers. On two occasions, the braves did turn on their pursuers and pitched into them. During the larger of the two attacks, near Harney Lake on June 23, Company I had to beat back more than 100 charging, screaming men in warpaint.[22]

Pender reported the fight to Fanny, not to make her fear for his safety but to acquaint her with the hard facts of active service. "Do not be alarmed," he told her, "for we are in no danger, for even if they [the warriors] choose to fight any more, they have but a few poor guns & we have arms that will kill five hundred yards away."

Apparently, Fanny had asked him to avoid exposing himself to danger. He replied that even under the best conditions, a soldier's life carried risks. Moreover, an officer had responsibilities he must discharge under all circumstances: "While in the army one had better do his own duty whatever it may be, and he will have the approval at least of his own conscience. I know my wife too well to think that she would like to see me shirking hardship or even danger when it becomes necessary to encounter them." Perhaps it was a matter of pride. If Fanny did not "think I was as much of a man as any one else, she could not respect me.... Fighting is supposed to be my profession, and any wife must get used to the idea."[23]

Yet he never got used to the idea of being apart from his family for long periods. Loneliness and homesickness dogged him throughout the Oregon expedition and caused him to pour out his feelings in his home letters. He inquired often of Fanny's health for, saddled with what was called a "delicate constitution," she suffered from a variety of ailments ranging from cramps and hemorrhoids to intestinal ills that would develop into colitis. He begged her to keep him informed of Turner's and her activities, no matter how mundane they seemed, and he spoke longingly of their home life at Fort

Vancouver. At times, their estrangement seemed unbearable. From one especially lonely bivouac, he wrote, "Oh! at night how I would like to have you, even between my rough blankets and hug you to my heart."[24]

By August, Pender's ability to tolerate the seemingly never-ending mission had worn threadbare. Not only was he homesick and weary of pursuing an elusive foe, his relationship with his immediate superior, Captain Andrew Jackson Smith, had turned so sour that the two communicated only through a third party such as David Gregg. Pender considered Smith an obnoxious Yankee as well as a pompous martinet who treated his subordinates with condescension. Then, too, months before, during a dance at Fort Vancouver, the captain had behaved toward Fanny Pender with undue familiarity; the incident continued to stir resentment in her jealous husband.

The rigors of the campaign heightened the tensions between the two, and at some point, it came to a head. Either verbally or with their fists the two "pitched into" each other, Pender giving Smith "as good as he sent." It is not known how the altercation ended, but thereafter each showed the other more consideration and respect.[25]

Late August found Major Steen's command still wandering through the wilderness in search of a foe lost to view. Provisions were running low, as was the patience of everyone involved. Pender was so demoralized that he was seriously considering transferring to another arm of the service, or even tendering his resignation. In answer to Fanny's despondent letters, he wrote: "You are not more tired of the [passing] days than I am of the whole Army...."[26]

All that sustained him was the thought that by abject necessity the expedition would soon end, permitting him to return to his "good Smart & pretty" wife and infant son. In this view he was correct, for before month's end Steen finally gave up the mission as a lost cause and led his exhausted, grimy, irritable troops back to Fort Vancouver. Upon reaching the garrison, Pender fell into Fanny's arms. Within a week she was carrying their second child.

His active campaigning ended, Pender returned to the life of a garrison soldier, although not at Fort Vancouver. By late September they had returned to Walla Walla. Their tour there was briefer than their first had been, but it ended happily enough, especially for Fanny, for in early November Pender gained an assignment that would keep him out of the field indefinitely. He was detailed as the chief administrative officer of his regiment. The position entailed a move to San Francisco, headquarters of the 1st Dragoons, a small city that, in comparison to his most recent duty stations, must have seemed like a metropolis.[27]

* * *

Two days before Pender's staff appointment, Abraham Lincoln of Illinois, the "black Republican" candidate in a four-way race for the White House, received enough electoral votes to become the 16th president of the United States. Hearing the news, and the clamor it caused among his Southern brethren in the army, Pender feared that secession was a foregone conclusion and civil war a clear possibility.

Although forced to confront the national crisis for perhaps the first time, he could not say how it would affect him. If his state left the Union, he would go with it, would resign his hard-won commission, and would relinquish his plum position at regimental headquarters, all without a second thought. But at first he doubted that North Carolina would be drawn into secession, even if the Deep South quit the Union as a body. Thousands of unionists hailed from the state, and Pender would have been hard-pressed to deny that he was one of them.

His dilemma was thrown into high relief after December 20, when the fire-eaters of South Carolina, in convention in Charleston, voted their state out of the Union. Early in the new year, while Pender tried to concentrate on the paperwork pooling on his desk, six other states in the lower South followed suit. Pender found the trend toward disunion unnerving, but he clung to the knowledge that the upper states, including North Carolina, had refused to secede, their officials pleading for time in which a political firestorm, and untold bloodshed, might be averted. Well into the new year of 1861, Pender continued to side with the cooler heads and hoped against hope that they would prevail. Fanny Pender, whose family had Whig ties, adopted the same stance as her husband.

The worsening crisis may have distracted the adjutant of the 1st Dragoons more than he knew. On January 31, less than three months after taking up his duties in San Francisco, he was relieved of them and returned to the field. He was ordered to report to the cavalry school of instruction at Carlisle Barracks, Pennsylvania. At that venerable post, the enlistment rendezvous of the mounted arm, he would assist in recruiting for his regiment, soon to be renamed the 1st United States Cavalry.[28]

Once again, and for the final time, Pender packed up his family and accompanied them on the disagreeable trip across the continent. When he reached the east coast in late February, he went not to Pennsylvania but to Washington, where he found preparations for Lincoln's inaugural in full swing. After checking Fanny and Turner into a hotel, he reported to the adjutant general of the army, from whom he sought a delay in reporting to Carlisle Barracks. Permission was granted, as was his request to escort his family to North Carolina.[29]

A few short days before the president-elect took the oath of office, the Penders were aboard a train bound for Good Spring, where Fanny saw her family for the first time since her wedding. She and her husband were warmly received, but 15-month-old Turner, making his introduction into Shepperd society, was clearly the guest of honor.

Among his in-laws—some of them disunionists, all of them proponents of state rights—Lieutenant Pender was bombarded with the burning question of the hour: when was he going to resign from the army and take up the defense of North Carolina? The last vestiges of caution prevented him from making an unequivocal reply. No one, not even Congressman Shepperd, could say for certain that their state would become a part of the government that had been formed in Montgomery, Alabama, early in February. For one thing, even as the Confederate States of America was being formed, North Carolina had been well represented at an eleventh-hour peace conference in Washington. When that effort collapsed under the weight of uneasy compromise, a majority of the state's voters had rejected a call for a secession convention.

Pender was also aware of recent events that seemed to signal a peaceful settlement of the slavery question, an issue closely linked with secession. The same day that North Carolina rejected a convention, the U. S. House of Representatives had passed and sent to the Senate an amendment prohibiting the federal government from interfering with slavery in states where it already existed. This act was known to have the support of the president-elect.[30]

But Lincoln had recently expressed other views that Southerners would not find so acceptable. In his inaugural address of March 4, he had made clear his belief that "in view of the Constitution and the laws, the Union is unbroken; and, to the extent of my ability, I shall take care, as the Constitution itself expressly enjoins upon me, that the laws of the Union be faithfully executed in all the States." Speaking directly to secessionists, Lincoln observed that there would be no violence "unless it is forced upon the national authority.…

In *your* hands, my dissatisfied fellow countrymen, and not in *mine*, is the momentous issue of civil war."

Perusing the text of the presidential message in the local papers, Pender doubted that the issue was as clear-cut as Lincoln chose to portray it. He was particularly skeptical that if war came the government would be the assailed rather than the assailant. Although Lincoln had not declared that he would attempt to reclaim federal property seized by the governors of the seceding states—an effort that would surely bring on war—he left no doubt that the government would "hold, occupy, and possess" the property that remained in its hands in the South. Pender saw in this statement the sort of threat to state sovereignty he had expected a Republican president to issue.[31]

During the first week in March, while South Carolina tightened the ring of troops and guns that enclosed the federal garrisons in Charleston Harbor, Pender made the most fateful decision of his life. On the 9th, the date of his reporting to Carlisle Barracks having passed, he wrote from Good Spring to the assistant adjutant general of the army, Colonel Lorenzo Thomas. He made reference to the furlough granted him in North Carolina and declared that he had not procured it under false pretenses, at the outset he "fully intended to report." However, "the course the President has indicated he shall pursue renders it impossible for me to serve in any position, that may at any time bring me into deadly conflict with that section of the Country to which I belong." He left no doubt as to his intentions when he signed himself, "W. D. Pender, late [of the] U. S. A."[32]

In compliance with existing regulations, that same day he addressed a note to Secretary of War Simon Cameron that began: "I have the honor hereby to tender the resignation of my Commission...." The action formally took effect 12 days later. "I shall never regret resigning," he informed Fanny, "whatever may turn up. I felt now as I felt then, that I could not serve in the U.S.A." and retain any claim to personal honor.[33]

Once he cast his lot with secession, Pender became anxious for his state to do the same, and annoyed when it continued to delay and temporize. By mid-April 1861, as one of the state's leading newspapers noted, "all eyes are now fixed upon North Carolina and Virginia. Will they submit to the coercion of Abraham Lincoln? Can they do it?" Virginia could not; the following day it passed an ordinance of secession that would be ratified by public referendum the following month. In North Carolina, however, the issue continued to hang fire. A month after Pender bade farewell to the army he had faithfully served for many years, the secession convention that had finally convened in Raleigh had yet to vote on the issue before it. "If they do not act and that soon," Pender wrote from Raleigh, where he had gone to obtain an appointment in the armies of the Confederacy, "N.C. is a doomed state—either to subjugation or eternal disgrace."[34]

By the time Pender wrote, North Carolina's governor, John W. Ellis, had called for the formation of 10 regiments for state defense and had spent several thousand dollars to equip and support them. Even so, as Pender told Fanny, "every one nearly admits that we are totally deficient in military progress, and that volunteers are bad enough at the best.... I am disgusted with North Carolina and am convinced that nothing can be done until we are badly whipt." His frustration eased and his embarrassment faded only after May 20, when the convention voted to send North Carolina out of the Union—the 11th and last state to so declare.[35]

Many historians, analyzing Pender's statements on the national mood, misconstrue his motives in opting to leave one army and join another. One of the most recent to discuss this matter, Gary Gallagher, pronounces Pender an eager secessionist and ardent Confederate. Nothing could be farther from the truth. Pender did not want to see his country ripped apart by war; he wanted only to defend his native state. "We fight for protection," he declared, while Northerners fought only for "revenge and stubbornness." Still, if only in a geopolitical sense—surrounded as it was by states that had already left the Union—North Carolina's secession was a matter of time. That being the case, Pender wished to see the die cast sooner rather than later. He feared the impression that delay would give the country and particularly the South: that the Tarheel State was reluctant to defend its honor against the usurpation of the federal government.[36]

As a regular army officer, educated and experienced in his profession, Pender could choose no other course than to continue his military career in the Confederate ranks. Advancement in his specialty mattered to him; no sooner had he indicated his intention to resign from the army of his nation than he sought rank—preferably higher than that he had achieved in the 1st Dragoons—in the forces of the South. When he received his first commission in those ranks, he described it strictly in economic terms. "Pay $1689.00 per annum," he told Fanny. "Little better just in these hard times than commencing on a small scale raising stock.... we will be pretty well off."[37]

Professional considerations aside, he did not go gladly into the armies of secession. He never admitted to a great devotion to Confederate nationhood. More than a year into the war, he called Fanny's attention to the irony of his situation: "Here I am not only risking my life in battle but by any of the various camp diseases in a cause which really primarily affects me but little...." In another letter, written a year later, he predicted that God would smite Yankeedom for forcing war upon the South, even "granting that we were wrong morally and politically." Nor did he believe in the economic grounds on which many Southerners justified secession; his distaste for slavery never weakened.[38]

Pender saw his course clearly and with unflinching honesty. He would fight for his state, his home, and his family, and he would do so in the manner of a professional soldier. But he would not delude himself into thinking that by leaving the U.S. Army and the Union he was embarking on a holy crusade.

Chapter Three

ACTIVE SERVICE

B efore war became a reality, even before his resignation took effect, Pender angled for position in the army he planned to join. In the second week in March he left Fanny, now seven months pregnant, in the care of her parents and her younger sister, Pamela, and entrained for Raleigh. There he had a brief audience with Governor Ellis and secured his support in gaining a commission with the provisional army of the Confederacy. Then he continued on to the capital at Montgomery.

On the 14th he presented himself at the office of Confederate Secretary of War Leroy Pope Walker. Although he did not at first see the secretary himself, he had a promising interview with Major George Deas of Walker's staff. Afterward Pender submitted a formal application on which he noted his West Point education, his service in Florida, New Mexico, and the Northwest, and the fact that he had been "mentioned three times for conduct in Indian engagements." He also displayed letters of recommendation from Ellis and other prominent North Carolinians. At least one of these had been written by Pender's father-in-law. The ex-congressman touted the loyalty, experience, and "high character of Lt. P. as a gentleman and an officer...."[1]

Having weighed his options carefully, Pender applied for a captaincy in the Confederate artillery. As he later informed Governor Ellis, such a position "is as much as any resigned officer of the same grade as myself" could hope to procure. It represented a promotion from his old rank, something he believed he had earned if only because he had not waited for his state to secede before entering the lists. He sought a berth in the artillery because his prior service in that arm, brief as it had been, recommended him for the position. While he no longer craved the life of a dragoon or cavalryman, he had not rejected mounted service completely. He told his wife that he might try for a position in the horse artillery, which traveled with and fought alongside an army's horse soldiers.[2]

Despite his preference, following the interview Major Deas informed him that he would gain a position in the infantry as soon as one became available. Pender put the best face on the outcome. As he informed Fanny, because his prior service was distinguished enough to stand him in good stead with the authorities in Montgomery, "I shall be pretty well up the list of captains." The pay that accompanied the position amounted to $1,350 per year. While not a munificent sum, it was more than he had earned in what was already becoming known as the Old Army. Thus, he could rate his visit to the capital as "very successful so far as I can tell."[3]

He remained in Montgomery for a week, during which time rumors of assignments and postings swirled about him like chaff in a storm. One report had Colonel William J. Hardee, tactical theorist, former commandant of cadets at West Point, and one of the most distinguished officers to have switched allegiances thus far, seeking his services at his Savannah headquarters. When that prospect fell through, Walker's office announced that he would go to Pensacola Harbor, where Florida troops under Brigadier General Braxton Bragg were trying unsuccessfully to reduce Fort Pickens, one of two federal garrisons in Southern territory fated to remain in Union hands throughout the war.[4]

The day the Pensacola assignment was broached to him, March 16, Pender learned that he was to be commissioned a captain in the Confederate service—not in the infantry, as he had supposed, but in the artillery, after all. He was happy that his services had been accepted so quickly—happy, too, at the prospect of leaving Montgomery, "for it is not pleasant to loaf in a large city much less in a small one." He was nevertheless impressed by the hum of activity that pervaded Walker's office, an indication that the fledgling army was quickly getting off the ground.

Another indication was the arrival in Montgomery during Pender's stay of a highly touted addition to the army: Brigadier General Samuel Cooper, a New York native who had been the adjutant general, U.S.A., before accepting the dual position of adjutant general and inspector general of the Confederate forces. "When such men as Col. Cooper gives up such a position ... to join us," Pender mused, "it looks like [war in] earnest." The presence in Walker's office of Major Deas, a Pennsylvanian by birth, emphasized the point.[5]

By March 17, Pender was about to depart Montgomery for Pensacola when Secretary Walker canceled the assignment without explanation. Instead, the newly minted captain—undoubtedly to his displeasure—was put to work in the War Office until a permanent posting could be offered him. In the interim, he received formal notification of his appointment as captain of artillery, to rank from the 16th, and he duly noted his acceptance of it.[6]

His situation was finally settled on March 21, when General Cooper, in one of his first acts in his new post, ordered Pender to "proceed with as little delay as possible to Baltimore, Md., on duties connected with the recruiting service." Thus the responsibilities he had refused to assume at Carlisle Barracks were to be thrust upon him in Maryland.[7]

During a private audience with Walker, Pender was told that he would take the place of an officer whom Brigadier General P. G. T. Beauregard, the commander in the tension-filled city of Charleston, had failed to send to Baltimore as ordered, "for the special service." Walker further informed Pender that once in Maryland he would answer to U.S. Senator Louis T. Wigfall of Texas, who for some weeks had been trying to raise troops for the Confederacy in that border-state metropolis. Following the interview, Walker wired the fiery Texan that Captain Pender would help him inspect likely recruits and oversee their shipment to training camps farther south. The secretary added: "Such money as he may require within the scope of his business you will arrange for him to have."[8]

Pender spent a couple of days tying up affairs in Montgomery before boarding a northbound train. He reached Baltimore on Sunday evening, March 24. Next morning he headed back south and spent the balance of the day conferring with Wigfall, who was lingering in Washington despite having resigned his Senate seat five days before.

Pender returned to Baltimore on the morning of the 26th. From there he wrote Fanny of his duties: "I am sending men South to be enlisted in the Southern Army. I merely inspect and ship them. I do nothing that the law could take hold of if they [Union officials] wish to trouble me." Although United States Army troops patrolled the city's outlying districts, "Baltimore is strong for secession, and I am backed up by the sympathy of the first [i.e., the leading] men here. The police, Marshall [sic], and nearly all are with us.... Do not fear for me whatever you may see in the papers, for rest assured that in the first place I shall be prudent and in the second I am well backed."[9]

Despite the support given him by Wigfall and local secessionists, during the sixteen days Pender toiled in Baltimore he failed to recruit enough troops to fill the regiment of infantry the senator had promised to deliver. Pender met with numerous able-bodied young men who professed to sympathize with the Confederate cause. Relatively few, however, were willing to enlist absent unmistakable signs of war. By April 3 he had sent only 126 enlistees by boat to Montgomery, barely enough to man two of the ten companies a regiment comprised. Still, he enjoyed his experience in the city. He lodged in a comfortable home on Exchange Street, received the praise and encouragement of local people on a daily basis, and dined with "one or two nice gentlemen." He supported his family by sending Fanny a portion of the first paycheck he received as a Confederate officer: seventy-seven dollars and fifteen cents, covering two weeks' service. To his wife's great pleasure, he even attended Sunday services at an Episcopal church and found the rector's sermon "delightful."[10]

Originally it was intended that he should stay in Baltimore for "some weeks." Instead, he abruptly ended his visit on April 11 in response to a telegram recalling him to Montgomery. His timing was fortuitous; on the steamer that carried him down the Potomac he spoke with a Confederate peace commissioner just returned from Washington. The man relayed confidential information that Fort Sumter, South Carolina, was to be fired on within 24 hours.[11]

The informant spoke the truth; at 4:30 the next morning, Beauregard's land and water batteries began to pound the garrison in Charleston Harbor. When the bombardment ended 34 hours later with Sumter raising a white flag, the news had already spread war fever across the country. Suddenly the conflict that Pender had observed taking shape over the past decade was at hand.

*   *   *

Stifling the urge to stop over at Good Spring to visit his very pregnant wife, Pender proceeded to Montgomery, which would remain the capital of the Confederacy until the government relocated to Richmond in late May. Yet he never reached Alabama; he was in Raleigh, conferring with representatives of Governor Ellis, when Secretary Walker rescinded the earlier order and permitted him to remain in his home state. The reprieve enabled him to make the trip to Good Spring, where he found Fanny in tolerable health and good spirits as she neared the end of her term. Her husband nevertheless worried about her delicate constitution, which seemed to assure her of a difficult delivery.[12]

He was still worrying when, on or about April 25, he returned to Raleigh at the urging of the governor, who had recently defied the federal government with warlike rhetoric. In the wake of the Sumter crisis, President Lincoln had called on the governors of every state but South Carolina to furnish militia to help the federal government deal with "combinations too powerful to be suppressed" by local marshals or the regular army. In refusing, the fiery but sickly Ellis had denounced the president's action as a "wicked violation of the laws of the country." Now the governor feared an invasion of his state, something he would not permit to happen without putting up a fight.[13]

Upon his arrival in Raleigh, Pender found the governor in urgent need of his talents as a drill instructor. Ellis wanted him to command the camp of instruction that had been established upon the city's fairgrounds as a rendezvous for local recruits. Enough volunteers to man the 1st North Carolina State Troops, one of ten regiments raised by the legislature in response to the national crisis, had reported to camp but without the uniforms, arms, equipment, and officers needed to make soldiers of them. Willing to serve his state in any capacity, Pender accepted the appointment, thereupon becoming a lieutenant colonel of state troops in addition to a captain in the Confederate service.

As he headed for the fairgrounds, he hoped that the military prowess of the 1st North Carolina would be such that he would have to do little more than tap its potential, but he feared that he had much work to do. He wanted to win high rank in the outfit. Despite being raised by the state, the 1st would elect its own officers including its colonel and, as the ambitious drill-master informed his wife, "I have determined to accept it if I can get it."[14]

Upon arriving at the regimental rendezvous, his worst fears were realized. Almost at once he saw that he would have to create a regiment from scratch, and without delay. Very few of the inhabitants of the training camp, which included a company from Pender's home county, had military experience—not even a nodding acquaintance with the profession. The majority knew nothing of soldiering beyond the patriotic gore that filled their history books. Many had the notion that war was a game, a tournament, even a picnic. Everyone wanted an opportunity to pitch into the mudsills and mechanics of the North; a few feared that political maneuvering would end the crisis before they could see action.

The false confidence and misplaced enthusiasm Pender encountered at the training camp bothered him more than the recruits' ignorance of things military. The fact that the 1st North Carolina had enlisted for only six months' service told Pender—who was certain that the coming conflict would be long and destructive—that the volunteers were playing at war. The basic problem was hubris: "The Southern people—as a class—think our southern men equal to ten Yankees." Another problem was a reluctance to get one's hands dirty: "The idea of their being brought together and having to submit to inconvenience to prepare them for service is something they cannot see the use of."[15]

From the first he made himself unpopular in camp by drumming into the recruits the basics of their adopted profession. Although he was largely responsible for the enviable reputation the 1st acquired even before leaving its state—Brigadier General Gabriel Rains, an old veteran, would describe it as "the best regiment" he had ever inspected in North Carolina—Pender's training regimen prompted disgruntled men to slip out of camp under cover of night, never to return. "A part of the boasted Edgecombe Company have left," he admitted to Fanny on April 28, "and more speak of leaving.... I shall not be surprised at any time to find our Camp deserted."[16]

The situation improved, and Pender's burden lightened, when, at month's end, Daniel Harvey Hill, a West Pointer and former superintendent of the North Carolina Military Institute, arrived in camp along with other experienced officers including former artillery lieutenant Stephen Dodson Ramseur. With their coming, Pender's state of mind improved enough that he could tell Fanny not to "trouble yourself about me, imagining that I am dissatisfied.... I am [as] well off as any one these times. We all have our troubles and annoyances, every one of us." He transferred his ire from the 1st North Carolina to Governor Ellis, whom he accused of refusing to spend the full amount of the military preparedness appropriation the legislature had enacted. "I have never seen," he huffed, "a public officer as mean in money matters."[17]

On May 4, the men of the 1st North Carolina elected someone to command them. Despite his initial decision to seek the colonelcy of the outfit, Pender was thankful that the honor went to D. H. Hill. By now he had repented of his rashness. The idea of commanding this gaggle of volunteers having lost its charm, he had "made up my mind [that] nothing should tempt me again to commit myself."[18]

When Hill took over Pender's recent duties, the latter cast about for another position in which he could help his state and, at the same time, advance his career. By mid-May he had written to the adjutant general of North Carolina, William J. Hoke, asking to be relieved from duty at Raleigh. His plan was to apply to the government in Montgomery for authority to recruit a company in the Good Spring area. Although a unit that small would not raise him above his captaincy in the Confederate service, he could organize and train it close to his wife's side as she endured the final weeks of her pregnancy.

His plans were dashed when, before he could contact Montgomery, Ellis ordered him north to Garysburg, not far from the Virginia line, where one of the six training camps that had been established throughout the state was located. Once there, he was to whip into shape one of the 12-month regiments being raised by private individuals rather than by the state authorities, the 3rd North Carolina Volunteers. Although Pender did not hesitate to obey, the thought of trading one collection of raw recruits for another did not thrill him. But then the governor, the adjutant general, and other state officials began to heap praise on him. They managed to persuade him that only he had the experience, the know-how, and the personal magnetism to turn the 3rd Volunteers into an outfit of which the Old North State would be proud.[19]

Appeals to Pender's fitness for high command—especially at this early stage of the war, with his service as a lowly subaltern so fresh in his memory— were highly effective. In fact, he freely admitted that ego and vanity posed problems for him: "I like the approbation of others and let it affect me." When a state judge, a friend of his family, telegraphed him to ask if he would consent to lead one of the regiments of state troops should the command be offered him, he confided to Fanny that "it makes one proud to think that my wife's husband is of enough consequence to be asked to take a Colonelcy when so many other ones are seeking it."[20]

For a time, he considered his susceptibility to flattery a harmless vice. Only later would he come to see that "I love too much the applause of men." Meanwhile, an associated weakness—his love for the applause of women—would cause problems of a different kind.[21]

*   *   *

To Pender's mind, in many ways the 3rd North Carolina Volunteers was the 1st North Carolina State Troops all over again. But although he encountered in Garysburg the same problems that had frustrated him at Raleigh—untrained but overconfident enlistees, resentful muttering on the drill-field, complaints and desertions—he came to see potential in the raw material at his disposal. The men were unmilitary, but they were also patriotic, determined, and eager for the fray. Many of them were also good shots, as target practice indicated, and they learned drill-field maneuvers with relative ease. In time he came to consider the 3rd "the best Regt. yet formed."[22]

Even more than the quality of the rank-and-file, Pender was impressed by the caliber of several men who would become line officers in the regiment. Only a few were from the planter aristocracy, which Pender considered a source of effete, feckless youth. Most were members of the upper-middle class, many of them professionals—lawyers, physicians, educators—who in the stratified society of rural North Carolina wore the mantle of leadership like a tailored suit. The list included Alfred Moore Scales, Thomas Ruffin, Thomas Setter, J. H. Hyman, and John Graves.[23]

These and other prominent recruits not only looked to Pender for training but thought highly enough of him to ask him to stand as a candidate for command of the regiment. When Pender did not immediately decline, Scales—a man of political prominence, having been both a state legislator and a United States congressman—entrained for Raleigh. There he sought the assistance of officials, including former Senator Thomas L. Clingman, in gaining Jefferson Davis's approval of Pender's permanent transfer from Confederate to state service.

When Scales returned to Garysburg with the president's consent, Pender felt duty bound to accept the colonelcy if offered to him. On May 25 he was unanimously nominated for the position by the officers, and two days later he won the position by vote of the full regiment. Soon he was heading back to

Raleigh to confer with Ellis on matters relating to the equipping of the outfit. He received his commission in the governor's office on the 27th, along with Ellis's congratulations and his promise that the 3rd Volunteers would never lack his moral or material support.[24]

The new colonel returned to Garysburg via Good Spring, where his recent run of success and satisfaction culminated in the birth of his second son on May 28. The boy remained unnamed for a brief period before the parents agreed on William Dorsey Pender Jr.[25]

Pender's duty schedule was such that he could remain with his growing family for no more than a couple of days. One day after "Dorse" Pender came into the world, his father's regiment was ordered from Garysburg to southeastern Virginia. The transfer had been prompted by fears of an enemy invasion of the territory immediately south of Hampton Roads.

Even as troops under Brigadier General Irvin McDowell were preparing to march from Washington, D.C. to Richmond, other Yankees, most of them led by a politician-general, Benjamin Franklin Butler, had reinforced Fort Monroe and other points on the Virginia Peninsula. Although most of the bluecoats held the north shore of Chesapeake Bay, where few defenses opposed them, the Confederate commander at Norfolk, Brigadier General Benjamin F. Huger, feared that they would soon cross "to this side, where we have guns."[26]

Huger's immediate concern was the Suffolk area, where the Norfolk & Petersburg Railroad intersected the railroad that linked Portsmouth, Virginia, and Weldon, North Carolina. Both lines had strategic value for the Confederacy, but neither was guarded in strength. Thus, when it left Garysburg on May 29, the 3rd Volunteers made directly for the vulnerable sector, pitching camp next day near the rail junction. Pender went directly from Good Spring to Suffolk, joining his outfit there on the 30th. He noted that when the 3rd arrived it relieved a few companies who had been trying, without much success, to cover the length of both railroads.

The threats his regiment suddenly faced made Pender aware that he was finally at the front, or at least very near it. Another sudden realization gave him less satisfaction. Not long after the 3rd set up camp, General Huger arrived to inspect it, making Pender conscious of his inferior rank. "The nearer to the scene of active operations we get," he told Fanny, "the less my importance grows."[27]

The 3rd remained for only a month in its camp at Suffolk, which Pender described as offering "fine shade, fine spring water, and good drill ground." Short as it was, that period produced events that affected the life of the regiment and its colonel. Within a week of the 3rd's arrival, Pender assumed an enlarged command, consisting of "one cavalry camp, besides our own, and… several post[s] besides this." When confined to regimental duties, he drilled his regiment as unremittingly as he had the 1st North Carolina, provoking the displeasure of many men but gaining the grudging respect of as many others.[28]

He devoted much time to helping his officers become conversant with their responsibilities. He was especially solicitous toward his older brother, David, who, via a pardonable exercise of nepotism, had become commissary officer of the regiment with the rank of first lieutenant. Although Pender believed his brother would become an efficient supply manager he was alternately amused and aggravated by David's acute homesickness. David found his estrangement from his wife, Mary, especially painful—a condition with which Dorsey Pender could sympathize. "Poor David," he wrote Fanny, "is the most miserable man you ever saw. He broods over the future all the time. Oh! how blest I am, [that] he who deserves so much happiness should have so much misery and I who am less deserving should be so blest." By mid-June, David was considering giving up his commission and returning home. Pender was grieved by the possibility, but he may have had a replacement—another relative—waiting in the wings. On several occasions he assured Fanny that he was doing all in his power to add her younger brother, Jake, to his staff. His efforts eventually paid off, but not until the fall of 1862.[29]

At Suffolk, the 3rd Volunteers not only learned the fundamentals of soldiering, it became a cohesive unit in which officers and men worked closely toward a common goal. On June 1 the outfit was sworn into Confederate service for a year; but when the Confederacy's field forces were reorganized the following spring, the 3rd, like every regiment in the army, was required to serve for the duration of the conflict. A few days after muster-in, the outfit was presented with two small Confederate flags made by a local woman. Pender elected to use them as file markers, but soon afterward he asked Fanny and her sister Pamela to make two full-size, silken banners bearing the regiment's name. When the task turned out to be beyond the sisters' capabilities, Pender purchased a gilt-fringed battle flag from a manufacturer in Richmond at a cost of sixty dollars in Confederate money.[30]

Flags were not the only gifts the local people bestowed on Pender and his men. Soon after reaching Suffolk, he was presented with a fine horse, complete with a full set of tack, the gift of two prominent businessmen. The steed, the first of several Pender would acquire in the army, he named Jim. The gelding was "really a very fine horse—goes well under the saddle and splendidly in harness." When informing Fanny of the gift, whose value exceeded four hundred dollars, he not only stressed his gratitude but took a swipe at his own family. He was more than a little chagrined that "rich relatives" had permitted strangers to furnish him with resources critical to his military service but which he himself could not afford. "Put not your trust in relatives," he warned his wife.[31]

In addition to showering their guests with tokens of esteem, the locals invited Pender and his officers to a series of collations and dances staged in their honor. Pender much appreciated these displays of hospitality, especially when comely young women had a hand in them. The praise they lavished on him, his regiment, and its camp, went directly to his head. In time, Pender began to suspect that he was a social lion.

This bit of self-delusion was harmless enough on the surface, but it had the power to do him harm. He made matters worse by telling Fanny about his socializing. One of his motives in doing so was to impress his wife with the esteem that he commanded in Virginia—"the idea," as he put it, "that Mrs. W. D. Pender's husband, altho' poor is considered a man of some merit." Another motive—perhaps an unconscious one—was a desire to arouse Fanny's jealousy. If so, he missed his mark by a wide margin.[32]

Beginning with one he wrote the day he reached Suffolk, his letters to Good Spring contained references to unmarried women and the attentions they paid him. "There are lots of beautiful girls here," he observed on May 30, adding that "when I have nothing else to do, I can look at something beautiful or fine." On June 2 he reported that he had "dined today with the most beautiful girl in Suffolk—and it has [a] great many very pretty ones." In the same letter he took pains to assure Fanny that "every woman I see has to undergo a comparison with you and none will stand the test, none ..." But his protestations of love did not prevent him, less than a week later, from bragging that local hostesses took turns keeping "my table covered with flowers and smile on me in the most bewitching manner."[33]

Why he wrote so proudly and so often of his romantic escapades to the woman he professed to adore, and who had just given birth to their second child, appears to defy reason. If he did not realize that Fanny would take offense, he was surely the densest of husbands. Perhaps he was merely showing off in a manner he considered humorous. He may have reasoned that his wife would see his behavior for what it was, a harmless fling. If she chose to regard it as something more serious, chances were she would not comment on it. After all, Fanny prized decorum almost as much as he did.

In fact, for some weeks she tolerated the ego massaging he indulged in at her expense. But on the evening of June 24 he went too far, and he made the mistake of recording the incident in detail. That evening he attended "a little gathering" in Suffolk, "and had a very nice time dancing and flirting with a very nice girl. I am trying to get her to knit you a sac for the hair, but she said that she is not going to work for my wife, but will do anything for me...."[34]

At least one of Pender's biographers believes that the colonel's head had been turned so completely by the "beautiful girls here" that he was seriously considering an extramarital affair. No evidence supports the theory, although Pender acted with amazing indiscretion and treated his wife with a degree of thoughtlessness uncommon in officers and gentlemen. No wonder that Fanny stopped writing to him for sometime after receiving the account of his flirtation. Her silence worried him, but he felt better when he received a letter from her on July 2. Curiously, it was headed "Read to end." He did so, to his sorrow.[35]

Fanny began by answering some questions her husband had put to her in a recent missive, including inquiries about her health (she had just recovered from an illness that had kept her bedridden for weeks). In reply to his complaints that she wrote him too infrequently, she explained that while he could write letters in the quiet of his tent, "I never sit down to write a letter that I do not have to get up half a dozen times to perform some little service either for the baby or for someone else. And often, I attempt to write with both children screaming in my ears...." For all that, "I never intended to neglect you."

She did intend to set some matters straight between them, though. She continued in a tone mostly sober and a bit sarcastic: "I have never in the whole course of my married [life] done anything deliberately that I knew would pain you—your will has always been my law—and I have ever tried to obey to the very letter the commands of my Lord and master...." It appeared, however, that she alone remembered their wedding vows. She repeated the words in which he had described his flirtation, and asked:

> ...why you wrote me such a thing as that? Was it to gratify your vanity by making me jealous, or to make me appreciate your love still more? You

are very much mistaken. I feel indignant that any woman should have dared to make such loose speeches to my husband and that he should have encouraged it by his attentions, for you must have gone pretty far for a woman to attempt such a liberty.

My dear, ever dear Husband, do not think this is only a little jealous feeling.… I never thought to hear that he, whom I loved above all the world, whom I respected and esteemed till now, would stoop to listen to such improper language—do you think the lady would have made such a remark in my presence? Then it was not proper for you to hear. I never expected to hear you admit that you had been flirting. What would you think to hear me use such an expression?

…I know you love me, my dear Husband. I have had too many sweet and precious proofs of it to doubt it now.… I have forgotten all the anger I felt at first—but I can never forget that letter—nothing you have ever written in this whole of our married life—ever pained me so acutely or grieved me so deeply. I know you are sorry for it now, for you must feel it to be unjust, but it is enough to know that you could, in any mood say so much to pain me.…"

Your faithful Wife.[36]

Contrary to Fanny's belief, her husband had not repented of his flirtation, in which he professed to see no wrong. When he wrote in reply to her admonition, he tried to portray himself as the aggrieved party: "If you knew what I have suffered since receiving this letter.… That letter was in my mind awake and sleeping, and again and again would my grief have to be relieved by tears. If you had simply said I do not love you I could have stood it, but to accuse me of dishonorable acts.… if you knew how much I suffered you would believe me sincere [in] what I've said."[37]

In these words he implied that the sorrow she had provoked in him was apology enough for any pain he had inflicted on her, however unintentionally. Her reaction was far out of proportion to his alleged offense. Thus he, more than she, was being treated unfairly. He dramatized his contention that she had wronged him by returning her letter, believing that the gesture "would be better than writing you an unkind one myself."

Pender feared (or professed to fear) that her angry letter— more than the act that had provoked it—threatened their marriage. He told Fanny that for a time after reading her missive, "I had about made up my mind that we were henceforth to be as strangers"—whatever that meant. His was a classic attempt to shift blame, to accuse the accuser, to muddy the waters—an action perhaps more reprehensible than his flirtation. At least, however, he did not carry out his implied threat to end their marriage. He was willing, he told her, to allow the whole thing to blow over ("honey let it pass") and to refrain from any future extracurricular activities—or at least from mentioning them. Two weeks after receiving her "Read to end" letter, he attempted to put an end to the subject: "Say nothing more about [it], and rest assured [that it would not drive a wedge between them]." To this proposal his long-suffering wife apparently assented.[38]

*   *   *

While Colonel Pender was skirmishing on the homefront, action of another kind was sweeping Hampton Roads. On June 10, a week after he began to instruct the 3rd Volunteers in a variety of battlefield evolutions, another regiment he had helped train—the 1st North Carolina State Troops—helped win for the Confederacy the first land battle in the Virginia theater. Through pluck and determination, D. H. Hill's men met and repulsed an advance by a Union force twice as large as they. General Butler had sent the sizable detachment to seize a strategic outpost near Big Bethel Church, ten miles above Fort Monroe. Hill's success was notable not only because it showcased Confederate might but because it validated Pender's efforts to make the 1st North Carolina (which thereafter would be known as the "Bethel Regiment") combat-ready.

The victory nevertheless left Pender with two regrets: that his regiment had not had a hand in it; and that one of his West Point classmates, Lieutenant John T. Greble of the 2nd United States Artillery, had died in the fighting. Pender considered the Philadelphia-born Greble, the first Regular Army officer to give his life in the conflict, a "noble fellow" whose heart was not fully with the Union cause.[39]

Instead of waging glorious battle, the 3rd Volunteers continued to drill, to take target practice, and to tend to camp chores. In its free time, the regiment, as also its colonel, followed newspaper accounts of operations in northeastern Virginia and in the Shenandoah Valley. In both theaters, Confederate recruits were opposed by larger if no more experienced Union armies. Given the numerical odds his comrades-in-arms faced, Pender was not sanguine about their long-term fortunes. Still, their commanders were officers of proven ability: General Joseph E. Johnston of Virginia, a stalwart of the prewar army who commanded in the Harpers Ferry vicinity, and Brigadier General Beauregard, who had left Charleston to lead the troops massing near Centreville and Manassas Junction to block access to Richmond. Inspired leadership could neutralize at least some of the enemy's advantages. It had done so at Big Bethel, prompting Pender to tell Fanny that "we certainly have cause to thank God for … his goodness and Divine Protection."[40]

If his regiment could see action under Johnston or Beauregard, Pender believed it could do the Confederacy some good. By late June he was thinking that, man for man, the 3rd Volunteers was as good an outfit as any North Carolina had sent to the war; it lacked only the validating experience of battle. Even so, he worried that its potential was being compromised by inadequate support from Raleigh. Despite the governor's promise to keep the 3rd well supplied, it continued to lack the most basic camp equipage. Pender had made out at least one requisition that the state appears to have ignored. It called for 120 tents and 850 shoes, knapsacks, haversacks, canteens, camp kettles, and mess pans, plus smaller quantities of axes, spades, and other fatigue equipment, "none of the above articles having yet been issued to the Regt."[41]

By June 12 he had determined to secure those items on penalty of resigning his commission. That morning he started for Raleigh to "have a row" with the governor, but events conspired to keep him at Suffolk. In his stead he sent Captains Scales and Ruffin, both of whom enjoyed more clout in the capital. Their mission ended in success, at least to the extent that in subsequent weeks Ellis saw to it that the 3rd was as well supplied as any North Carolina unit serving away from home. Apparently Ellis, whose health had deteriorated under the burdens mobilization had heaped on him, could do no more than this. Even so, his renewed support showed quick results. On the 18th, a visitor to Suffolk told readers of the Raleigh *Register* about "the neatness and good order which characterizes The Camp," which he considered "abundant proof" of Pender's "efficiency as a commander."[42]

Having won his struggle with the governor and with no struggle with the Yankees imminent, Pender suddenly decided that his life was static and dull. Elsewhere, it was a different story. Activity of great consequence was occurring not only in the Shenandoah Valley and along the Manassas line, but in the northwestern corner of the state, where Brigadier General Robert Selden Garnett was operating against Union outposts at the head of a command that included two of Pender's classmates, Lieutenant Colonel J. E. B. Stuart of the Virginia Cavalry and Lieutenant Colonel John Pegram, a sometime-brigade commander.

Pender was jealous of the opportunity his mates enjoyed to win promotion and glory in an active theater while he whiled away the days guarding railroads that no Yankees cared to threaten. By June 28 he was telling Fanny that everyone at Suffolk "was getting tired of loafing, and if we stay here much longer, my trouble will increase, for some of the Regt. are getting to behave differently from what I could wish." Despite the growing unrest, he no longer thought of resigning: "They are the best set of men I ever saw, and I would not leave them for anything in the world, except my dear wife and children."[43]

Fortunately for everyone's peace of mind, on July 4 the 3rd Volunteers celebrated Independence Day by breaking camp and leaving Suffolk for points north and west. Crossing the James River, the men put down stakes along Pagan Creek, six miles south of the colonial village of Smithfield. There, having been assigned temporarily to a brigade commanded by Huger's artillery chief, Brigadier General John C. Pemberton, the 3rd traded guarding railroads for guarding cannons. Batteries of long-range guns, mostly 32-pounders, had been emplaced along the south bank of the James to prevent incursions by Yankees stationed at Newport News and other points on the lower peninsula.

Here the regiment was kept busier than it ever had been at Suffolk. At Pemberton's decree, it was fragmented to guard a four-mile stretch of riverbank. Each day Pender traveled from one point to another to keep tabs on his outposts, some of which were encased by earthworks. As he informed Fanny, the detachments "can see all the movements of the enemy by water, at Newport News. It would amuse you to see the curiosity evinced by our men at every movement of theirs."[44]

Pender and the main body of the regiment manned Camp Ruffin, which had been carved by painstaking labor out of a dense thicket near Isle of Wight Church. Pender called the result "anything but agreeable in looks or in comfort" and complained that the dead vegetation that had been excavated to make way for the camp "smells terribly in my tent."[45]

Despite his peripatetic service on the James, Pender's life quickly settled into the same monotonous pattern it had assumed at Suffolk. He missed his wife more than ever before. The day after pitching his new camp, he told Fanny that "it is certainly lonely enough [here] to satisfy a monk." Passing time failed to improve the situation. On July 11, he mused that "I did not believe such a lonely place could be found in Va."[46]

He welcomed any interruption in the flow of events. Despite the inconvenience it caused, he even rejoiced to appear as a witness before a court-martial sitting in Portsmouth. Within a week, however, he had returned to the tedious daily routine at Isle of Wight Church. To take his mind off the ennui, he pored over newspaper accounts of operations in other, active theaters, including western Virginia. There on July 11 the federals of Major General George B. McClellan overwhelmed General Garnett's force at Rich Mountain, securing western Virginia for the Union. Two days later the victors fell upon the survivors at Corrick's Ford, routing them, killing Garnett and two dozen of his men, and capturing 550 others including John Pegram. Writing of Garnett's and Pegram's fate, Pender noted that Corrick's Ford "was a sad day for the South. Two finer men and better officers are not to be found."[47]

He also paid close attention to reports of skirmishing by Johnston's troops in the Valley and by Beauregard's along Bull Run. Toward the latter site, more than 30,000 federals were marching, having left Washington on the 16th. Pender kept his fingers crossed: Corrick's Ford had been a blow to the Southern cause, but a defeat on Bull Run might sound its death knell. For one thing, it would curtail the efforts of the European powers—many of whom were sympathetic to the Confederacy—to intervene in the fight. Pender relayed to Fanny a rumor that "England [and] France are… certain to recognize our Confederacy. France is to lend money and England is sending troops to Canada. If it proves to be true we are certainly in luck and need not fear the result. I hope sincerely that something may turn up to cause peace to be made and that speedily." Perhaps mindful of his narrow escape from marital disaster, he added: "I prefer quiet and my family to war and separation."[48]

As if on cue, his wish was granted. On July 21, three days after he invited Fanny "to come down to see me" at Smithfield, she arrived for a three-week visit. The happy reunion appears to have smoothed over the rift his indiscretion had caused. It was also, as one biographer notes, "just the tonic for his depression." For a time, he could forget the behind-the-lines duty that had sidetracked his career. Instead, he could make Fanny at home in camp. He introduced her to each of his officers as well as to many of the enlisted men, and he drilled and paraded the regiment not only for its own good but also for her pleasure. On Sunday, he escorted her to and from a local church, an old habit he had forgotten. He confessed that he had not attended services during the past three months.[49]

Fanny's visit coincided with momentous news from the north. Within a day of her arrival, the camp was abuzz with news of a major clash of arms along Bull Run. On the 21st the raw but spirited troops of McDowell had attacked the left flank of Beauregard's line north of Manassas Junction. Beauregard's much smaller army would have been at the Yankees' mercy except that over a several-day period it had been reinforced by the bulk of Johnston's command, which, having given its enemy the slip, had hastened from the Valley aboard the cars of the Manassas Gap Railroad.

Suddenly equal to the enemy in strength and superior to them in tenacity, the Southerners turned back McDowell's flank drive as well as his subsequent advances elsewhere along the line. By late afternoon, following hours of inconclusive struggle under a torrid sun, the last of Johnston's troops to arrive turned the tide and sent the Federals on a slow, then a speedy and panicky, retreat toward the Washington defenses. By day's end, the new capital at Richmond had been saved, at least temporarily, and Confederate nationhood no longer seemed such a fragile vision.[50]

The fight near Manassas worked not only to the Confederacy's advantage but to Colonel Pender's as well. The fatalities among the nearly 2,000 casualties with which Johnston and Beauregard had purchased victory included Colonel Charles P. Fisher, whose 6th North Carolina State Troops had anchored the left flank during the critical phase of the battle. Fisher, a prewar railroad official, was not a professional soldier, but he had won the respect of his men by his fearless leadership. His death was felt so keenly in the ranks of the 6th that surviving subordinates appealed to Governor Henry Toole Clark, successor to the recently deceased John Ellis, to appoint a new colonel as quickly as possible. Ordinarily, the regiment's second-in-command, Lieutenant Colonel Charles E. Lightfoot, would have moved up to fill the vacancy, but he was not a North Carolinian; furthermore, unlike his superior, he had not distinguished himself at Manassas.[51]

By mid-August, when Fanny Pender reluctantly left Smithfield to return home, her husband had learned of the vacancy in the 6th and had decided to put in a bid for the position. Command of a front-line regiment that had served capably in battle appealed to him; to be sure, the job was preferable to guarding river batteries. Apparently, relatives or friends brought his name to the attention of the new governor. Clark, who hailed from Edgecombe County, must have expressed some interest, for by mid-August Pender was "on my way to Raleigh to secure if possible the Colonelcy of the 6th.... If I get the appointment I want to be at Manassas next week."[52]

He did get the appointment, despite the fact that Fisher's officers, who were not acquainted with Pender, failed to include his name in a list of recommended successors. On August 19, after meeting with the candidate—and apparently before receiving the list of recommendations—Clark announced Pender's assignment to the position, to rank from the 17th. The workings of the Confederate bureaucracy were so slow, however, that Pender's transfer from the 3rd Volunteers to the 6th State Troops was dated September 12.

He returned to Smithfield long enough to tend to last-minute administrative details and say his good-byes. All who saluted him or shook his hand in farewell expressed regret that he was leaving. Some of the officers, including Scales, Ruffin, and brother David, spoke of resigning and following him to his new regiment, even if they had to serve in it as private soldiers.

Despite the rigorous training he had put them through, despite the wails of complaint his regimen had provoked, the majority of the rank-and-file shared the sentiments of their officers. "I am convinced," Pender told Fanny with evident pride, "that 4/5 of the Regt. will hate to see me leave. All say that it will go to rack." This Pender doubted, but already his mind was on his new outfit at Manassas. By August 26, he was there in body as well as in thought.[53]

Chapter Four

CHRISTIAN WARRIOR

O n August 26, when he reached Camp Jones at Bristoe Station, four miles south of the recent battlefield, Pender discovered that the 6th North Carolina had gone downhill in the five weeks since the loss of its colonel. The first thing he noticed was the first thing he told Fanny about his new command—the health of the regiment was "terrible. Only about two hundred and thirty [are] fit for duty," dozens of others being "dangerously ill." He was also struck by the unmilitary appearance of the men, many of whom lacked essential clothing and equipment, and by the general lack of discipline and decorum. Morale, he told Fanny, was bad: "They had gotten despondent and truly they had enough to make them so. I find it hard to keep up my spirits with so much sickness and so many deaths. We have had six in the last week and several more will die."[1]

A major reason for the sorry state of the outfit in general, and for its long sick list in particular, was the lack of attention that Lieutenant Colonel

Lightfoot had devoted to the regiment. As Lieutenant Benjamin F. White of the 6th noted in his diary, Lightfoot would now be in Pender's position "had he been dilligent [sic] to care for the sick & attend to the rights and wants of the regiment." Beyond drilling the men to within an inch of their lives—even those who lacked shoes and had become disabled as a result—Lightfoot had been "totally indifferent" to matters that affected the outfit.[2]

Pender, himself a martinet, understood Lightfoot's emphasis on instruction. Although the 6th had a battle under its belt, its men were hardly veterans; they needed all the training they could get. At some point the Yankees, who had fled to Washington where they had been taken over by General McClellan, the hero of western Virginia, would recover their poise and nerve and retake the road to Richmond. Yet Pender also knew what Lightfoot apparently did not: that keeping the soldiers' spirits high and individual and corporate pride strong was at least as important as teaching them how to maneuver on a battlefield.

From the first, he sympathized with his regiment, this flock without a shepherd, as well as with the soldiers' dependents at home. By late September he was seeking outside help, suggesting that if Fanny "could get up a [benefit] concert in behalf of this poor Regt. it would be a good work for those who need it. They are mostly poor men, some of them with starving wives at home. Wives and children crying to them for bread and they unable to help them. What agony they must suffer."[3]

He sympathized, too, with "the anxiety of some poor fathers who come here to see their sick sons." He even decried the plight of the free blacks and slaves employed as officers' servants. "I am horrified," he told Fanny, "to see how *white men* calling themselves gentlemen neglect their poor helpless negroes in this camp. They have free boys in most cases forced from home—and in several cases when they get sick they are allowed to die without any care on the part of those who are responsible for their well being. Two have died here in the last four days and one more will certainly die before many days."[4]

At first, Pender could not say if the complaints lodged against his second-in-command were valid or simply the result of resentment and jealousy. In mid-September he advised Fanny that had Lightfoot "remained much longer in command, the Regt. would have been lost beyond redemption." Even so, the officer had "some good points. He is a nice gentleman and will carry out orders ... [and] is a good assistant." Over time, however, he came to consider Lightfoot more of a liability than an advantage. When the man was transferred to the command of a battalion of Alabama infantry in March 1862, Pender breathed a sigh of relief.[5]

With or without Lightfoot's help, the new colonel set about the task of rescuing the 6th North Carolina from neglect and melancholy. Under Lightfoot the regiment's camp included a single hospital tent; Pender ordered up several additions from the quartermaster depot at Norfolk. He saw to it that medical officers provided more diligent and consistent care of regimental personnel, black as well as white. At least three times a week, he visited the hospital to chat with its inmates as well as with visitors from home. To speed patients' recovery he ensured that they had access not only to the medications they needed but also, in common with their able-bodied comrades, to better-quality rations. As befit his growing interest in Christianity, he also took on the task of officiating at burial services, quoting from a bible that Fanny had given him and which he had begun to study in his spare time. Aware that religion could spur regimental morale, he made efforts to secure a chaplain, something the regiment had lacked for quite awhile.[6]

Pender worked hard to provide the basic resources the 6th lacked. Less than a week after taking command, he petitioned Governor Clark for shoes, tent flies, and miscellaneous camp equipage. Acting on the same impulse that had prompted him to suggest that Fanny stage a concert, he appealed to the womenfolk in the counties from which the regiment had been recruited. In newspaper notices and through word of mouth, he asked them to knit socks, undergarments, and other articles of clothing. His plea was heeded; by September attire of all types—some new, some used but clean—began to flow into Camp Jones, where they found grateful takers.[7]

Pender's efforts to revive regimental morale taxed his physical and emotional strength; so too did his long hours on the drill-plain. As autumn approached, he sometimes feared that "I have lost some of my energy and zeal." Yet he was buoyed up by signs that suggested the outfit was reviving. Its growing proficiency at drill convinced him that most of its men would perform capably in battle. Even so, he believed that the 6th lacked the potential for greatness he had observed in his old outfit: "The men are not so good a class and the officers are nothing like as intelligent" as Scales, Ruffin, and their colleagues.[8]

Pender's hard work on behalf of his command did not go unnoticed. In late September Lieutenant White commented that through recent improvements, there was "more cheerfulness in the regiment than I have seen" in months. Morale was also heightened by command identity. When addressing the troops, Pender made much of the fact that the regiment was a component of a powerful fighting force, the Confederacy's largest in the eastern theater. Once styled the Army of the Potomac, it would soon take on a more enduring name: the Army of Northern Virginia.[9]

At Bristoe Station, unlike at Suffolk or Smithfield, Pender was in contact with the army's leading lights, some with whom he socialized. At the end of August he took tea at army headquarters at Manassas with General Johnston and his visiting wife, an experience that thrilled their guest, especially after the couple recalled having met him, as a lieutenant of dragoons, at Fort Leavenworth. At about the same time, Pender made the acquaintance of another stalwart of the army, William Henry Chase Whiting of Mississippi, who had risen from major to brigadier general on the strength of his gallant performance in the late battle. Pender told Fanny that "what I have seen of Whiting I like very much." He had no inkling that within a few weeks he would be serving in the man's infantry brigade.[10]

Another person Pender thought highly of was within riding distance of his camp after September 19 when the 6th was moved to a new campground 20 miles closer to the Potomac River, near the village of Dumfries. Upon setting up the new home, "Camp Hill," Pender learned that his academy chum, Stephen D. Lee, was in command of a light battery (one of the finest artillery units in Confederate service, in Pender's opinion) that had bivouacked only three miles away. Thereafter, the friends visited on a regular basis; their renewed association reminded Pender that the young South Carolinian was a worthy comrade in every way—in fact, "the salt of the earth."[11]

Before long he was promoting Lee as a potential husband for Fanny's sister, Pamela, whom he had come to regard as "the dearest creature in the world except three—my wife and my children." Pender believed that two people so high in his estimation could not help but attract one another, "but to bring them together is the trouble." As it happened, friend and sister-in-law never met, let alone fell in love, a matter of lingering regret to the colonel of the 6th.[12]

*   *   *

The new camp was situated in an area of rolling hills—some well above 250 feet in height—that had given it its name. Camp Hill was watered by streams that branched off from Powell's Run, a source of excellent drinking water. Nearby Dumfries, an old river port 20 miles above the city of Fredericksburg, contained some of the finest specimens of eighteenth-century architecture in Virginia.

The area had strategic value because of its location astride a principal thoroughfare between Washington and Richmond: the Telegraph Road, along which, 17 years before, Samuel F. B. Morse had strung wire to carry current to his new communications device. In this picturesque locale, Pender and his regiment supported river batteries, including those at Freestone Point and Evansport, that challenged Union shipping in the Potomac. Pender realized that once again he had been assigned to something less than a frontline position. But he also knew that, with the physical and military health of his regiment still on the mend, it could stand a further respite from action—even if he thought he could not.[13]

A week after arriving, the 6th was called down to the river at Freestone Point, where an enemy landing was reported to be imminent. When no Yankees appeared, the foot soldiers stood around and the gunners contented themselves with shelling some vessels churning harmlessly upriver. The following day, as Pender marched the men back to camp, he began to suspect that his service at Dumfries would be limited to answering false alarms. He told Fanny that she need not worry about his falling in battle, for "nothing but a natural death can await me here."[14]

When he returned to the task of training his regiment, Pender found that the exercise took up only a part of his day, and other chores failed to fill the void. Saddled with an increasing amount of off-duty time, he spent much of it reading not only the bible but some religious tracts that Fanny had sent him. Then, the Reverend Adolphus W. Mangum, pastor of the Methodist church in Salisbury, North Carolina, reported for duty as regimental chaplain. Mangum would prove unsuited to military life and would leave the outfit after a little more than a month in the field. While he was on the scene, however, he appears to have directed and deepened Pender's interest in religion. Pender quizzed the chaplain so earnestly on theological matters that Mangum urged him, at an early date, to be baptized in his chosen faith.[15]

Under the chaplain's influence, Pender entered more fully into his quest for religious knowledge. Tracts with titles such as *Confession of Sins, The End of Controversy Controverted,* and *Double Worship of the Church* became his favorite reading material. These were publications of the Episcopal Church, for his wife's example was drawing him steadily, although not without some hesitation, to her religion. At first he asked her: "Why—for I cannot see why—could I not be equally safe in some other Protestant Church[?] I want to be fixed upon these points."

On one point, however, he had made up his mind: "I want to become a member of some church for I do not feel safe, of retaining even what little progress I may have made without some external help. The open profession [of religious faith] has, I should think, a tendency to do away with that fear of the laughter of the unworldly, which I believe all feel more or less at first." Regardless of others' reaction, he was ready to make such a profession—"I want to be a Christian"—and the idea of sharing one religion with his wife had great appeal.[16]

After digesting Fanny's replies to his questions, and following further sessions with Mangum, who advised Pender that he "had good grounds for hope" of salvation, he made his second momentous decision in seven months. On the last day of September he informed his wife that "I have come to [a decision] that I know will give you great happiness. I have determined to be baptized as soon as I can get an opportunity. If I can find no minister I shall try to go to Fredericksburg. I know honey that I am not worthy, but if I wait I may never… take that first step."[17]

Having made up his mind, he tried to explain why: "I feel sincerely desirous of doing what is pleasing in the sight of God. His image is continually in my mind, and wrongdoing grieves and worries me, and I sincerely try to do better. I love our Savior—not as I should, however." He realized that he was capable of unchristian behavior on a daily basis. He had a tendency to berate officers and men for failings real and imagined; he could be strict to the point of insult with his subordinates; his vocabulary contained too many swear words; and vanity, jealousy, and the sins of the flesh sometimes had a hold on him. Still, "I desire to put away all covetousness and sin and I believe in the Apostles' Creed, and I feel that the connection with the church will be a great help to me," not only as a man but as a soldier.[18]

To perform the sacrament, Pender went looking for an Episcopalian chaplain. He found one in the camp of the Hampton Legion, an infantry-cavalry-artillery unit from South Carolina. After listening to Pender's wishes, the Reverend A. Loomis Porter of Charleston agreed to officiate. He suggested that the rite be performed in the presence of the entire 6th North Carolina for the benefit of its unbelieving members. Reluctantly or readily, Pender agreed. The ceremony was performed at Camp Hill on Sunday, October 6, following the regular Sabbath services. The 6th was drawn up as a body to witness the ceremony, while S. D. Lee (who was not himself a Christian, though he would become one in later years) served as a witness, as did another of Pender's West Point classmates, Colonel Benjamin Alston of the 4th Alabama Infantry.[19]

In later weeks, Pender was disappointed, although not surprised, to find that the ritual had failed to make him a model churchman. On numerous occasions he feared that he was retreating, rather than progressing, in his faith. The thought that he was backsliding left him disgusted with himself. "I am not a Christian," he admitted one week after his baptism, "but do the best I can." Two months later he was still lamenting his weaknesses, telling Fanny that "if I do not have faith it is because I cannot." In late November, he gave way to gloom: "I have almost despaired of ever becoming a [true] Christian. I try but fail to arouse myself to that earnestness that one should have." His only hope was that "I may live long enough to become stronger in faith and good works."[20]

He attempted to bolster his faith by immersing himself in the bible and by regular attendance at Sunday services. He had to leave Camp Hill to do so, for his strenuous efforts to locate a successor to Chaplain Mangum remained unsuccessful throughout the winter. When not in church, he carefully examined the tenets of his faith until able to persuade himself (perhaps a bit belatedly) that Episcopalianism was the true church, the most direct conduit to God's love and man's salvation. Thereafter he worked hard to communicate his spirituality to believers and nonbelievers alike. The example he set attracted the notice of his subordinates. Lieutenant White, writing two months after Pender's baptism, included his colonel in a list of "Christian warrior[s] fighting in a just cause."[21]

Hopeful of sharing his commitment to God with those close to him, Pender began preliminary attempts to convert his brother, David, and his body-servant, Joe. Speaking of the young African-American who attended him, Pender wrote: "If I could bring him to a true Christian condition I should feel that I had done some good in this world." In neither case did he achieve quick results, but he did not stop trying.[22]

His conversion progressed steadily enough that by the spring of 1862 he was ready to take communion in the Episcopal Church, a perquisite to which was confirmation. He did not, however, let anyone but Fanny know the step he planned to take. Not even his superiors, who granted him a one-day leave, knew the motive behind it. His public baptism had generated much comment, both in the army and in the newspapers. Pender, who closely guarded his privacy, regretted the publicity. For that reason he had dissuaded Reverend Porter from publishing an account of his conversion, declaring that "I do not sincerely consider myself a fit subject for any such publication," being "a great sinner and not worthy to be held up to others as a light....."[23]

Feeling as he did, he preferred to be confirmed out of sight of the army. On May 25, he slipped away from camp, rode to the Confederate capital, and was confirmed by the Episcopal bishop of Richmond, John Johns, in a ceremony conducted in an all-but-empty church. Afterward he wrote Fanny of his hope that the ritual would inspire him to overcome temptation, repent of his sins, and become a Christian in deed as well as in name. He realized that, like baptism, confirmation was merely an outward sign of his commitment to strive in God's service. He was well aware that "it is much easier to conform to the outward forms than the inward ... but by God's help I pray I may come in the future to everlasting salvation."

Although he had far to go to realize that hope, his journey toward light and truth was one of great potential. In the end, according to those most familiar with his spiritual quest, he gained the long-sought prize. Looking back after the war, one of his chaplains observed that "no one ... could have manifested higher rank as a Christian, a churchman, a friend, or a soldier, than General Pender."[24]

* * *

Leading a regiment of soldiers, many of them nonbelievers, tested Pender's Christian resolve. At times he was able to resist temptation and avoid sin. When his subordinates passed the bottle during a campfire chat, Pender, who did not have a drinking problem but believed that self-denial should extend to spirituous liquors, refused the libation. At other times, his new-won piety failed to sustain him in a pinch. When an officer or enlisted man failed miserably in his duties, Pender occasionally unleashed the sharp tongue he had vowed to keep in check, to the point of engaging in "unclean conversation." Invariably, such lapses shamed and depressed him and made him vow to improve at all costs. As part of his penance, he would force himself to seek out and apologize to anyone he had offended through word or deed, even if he had to ride a mile or more to do so.[25]

As autumn wore on and winter closed in, the regiment's sick list began a slow but steady decline, one that accelerated when warm weather returned to northern Virginia the following spring. As of late August 1861, Pender could report regimental health "somewhat on the mend," although only 280-some men were carried on the rolls as present for duty. Six months later, the number had doubled. Yet no matter how many took to the drill-field, they rarely performed up to their commander's exacting standards. Only when, late in the fall, General Johnston visited the 6th's home and reported himself pleased with what he found there, did Pender admit that his outfit was up to the mark "in drill, discipline, [and] polish." Unnecessarily, he told Fanny, "I take something of the praise to myself."[26]

At intervals, poor performances at regimental and battalion drill led Pender to question whether the 6th was in fact improving except in health. On one such occasion he wrote Fanny in disgust that "I can say heartily I wish I were back with the 3rd, and if I were to consult my own feelings I would leave them [the men of the 6th] to their fate, and that would be the worst calamity I could visit upon them. But one thing is certain, so long as I am here they shall know that I am Colonel."[27]

Thanks to his unceasing quest to maintain image and decorum, the regiment at least had a good-looking camp. When, in mid-November, the 6th was ordered to construct winter quarters, the log huts and stockaded tents that sprang up along the outskirts of Dumfries bespoke order and neatness. Camp Hill began to attract favorable attention, not only from Johnston but from General Whiting, who commanded the three brigades that occupied the Dumfries vicinity, as well as from lesser-ranking officers and civilians. Whiting was especially lavish with his praise, informing Pender that his regiment's encampment "was the neatest in the [Confederate] Army of the Potomac." He singled out the colonel himself by disclosing that, as Pender told Fanny, "he had chosen me for the position I occupy—left flank [of Whiting's command]—and that I only had to prove myself as good a soldier in the field as in the camp and he should be satisfied...."[28]

Had such praise come Pender's way months before, it would have swelled his head. Now he told his wife that "I hope it does not increase my vanity, for of a surety I feel that what I do is through God's mercy." He added an example that must have warmed Fanny's heart: "Yesterday I experienced a palpable assistance from Christ, for evil thoughts were taking possession of me. I prayed to Him and the temptation left me at once. Should not such manifestations encourage me[?]"[29]

As cold weather began to shut down operations on the Potomac and limit outdoor activity, Pender spent increasing time reading the bible and his tracts, as well as in writing letters home. He had always been a frequent correspondent, but now he outdid himself. He sent Fanny at least one letter every five days, and sometimes three or four letters—including several-page narratives—in the same week. He inquired about her health and that of her family; about her day-to-day life; and, especially, about how their sons were getting along. He expressed an interest in every aspect of the children's lives, from the temperature of the baby's bath water to the manner in which Fanny punished Turner for sins of commission and omission. He was concerned that neither child should grow up spoiled or lazy. He was also determined they should know that their mother and father loved them to the point of doing anything for them that would not adversely affect their upbringing. He agreed, to an extent, with Fanny's desire that "we may not have any more children, at least for years. In the course of time I should like to have a sweet little flame haired Fanny, to make some man happy in the future, as you have done me." In fact, they had both expressed a little disappointment that neither of their first two children had been a girl.[30]

In reply to news from home and the occasional gift box that Fanny sent him, Pender regularly provided details of his life in camp, on court-martial duty at Dumfries, and in active operations—such as they were. Time and again during the winter the military grapevine had Yankee raiding parties on the verge of attacking the batteries the 6th had been assigned to defend. Fears that the rumors would prove true drove General Whiting to keep his troops, Pender's outfit included, in a near-constant state of readiness.

Although Pender admired Whiting and considered him coolheaded in most situations, he thought his superior was overreacting in this case. Pender reasoned that an offensive against the upper Potomac would serve to distract McClellan's troops—who were still organizing and training inside the Washington defenses—from their ultimate goal: "It seems almost impossible to believe that after making such tremendous efforts and sending so much money, they will give up the idea of 'on to Richmond'."[31]

Although Pender's argument was sound, it also depressed him. It made him realize that, eight months into the war, he had yet to be sent to the front. Would he ever be? A related thought was that, deprived of serving in an active theater, he enjoyed no opportunity for promotion. Yet he sometimes sounded ambivalent about the matter. On one hand, he was uncertain whether he could handle higher rank with honor to his state and to himself. Writing to

Fanny on November 12 from the site he had renamed Camp Fisher in honor of his fallen predecessor, he feared that "I have vanity enough, but singularly to say, not enough confidence" in his abilities. On the other hand, less than a fortnight later he was complaining that, despite the efforts of his brother, Robert, to secure a brigadier's rank for him in North Carolina's forces, "Gov. Clark threw cold water upon my efforts...." It seemed that the "old Foggy [sic]" had replied that "I ought to be satisfied to have risen from Lieut. to Colonel." Pender tried to put the matter behind him, insisting that "it does not trouble me at all." In fact, it troubled him a great deal. He may have doubted his fitness for higher command, but he disliked the idea that others felt the same way.[32]

The winter of 1861-62 may not have found Pender furiously busy, but he managed to keep himself and his men occupied. He drilled the outfit when weather permitted; inspected their huts, hospital tents, cook shacks, and picket posts; and led their officers through tactics recitations. As time permitted he conferred with superiors such as Whiting to keep posted on issues affecting the entire army. When not on regular duty, he sent recruiting parties back to North Carolina to fill the gaps that sickness and disability had created in the ranks of the 6th. His efforts sometimes met with opposition from state officials as well as from the commanders of other outfits in need of enlistees, but through patient negotiation Pender cleared away every obstacle.[33]

Occasionally he battled illnesses of his own, including dysentery and constipation. He continued to seek a replacement for Chaplain Mangum, writing directly to Bishop Thomas Atkinson of the Diocese of North Carolina for aid in his search. He labored to prevent the regiment's new sutler, Mr. E. L. Fant, from selling liquor to the men in violation of army regulations and Pender's own well-publicized prohibition. And he sought promotions for deserving officers and commissions for worthy non-coms.[34]

He also did a certain amount of socializing—although, presumably, no longer in the manner that had caused so much trouble at home. In fact, the only women he admitted to consorting with at Dumfries were, as he told Fanny, "one married lady middle aged and one old maid so you need not be jealous." Because active operations were few and far between at Camp Fisher, Pender was able to dine regularly with Stephen Lee; General Whiting; Major General Gustavus Woodson Smith, a division commander in Johnston's army and one of Pender's instructors at West Point; and old friends such as James

Howard of Maryland, with whom Pender had served at Fort Vancouver and who now commanded a Confederate artillery unit.[35]

The happiest visit paid him in winter quarters—the more so as it occurred soon after he passed a lonely Christmas—occurred when, early in January, Fanny, Turner, Dorsey, and the children's nurse arrived at Dumfries. The joy Pender experienced at being reunited with his family lasted throughout the six weeks they were able to stay with him. Then the visit ended abruptly, when unusually heavy activity in the Potomac renewed fears of an attack, prompting Pender to send his loved ones beyond harm's reach.

While his family remained, Pender enjoyed squiring everyone around Camp Fisher and its environs. After February 3, Turner could frolic in several inches of snow. When the frosty weather drove them all indoors, the family fit snugly in the headquarters hut Pender's men had built for him. The "popular house," as some called it, sported two rooms, a window, and two doors.[36]

Fanny and he spent hours alone in the room that held his bed. By the time she left his side, she was expecting. This did not surprise her husband. "Surely if you do not want children," he advised her, "you will have to remain away from me, and hereafter when you come to me I shall know that you want another baby."[37]

His humor masked a real concern over the outcome of her pregnancy. Coming so soon after her last, and especially in view of the difficulties she had experienced in carrying both boys, her condition pleased neither of them. When Fanny miscarried some weeks after returning home, her husband pronounced it "the best thing that could have happened except not to have gotten in that condition…." He added that "it would have worried me very much if you had gone on to maturity in that condition, for I should have known that you were very unhappy." It is possible that Fanny took steps to end the pregnancy, for when Pender learned of the miscarriage he observed solemnly that "you did the next best thing you could."[38]

Especially in view of his recent conversion, Pender felt guilty about the sexual side of his nature and struggled to keep carnal urges under control, fearful of the result. In July, following Fanny's return home after her first visit to the army, she had suffered urological difficulties for which Pender blamed himself, apparently suspecting they had been caused by their recent love-making. "The thought that you had been suffering as you must have been," he wrote after her departure, "made me feel very sad indeed … and I have to reproach myself for it. Honey, the same that causes you so much trouble is my stumbling block in this world. When I think I am getting better it … stares me in the face to my great mortification, for I do feel humbled and mortified to think that the most dangerous of all our passions and the most sinful when indulged, should be the one that I cannot conquer.… It is the greatest curse it seems to me that could have been laid on man." Still, he would strive to break the hold that carnality had on him "in thought as well as act."[39]

*   *   *

When Fanny and the children left the army in mid-February, Pender took leave to accompany them to Richmond. At the railroad depot he parted with them amid a tearful round of farewells. Afterward, unwilling to return to a lonely camp, he lingered in the city. There he renewed acquaintances with an academy classmate, Custis Lee, with whom he lodged for a few days. Despite his preference for a field command, the honors graduate of the Class of 1854 had been assigned as aide-de-camp to Jefferson Davis. Pender suspected that the posting owed to the influence of Lee's father, who, following an unsuccessful field campaign in western Virginia, was serving a second stint as Davis's military advisor.

Having failed to suppress his appetite for higher rank, Pender, with his roommate's help, made the rounds of the Confederate War Department, inquiring about available commands, seeking contacts to play and wires to pull in his own behalf. His attempts availed him nothing, but his presence in the capital did permit him to inspect the fruit of a rumor-mill that, by virtue of its position at the nerve center of the Confederate government, was more likely than most to yield accurate information.[40]

One of the rumors he picked up in the capital centered around a conference held earlier that same day, February 20, and attended by President Davis, his Cabinet, and General Johnston. Supposedly, the conferees were considering a proposal that Johnston's army pack up and withdraw from its camps at Manassas, Bristoe Station, and elsewhere on the fringes of last July's battlefield. Apparently the army leader was concerned that, with McClellan's huge command flexing its muscles a few miles away at Washington, he might find himself attacked before he could retire to more defensible positions below the Rappahannock River.

At first Pender could not determine the credibility of the rumor, but by fortuitous timing he was able to confirm it a few hours after hearing it. Later that same day, he chanced to meet Johnston, fresh from Davis's office, in the lobby of a downtown hotel. When Pender repeated the rumor in the general's presence, an open-mouthed Johnston realized that "an accurate report of what had been considered in the utmost secrecy behind guarded doors, had reached the hotel" within hours of the meeting.[41]

Fearing that a general movement was imminent, Pender returned to Dumfries the next day. As he suspected, Camp Fisher offered painful reminders of his family's recent presence, some of them physical—Dorsey's cradle, for instance, remained in the bedroom. "I think I shall let it stay," he wrote Fanny. "It will only remind me still more forcibly of what happiness I did enjoy and how cheerless I am …. My dear wife I believe I never missed you as I do now. May God protect us from all danger and allow us to meet again and not soon be separated."[42]

For several days after his return from the capital, nothing occurred to mar the regularity of life in winter quarters, making him wonder if Johnston's proposal had been rejected. Then, at the end of the month, General Whiting issued a series of orders that suggested an imminent move. At his superior's direction, Pender requisitioned extra equipment that would be needed on the march. The items arrived in record time, another clue that a movement was afoot. By February 28 Pender had placed his outfit—now more than 400 strong, with 104 other men still on the sick list—on notice that a march would soon begin. Leaves were canceled, excess baggage was sent to the rear and packed in wagons, and ammunition was distributed.

Despite the rapid preparations, not till the evening of March 7 did the 6th North Carolina strike tents, dismantle or burn their cabins, and move out in the direction of Fredericksburg. All around, other elements of the Confederate Army of the Potomac followed suit, trudging south in the glow of blazing huts and storehouses crammed with rations that must be denied to the enemy. It was apparent that Davis and his advisors had given Johnston's withdrawal a belated go-ahead. Thinking about it as he rode at the forefront of the 6th, Pender decided he should not be surprised it had taken so long to come about—politicians never made up their minds in a hurry if they could help it.

The movement proceeded at a comfortable pace, one that even the recruits in the ranks found tolerable. This was fortunate, for the roads were muddy, in places churned into a gumbo by wagons and battery teams, and crossing the Rappahannock via the few remaining foot and rail bridges required an unusual amount of time. It was evident that the army had stolen a march on its enemy, for careful observation revealed no pursuit worthy of the name.[43]

By midafternoon on the 10th, Pender's men were filing onto an expanse of cleared ground amid farm fields two miles west of Fredericksburg. Nearby the other regiments in Whiting's brigade also went into bivouac. The 6th's commander dubbed his parcel of earth Camp Barton. It became a camp in fact as well as in name when the regiment's tents arrived later in the day. Pender supervised their erection in neat rows, or company streets. Then he sat down at his writing-desk to inform Fanny of his new venue, assuring her that "we are delightfully situated here, about the right distance from Town, nice camp, lots of troops, etc. The only drawback is the 11th Miss. Regt. is too near for quiet...."[44]

The regiment remained in its "nice camp" for four weeks. During that period it increased in size with the coming of more recruits from North Carolina, and in health as men returned from the hospital. The fall-back to Fredericksburg suggested that Johnston wished to avoid a clash of arms. But if the portents were wrong, the 6th was able and ready to fight, something it could not have done a few short months ago. As one of Pender's officers recalled after the war, "the condition of the Sixth when it left ... for Fredericksburg in March 1862, was a vindication of the wisdom of Governor Clark in appointing Pender to succeed Fisher."[45]

Pender himself was in something less than a fighting mood. For much of the time he spent near Fredericksburg, he suffered from a nagging cold, which prevented him from taking the drill-field at Camp Barton. Castor oil eventually relieved most of the symptoms, although the cold, rainy weather that had begun to predominate aggravated a sore throat that left him hoarse for days at a time.

The ailments did not prevent him from making a quick trip to Richmond to see about replenishing his regiment's supply of muskets, cartridges, and bayonet sheaths, but the trip gained him only half the materiel he had gone there to procure. The result so heated his temper that, upon returning to camp, he lashed out at any officer and enlisted man who crossed his path. As always, when he retired to his tent he knelt in prayer, repenting his sins, asking God's forgiveness, and pledging to fight weakness more effectively in the future.[46]

Perhaps his physical ills sapped his desire for battle, for his mind turned to thoughts of peace in a reunited nation. He wished he might return to Good

Spring, take his wife and children in his arms, and stay with them forever. "But," he reminded himself as well as Fanny, "the Lord only knows when this horrid war will end...." He prayed for that day to arrive sooner rather than later. The same prayer was on his lips every night as he climbed into bed, and he recited it each weekend when he traveled to Fredericksburg to attend Sabbath services.[47]

By late March, his prayers had a sense of urgency to them. He had a strong feeling that his time away from the battlefield was about to end. Heretofore he had devoted much attention to the first half of the term "Christian warrior." Now he was going to have to emphasize the second half.

Chapter Five

"GENERAL PENDER, I SALUTE YOU!"

In the last days of March, as the 6th North Carolina lolled in its camp outside Fredericksburg wondering when a battle would come its way, McClellan's Federals were hard at work to provide an answer. The Union commander's original plan of campaign—to turn the Confederates out of the Manassas-Centreville line by moving against their rear via Virginia's Middle Peninsula—had been foiled when Johnston withdrew below the Rappahannock. But by mid-March, only a few days after the Union ironclad *Monitor* had battled its Confederate counterpart, *Virginia* (the former U. S. S. *Merrimack*) to a draw in Hampton Roads, thereby securing the waterway for Union shipping, McClellan devised a new strategy.

Now he would operate against the Rebel rear by way of the lower peninsula. He would ship his 105,000-man army and a vast quantity of rations and materiel by transports from Alexandria and points nearby to Fort Monroe, from which point he would make an overland march on Richmond. Before the month was out, the mammoth logistical undertaking was underway, with troops disembarking at Ben Butler's old stamping ground and massing for a march up the Peninsula. Barring their path were a few defensive positions, including the soon-to-be-abandoned works at Big Bethel, and the fortified port of Yorktown. About 15,000 Confederates under Major General John Bankhead Magruder held the Yorktown line, which stretched as far north as Virginia's colonial capital, Williamsburg. Whether Magruder's tiny command could slow the Yankees down remained to be seen; it could not stop them.[1]

For some time, Pender and the other residents of Camp Barton remained blissfully unaware of McClellan's coming. During the last week in March and the first days of April, Pender put his energy into making his outfit look good during a series of reviews called by his superiors. As he rode proudly in advance of the outfit, he tried his best to look like general officer material. He sported a well-tailored but unostentatious uniform comprising a double-breasted frock coat of woolen twill carrying black leather shoulder straps of the kind Yankee officers wore and with gold braid rippling along the sleeves; kersey pants in royal blue; and a gilt-spangled kepi tilted at a rakish angle on his forehead. Behind him came his officers and enlisted men in a long, orderly column. Although not as sartorially splendid as their commander, the rank-and-file displayed freshly brushed uniforms and carried shoulder-arms with metal parts so carefully polished as to reflect the spring sunlight.

Smart attire and well-aligned ranks produced desirable results. On March 25 Pender rejoiced that "Gen. Whiting had out eight Regts. today in review, and mine was the largest of them all, 500 men." The 6th's turnout—twice the number that had been fit for duty when he took over the regiment—paid tribute to the improved medical care he had instituted. As he informed Fanny, "all said I had the best Regt. I felt very proud of it...."[2]

The following week, the 6th joined 11 other outfits, plus three batteries, in parading before Johnston himself. Pender was gratified when one of the commander's staff officers mentioned having heard the regiment "complimented [a] great deal during the day." Pender exulted that "it has the reputation of being about the best in the service. Now if we can only maintain our reputation in battle." He added, pointedly: "I sometimes feel quite anxious when I think of how we should behave on that occasion."[3]

Pender's comments about his regiment's showing reflected a degree of pride in himself that suggests he was not yet free of vices. But he was also capable of acts of kindness and charity, showing himself to be worthy of grace. In the last days of March the wife of a soldier from Alamance County, North Carolina, found her way to Camp Barton after walking the two miles from Fredericksburg in the rain and mud. She had come to visit her husband in the hospital, only to find he had died of his illness a few days earlier. When Pender learned of the widow's plight and the fact that she had spent her last cent to reach Fredericksburg, "I sent her back in the ambulance and gave her $5—I knew I should spend it better that way than any other.... Wasn't her case a hard one[?] Many is the poor heart that will be broken by this war."[4]

Two days after his good deed, he sent Fanny premature news of a great Confederate victory in West Tennessee. But Confederate fortunes would never rise as high in the western theater as they would in Virginia. Next day counterattacks turned the battle of Shiloh into a Union triumph. In the same letter Pender made his first written reference to the invasion force on the Peninsula, noting that "McClellan is there with nearly all of his army" but adding that "we have an insignificant role to play here." He predicted that the blue tide would recede when it struck Magruder's defenses, and without assistance from Johnston.[5]

He may have written in this vein to keep his beloved from worrying about him. In reality, he must have hoped that his regiment would be sent to reinforce Yorktown, thus bringing on his long-deferred baptism of battle. If so, he was not disappointed. Early on April 8 he received orders to leave at once for Fredericksburg. Before noon the 6th North Carolina had dismantled Camp Barton and had taken to roads that would eventually carry it to the Peninsula.

Through the rest of the unusually raw and rainy day, Pender's outfit brought up the rear of Whiting's division as it trudged alongside the tracks of the Richmond, Fredericksburg & Potomac Railroad. By the time they reached the village of Bowling Green, ten miles from their old camp, on the afternoon of the 9th, the men were being pelted by hail. That night they bivouacked in the open, with only a blanket or two to ward off the cold. Pender, determined to share their hardships, slept on the ground in their midst.[6]

Next day the march resumed in the direction of Milford Station. When they reached the depot, footsore men gladly obeyed Pender's order to pile into boxcars that would carry them to Ashland Station, near Hanover Court House. Although protected from the elements at last, the riders shivered in the unheated cars. By the time they reached Ashland, where they disembarked at midday on the 10th, the weather had managed to worsen. When he "got thar," wrote a semi-literate private in the 6th, "I was wet and nearly frosen… and it was a snowing a little…."[7]

Pender sympathized with his men's ordeal but suspected it had just begun. At Ashland, while other regiments marched farther south, the 6th was ordered into bivouac. It remained near the depot, without further orders, for four days. During that time the weather improved, but the men's comfort did not, for no tents, cooking facilities, or firewood were sent to them. "Somebody," wrote Lieutenant White, "has a large amount of sin to answer for."[8]

On April 14, Pender, who had learned that McClellan's people were "making their grand move" on Yorktown, was permitted to resume the march south. The journey continued for five memorable days and covered 75 miles. The pace was so grueling that dozens of men collapsed by the wayside, unable or unwilling to go on. Unceasing grumbling ran the length of the column as it moved to and across the James River and began to descend the Peninsula. Everyone wanted to know why they could not ride the rest of the way to Yorktown as they had to Ashland. Pender continued to sympathize, but he did not blame the authorities who had decreed the regiment must travel by shank's mare. He was aware that the Confederacy's rail system was so overtaxed it had to give priority to shipments of guns, ammunition, and supplies.[9]

By the 18th, journey's end was in sight. That morning the 6th North Carolina marched through Williamsburg, past the venerable College of William and Mary. By evening its men were occupying a sector of the defensive line that stretched from Yorktown across the length of the Peninsula. Although he turned out to be mistaken, Pender supposed a clash of arms— perhaps the war's climactic encounter—was imminent. If so, he wrote Fanny that night, he was confident of the result: "We all believe and hope we shall whip them. In all the skirmishes that have taken place—and they occur nightly and daily—we have had the best of it."

He tried to keep the mood upbeat, but his calm demeanor faltered noticeably toward the end of his letter when he confided that "I try to prepare myself for the worst, but I am a great sinner and can only trust in the great mercy of God and the atoning power of the Blessed Saviour…. The Lord be merciful to us…. My love to all…."[10]

* * *

Pender had arrived not on the verge of an attack but in the midst of a long, enervating siege. The booming of cannon and the rattle of musketry that greeted his ears that first night occupied his every waking minute thereafter. Obviously, Johnston's army had not arrived too late to save Yorktown.

Later it was learned why the little garrison had not been overwhelmed long ago. Upon the Yankees' approach, May 4-5, General Magruder had used his limited resources to maximum dramatic effect. He had marched his troops round and about their works in full view of the enemy before sending them circling back to their starting point. The impression given was of never-ending columns of infantry and artillery. McClellan had been duped into halting his drive on Richmond and laying siege to Yorktown until able to reduce the town through bombardment.

For the next four weeks, Union fatigue parties dug investment lines and manhandled heavy ordnance—including massive 13-inch seacoast mortars borrowed from the navy—into position south and southwest of Magruder's works. For the majority of this period, the Confederates, now 60,000 strong, with Johnston in overall command, watched, waited, fired on their opponents at long range, and took fire in return.[11]

From his regiment's camp on the Williamsburg Road about a mile west of Yorktown, Pender began to assure Fanny that no battle appeared imminent. And should it come without warning, it was unlikely that he would be directly involved in it, since his regiment—as was true of the rest of Whiting's brigade, under temporary command of Colonel Evander M. Law of the 4th Alabama—held a reserve position in the rear. By the 25th, in fact, rumor had many of McClellan's men bypassing Yorktown and marching directly to Richmond. Should the report prove true, Pender believed that the capital's defense forces would sally forth to turn back the invaders.

As the siege dragged on, conditions along the Confederate lines saddled the Yorktown garrison with a "great many hardships," but west of town, where Pender was encamped, "we are very comfortable.... We have no picket or trench duty. Nothing but to rest and enjoy ourselves preparatory to finishing the fight.... The reserve have to give the final decisive blow."[12]

The slow pace of the siege left Pender time for socializing with nearby units. One visit gave him particular satisfaction. On April 21 he rode to the camp of his old regiment, now known as the 13th North Carolina Troops (those regiments originally known as "Volunteers" had been renumbered and redesignated, while the original 10 outfits retained the name "*State* Troops").

The reunion, he told Fanny, was "truly flattering. They cheered me & stood around in groups to get a look at me." With pardonable exaggeration, he added: "Three hundred say they intend to join me, if allowed" to transfer to the 6th.[13]

The free time also enabled him to tend to affairs in his own regiment. At Yorktown he warmly greeted the arrival of a new chaplain, the Reverend Kensey J. Stewart, formerly of Alexandria, Virginia. Fame preceded the Episcopal clergyman, who during a confrontation with Union occupiers the previous year had been hauled from his pulpit during Sunday services for omitting the customary prayer for the health of the president of the United States. At first Pender considered the minister "eccentric, but I have no doubt is an able man." In the latter view, he was correct. In a deeper sense than his predecessor, Reverend Stewart became a spiritual advisor to Pender. It was at his urging that the colonel made up his mind to be confirmed in the church.[14]

By May 3, Johnston had decided to evacuate Yorktown before McClellan could complete his siege lines and pound the city with his big guns. The pull-out began after dark that evening and continued throughout the 4th. The garrison was the first to depart, while the troops farther west waited until they were able to fall in to the rear.

The task of guarding the end of the column fell to G. W. Smith's "Reserve Corps," of which Smith's old division (now led by Whiting), Whiting's old brigade (under Law), and the 6th North Carolina were components. Pender was aware that holding the "post of honor" was a dangerous assignment; at the outset of the withdrawal he entrusted to Reverend Stewart's care personal possessions including his pocketwatch and a letter to Fanny, to be handed her in the event of her husband's death.[15]

As the bulk of Johnston's and Magruder's forces trudged along the road to Williamsburg, Pender's troops remained stationary, ready to engage the enemy if McClellan mounted a rapid pursuit. Little Mac did not, but Yankee warships in the York River continued to shell the city's defenses, as they had throughout the siege. Hoping that the Lord would bless the evacuation with success, and seeking to take his men's minds off the deadly cannonade, Pender asked Stewart to hold an outdoor service. The chaplain was surprised, but he quickly agreed. Years later, he recalled: "I had a small table for an Altar; it was covered with a white cloth; above us were the old forest trees, through the tops of which, ever and anon crashed the huge ["lamp-post"] shells, from the gunboats.... Around this table, I had one or two lines of soldiers and officers kneeling upon one knee; behind them stood the rest; our music was supplemented [by] the death rattle of a soldier in a nearby tent...."[16]

* * *

Not until the morning of May 5 did Pender and his men strike and pack tents and, along with a few detachments of horse soldiers, join the retreat column. To everyone's relief, the Yankees did not attack until around noon. Smith's corps had passed Fort Magruder and the other redoubts south of Williamsburg and struck the road to Richmond via New Kent Court House. One of Pender's subordinates recalled the escape as a near thing: "There was nothing between us and McClellan's advancing army but a few cavalrymen. Again and again, many times during the forepart of that day, as our army passed on, we would drop back and reform our lines across the road, prepared for the enemy's advance, but we had no fighting to do."[17]

Late that afternoon, a body of Yankee cavalry, the vanguard of a belated pursuit, appeared south of Williamsburg. Before they could overtake the gray column, J. E. B. Stuart, now a brigadier general commanding a brigade of horse, galloped down to oppose them. Behind him, detachments of the divisions of Major Generals James Longstreet and D. H. Hill countermarched through Williamsburg. Their men occupied the forts in that area and dosed the Federal infantry that had come up in the cavalry's rear with rifle- and cannon-fire.

While Stuart and his infantry friends mixed with the pursuers, Pender, his regiment, and the balance of the reserve corps kept moving north. That night everyone bivouacked near the hamlet of Barhamsville. They would remain within range of Williamsburg until Longstreet, Hill, and the army's wagon train were beyond possibility of being overtaken.[18]

Whiting's division was still at and near Berhamsville when at noon on the 6th reports came in of Union troopships anchoring along the York River a few miles to the northeast. The largest contingent was at West Point, at the confluence of the Mattapony and Pamunkey Rivers, only a few miles east of Whiting's bivouac. Late that afternoon hundreds of Yankees disembarked at Eltham's Landing. They did not advance far before going into bivouac, but their presence in close proximity to the Confederate line of retreat was intolerable. It was evident that McClellan, foiled at Yorktown, had sent part of his army by water to halt the Rebels short of Richmond.

The next morning, as Johnston's vanguard proceeded toward the

Confederate capital, 30 miles to the northwest, the bulk of Whiting's command, under the personal direction of General Smith, moved against the Yankees. Through the balance of the day, the Confederates attacked up and down the shoreline—mostly near Eltham's Landing—to prevent the enemy from moving inland. The blocking maneuver worked flawlessly. After a two-hour battle, the enemy was driven back to river's edge, where they remained, conceding defeat.[19]

One reason for Smith's success was the stability that Law's old brigade lent the Confederate right flank. Although not heavily engaged, the 6th North Carolina did its part in this effort, advancing in lines of skirmishers across fields and through woods under Pender's close supervision. Only a portion of the regiment came into contact with the foe, some of whom it sent running for the river bluffs. A few North Carolinians pursued; one of them, Private Bartlett Yancey Malone, had a high time "a scurmishing [sic] and a running from one place to another hunting the scamps."[20]

After the Federals fell back, Pender and his men supported artillery units, including S. D. Lee's battery, in taking positions from which to shell not only the enemy soldiers but their ships. Given the longer range of the naval guns, however, the contest was an uneven one from the start. After suffering a few casualties, Pender's men, as also the rest of Law's brigade, withdrew from harm's reach.

Early in the afternoon, the foe having been sufficiently chastised, Whiting's division disengaged and joined the retreat column, whose rear guard it again became. By evening the command had reached New Kent Court House, where it was beyond pursuit. There Pender sat down and scrawled a hasty note to Fanny, describing briefly the first battle of his Confederate career. The fighting, he said, had been fierce at times, "we with inferior numbers beating them badly." Although he had seen enough fighting "to satisfy me of my men's pluck," he had enjoyed no opportunity "to test my courage."[21]

Eighty years later, historian Douglas Southall Freeman agreed with Pender's self-assessment, noting that the fight of May 7 had provided "nothing to suggest the picture of a rising professional soldier with high aptitude for combat." That picture, however, was about to come into focus.[22]

*   *   *

The road to Richmond was crowded with troops, wagons, and artillery carriages, making for stop-and-start progress. The glacial pace with which Smith's corps headed north began to wear on Pender and his men. A close pursuit would have engaged their attention and energy, but none developed. By May 11 the Confederate rear guard was still several miles from the capital and Pender was bewailing the "monotonous time we are having[,] only marching 1½ miles yesterday and 4 the day before. I wish we were at our journey's end where we could have what few comforts" were available in a fixed camp, including clean clothes. Pender had worn the same attire, from cap to boots, since leaving Yorktown on the 5th.[23]

To take his mind off his discomfort, he conjured up a happy scene from a year ago. He reminded Fanny of the time "we were under the shade tree [at Good Spring] sitting on the grass, the happiest hours of my life." It had been a tumultuous period, a time of change and anticipation as they awaited the birth of their second child and Pender's first assignment as a Confederate officer. Still, they had managed to steal some time from the war to devote to each other. "I shall never forget it," he insisted, "and I do not wish to. It was complete earthly happiness."[24]

By the 17th, the 6th North Carolina was finally in camp five miles from the eastern outskirts of the capital, with the rest of Johnston's army all around. In their new positions the Confederates had ample time to improve existing defenses and build new ones, for McClellan was pursuing even more slowly than Pender's column had marched from New Kent Court House to Richmond. The colonel warned his wife not to believe newspaper reports that McClellan had forced his opponents to flee: "You see the enemy is on to Richmond with us, but do not think we have been running all the time from McClellan, for it is not so. Our Generals have been very anxious for him to attack us...."[25]

Pender used the time granted him not only to strengthen his share of the Richmond defenses but to try to determine his prospects for advancement. While at Yorktown he had predicted that "my claims for promotion are no better than they were six months ago so far as I can see." Still, "if the war lust & I live I shall be promoted some of these days." He tried to convince Fanny that "I do not feel any uncomfortable uneasiness about the matter.... I want promotion as much for your sake as anything else. I should like for those who have known you, to know that you are the wife of a general & [promoted] from supposed merit & not political influence."[26]

Here he was being disingenuous, and his wife probably suspected as

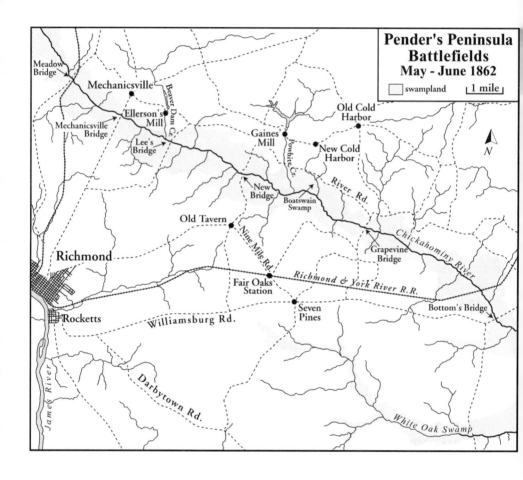

**Pender's Peninsula
Battlefields**
May - June 1862

☐ swampland   ∟1 mile⌐

Meadow
Bridge

Mechanicsville

Ellerson's
Mill

Mechanicsville
Bridge

Lee's
Bridge

Beaver Dam Cr.

Old Cold
Harbor

Gaines'
Mill

New Cold
Harbor

Powhite Cr.

New
Bridge

Boatswain
Swamp

River Rd.

N

Old Tavern

Nine Mile Rd.

Grapevine
Bridge

Chickahominy River

Richmond

Fair Oaks
Station

Richmond & York River R.R.

Seven
Pines

Bottom's Bridge

Rocketts

Williamsburg Rd.

James River

Darbytown Rd.

White Oak Swamp

much. The prospect that he might not be promoted—at least not for some time—*did* leave him uncomfortable and uneasy. Despite his awareness that to do so was a sin, he continued to harbor large reserves of ambition and pride. He wanted to be a general for his own sake, not for Fanny's. For this reason he overreacted to a rumor that made its way to his camp: that General Whiting had been ordered to name a permanent commander for his old brigade. Colonel Law had filled that position capably at Eltham's Landing, but Pender believed that, even though Law was senior to him by date of commission, "I am by right entitled to" the post, unless a general officer was assigned to it.

He felt so strongly about the matter, he wrote that if he failed to gain the position, "I shall deem it due my self respect to resign and look out for some other position…. I am entitled to the Brigade…." Subsequent events, however, made his threat sound not only petty but empty. In time Law was given *de jure* as well as *de facto* command of the brigade. Pender kept his commission and said no more about the whole thing.[27]

If not entitled to it, the quickest way to prove oneself worthy of the position was to distinguish himself in battle. That opportunity came Pender's way as May rushed to a close. On the 22nd, the Union's Army of the Potomac finally settled into place astride the Chickahominy River, the last natural barrier to Richmond. Thereafter, McClellan maneuvered as if he planned to lay siege to the capital as he had to Yorktown. The thought gave his adversaries pause. Given McClellan's great advantage in manpower, entrenching tools, and heavy ordnance, Richmond's fall was a *fait accompli*. And this time Johnston would not evacuate to save his army—his civilian superiors would never permit it.

After considering his options, Johnston hoped to forestall a slow, painful defeat by landing a quick, devastating blow. His enemy's position gave him an opening. Unwisely, McClellan had split his army, placing two of his corps south of the Chickahominy while the other three occupied the north bank in order to link with a sixth corps, reported to be marching down from Washington. The Union army's awkward stance left each of its wings beyond easy supporting range. The mistake was made to look worse by heavy rains that fell on the 29th and 30th, which raised the Chickahominy so high as to be nearly impassable.[28]

Originally Johnston planned to strike the heavier wing, thus preventing its link-up with the approaching reinforcements. However, on the 28th, before the plan could be put in motion, it was learned that the sixth corps would not be coming to McClellan's assistance after all. At the last minute the Washington authorities had diverted it to the Shenandoah Valley. There Brigadier General Thomas J. Jackson, who had won the nickname "Stonewall" for his tenacity at Manassas, had been sent to divert Union attention from the Peninsula. The strategy had worked brilliantly. Jackson's ability to range almost at will through the Valley, marching, attacking, and feinting seemingly everywhere at the same time, had frightened Abraham Lincoln into foreseeing an attack on Washington. Thus the president made a last-minute decision to withhold from McClellan the additions he believed he needed to take Richmond.[29]

The changed situation told Johnston that he need no longer risk attacking above the river. On the 30th, he led the bulk of his recently reinforced army, including Whiting's division, toward the isolated positions of the Union Third and Fourth Corps south of the Chickahominy. The remaining Confederates would launch limited attacks to hold in place the Federals on the other bank.

For Pender, the operation that would deeply involve him in battle for the first time as a Confederate officer began in the early hours of May 31 as Whiting's division—recently expanded to six brigades and which, for the operation, had been attached to Longstreet's command—moved out along the Nine Mile Road to form the left flank of the attack column below the river. The division would play a critical role in a fairly complicated plan. After Whiting and Longstreet enveloped the right of the Fourth Corps near Fair Oaks Station on the Richmond & York River Railroad, D. H. Hill's division would use the Williamsburg Road to launch a secondary attack farther south near a landmark known as Seven Pines. Meanwhile, the division of General Huger, just up from Hampton Roads, would protect the south flank by advancing along the road to Charles City.[30]

The strategy behind the movement was sound, but from the outset things went awry, pointing up the army's inexperience in combat. Longstreet and Huger took wrong roads, a giant traffic snarl slowed everyone but Hill, and instead of hitting home shortly after dawn Johnston's blow did not fall on either Fair Oaks or Seven Pines until early in the afternoon.

Whiting's division, Law's brigade, and the 6th North Carolina did not become fully engaged until about 5:00. By then Pender was ready for a fight. Nervous energy had consumed him since the evening of May 28, when his

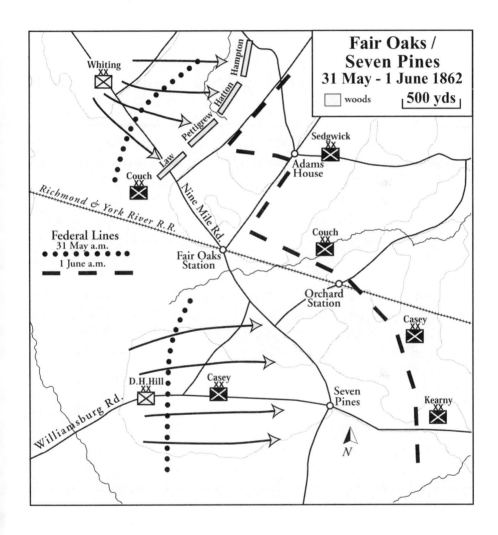

regiment advanced toward Meadow Bridge on the Chickahominy, only to be recalled to its old camp, courtesy of Johnston's revised strategy.

Tension climbed even higher this morning, when Pender, along with everyone else in Whiting's division, found the path to the Union right blocked by Longstreet's errant march. The traffic jam was not cleared away until early afternoon, when Whiting moved up the Nine Mile Road as far as Old Tavern. There he halted until, as per his orders, he got the word to attack southward in concert with Longstreet, Hill, and Huger.[31]

The battle effectively began at 1:00 P.M. when Hill's men attacked the defenses at Seven Pines. The assault smashed a division of the Fourth Corps and sent it staggering back on its supports. On Hill's front the fighting was savage, but an atmospheric phenomenon known as "acoustic shadow" prevented Whiting's men from hearing the racket until it had been going on for more than two hours. When the order to move finally came, Whiting hastened down to Fair Oaks Station, Law's brigade marching on the left side of Nine Mile Road and with the brigades of Brigadier Generals John Bell Hood and J. Johnston Pettigrew on the right. The rest of the division, Brigadier General Wade Hampton's and Brigadier General Robert Hatton's brigades, trudged farther to the rear, conforming their movements to those of the units in front.

En route to Fair Oaks the 6th North Carolina, the vanguard of Law's brigade, passed abandoned enemy camps where meals were still cooking over fires. Beyond the campsites, Pender led the men through a woodlot, on the other side of which they halted in the face of musketry and artillery fire. Quickly forming a line of battle, the colonel led his main body through an open field. In front was a line of skirmishers who attempted to draw the enemy's fire, thus revealing their position. Once he discovered that position, Pender expected to overrun it or blast its defenders into retreat.

In his eagerness to engage the foe for the first time, he advanced his men too far, too fast. When perhaps halfway across the field, one of his subordinates notified him that the flags of at least three enemy regiments could be seen off to the left and rear. A surprised Pender sent word to Colonel Law that he might need support. At the same time, having gotten his troops in a predicament, he vowed to get them out of it. In "as clear and musical a voice as was ever heard on the battlefield," he issued orders that realigned the ranks until they were facing the threatened sector. A minute later, in response to his command, the 6th North Carolina was following its colonel at the double-quick toward a position that was defended by cannons as well as by foot soldiers.[32]

The artillery opened on them with an unearthly roar, shot and shell whizzing above most of their heads and felling some men along the right flank. A few frightened rookies took off for the rear, but the majority of the regiment maintained cohesion, halting only when Pender noticed that some of Law's regiments were rushing to their support. His flanks now secure, he resumed the advance, urging the men forward by twirling above his head the German-made cavalry saber (model 1840) that he had wielded in the 1st Dragoons. In response, the 6th pushed to within 100 yards of the guns before a particularly well-placed salvo caused everyone to fall back.

Pender regrouped the survivors behind a little ridge at the edge of the field. There he found himself in command not only of his own troops but of soldiers from supporting units who had been separated from their comrades. At his order, a steady, accurate fire was soon raking the Union line. Meanwhile, other elements of Whiting's division, which had attacked defenses farther to the left, were reeling backward from heavy losses, including the death of General Hatton and the wounding and capture of General Pettigrew.[33]

Eventually the remainder of Law's troops, including some cannons of their own, reached the field in the rear of the 6th North Carolina. With them came a courier from Whiting who urged Pender, if at all possible, to make another attempt to take the Yankee battery. A colonel desirous of displaying his fortitude at the expense of his troops would have assented, but Pender could see that a new attack would only lengthen his casualty list. He was about to relay the news to Whiting when another officer, a stranger to Pender, galloped up and shouted that the battery must be taken. Before Pender could remonstrate, less prudent members of Law's brigade, including some from the 6th, got to their feet and raced for the guns—only to be driven back by shrapnel and canister. In their haste to return, they threatened to destabilize Whiting's line.[34]

Pender, his decision to forego a second attack thus validated, worked with other officers to restore order in the ranks. By the close of the afternoon, he had restructured and strengthened his part of the division perimeter. It was dangerous work, for it required him to move back and forth along the line while showing able-bodied men the best way to shelter themselves and helping move wounded comrades to the rear. The calmness with which he imparted orders and advice served to quiet the fears not only of his own soldiers but of men in other regiments of the brigade.

His conduct elicited favorable commentary from many onlookers, including Jefferson Davis, who had left Richmond to observe firsthand a battle that might decide the fate of his city. That evening, after the fighting had tapered off on Pender's part of the field, allowing everyone to breathe more easily, the colonel was surprised and flattered when the Confederate president galloped up and called out: "General Pender, I salute you!"[35]

General Pender. It was music to the ears of an officer with even a modicum of ambition. Pender must have reflected that his first battle, which had opened so badly, could not have ended more pleasingly.

GENERAL AND MRS. WILLIAM DORSEY PENDER. *This photograph was taken at the time of the couple's wedding in Good Spring, North Carolina, March 3, 1859.*

GOVERNOR HENRY T. CLARK OF NORTH CAROLINA. *In August 1861, he appointed Pender colonel of the 6th North Carolina. Three months later, when Clark blocked Pender's attempt to gain higher rank, the colonel referred to him bitterly as an "old Foggy."*

BALTIMORE, MARYLAND, IN 1861. *Pender's first assignment as a Confederate officer was a three-week stint of recruiting duty in this city of divided loyalties.*

UNION SIEGE LINES AT YORKTOWN, VIRGINIA. *Arriving at this besieged city in mid-April 1862, Pender noted: "We have a magnificent army here; the largest and finest we have ever had at [one] place."*

GENERAL JOSEPH E. JOHNSTON. *He commanded the principal Confederate army in Virginia from July 1861 until disabled at Fair Oaks (Seven Pines), May 31, 1862. On at least one occasion, Pender was a dinner guest at the general's headquarters.*

GENERAL WILLIAM H. C. WHITING. *Pender's immediate superior for several months in 1862, Whiting later saw his career decline due to erratic leadership, the result of alcoholism and drug use.*

CONFEDERATE PRESIDENT
JEFFERSON DAVIS. *A spectator
during the fighting at Fair
Oaks, he exclaimed at battle's
close, "General Pender, I salute
you!" Within days, Pender wore
the wreathed stars of a brigadier.*

MECHANICSVILLE, VIRGINIA. *Here on June 26, 1862, Pender performed with
distinction during his maiden effort in brigade command.*

GENERAL ROBERT E. LEE. *Johnston's successor in army command, he was Pender's* beau ideal *as a soldier. In turn, Lee considered Pender his most promising young subordinate.*

GENERAL STEPHEN D. LEE. *Pender described his West Point classmate and close friend as the "salt of the earth." Fanny Pender named their third child (whom her husband never lived to see) after the South Carolina-born general.*

GENERAL THOMAS J. ("STONEWALL") JACKSON. *Pender's longtime division and corps commander, Jackson was secretive and eccentric but a genius at warfare. Pender never warmed up to the man, whom he regarded as cold, aloof, and unconcerned with the welfare of his troops.*

REVIVALISM IN THE ARMY OF NORTHERN VIRGINIA. *Inspired by his devout wife, the once-irreligious Pender became a member of the Episcopal Church when baptized in the camp of his regiment in October 1861. Thereafter he strove to be a "Christian warrior" in both word and deed.*

HARPERS FERRY, VIRGINIA. *This Union garrison surrendered to Jackson's troops on September 15, 1862, an outcome that Pender's energy and determination helped bring about.*

CONFEDERATE TROOPS AT SECOND MANASSAS. *This was another battle in which the hard-driving Pender played a prominent role. Afterward he noted humbly that "I flatter myself I did good service."*

GENERAL AMBROSE P. HILL. *As commander of the Light Division and later of the Third Corps, Army of Northern Virginia, he relied heavily on Pender's fiery spirit and tactical acumen. No one mourned Pender's mortal wounding at Gettysburg more than he.*

CONFEDERATE ATTACK ON CHANCELLORSVILLE. *Pender's dramatic performance here on May 3, 1863, won favorable notice throughout the army and secured his promotion to major general in command of the army's premier division.*

THE LIGHT DIVISION ON THE MARCH. *As he neared Gettysburg, Pender marveled at the stamina and spirit of his men; "I never saw troops march as ours do; they will go 15 or 20 miles a day without leaving a straggler and [w]hoop and yell on all occasions."*

Chapter Six

BARRING THE DOOR
TO RICHMOND

For all the casualties it inflicted—more than 6,100 in the Confederate ranks, something over 5,000 for their opponents—the May 31 fighting at Fair Oaks and Seven Pines was basically inconclusive. Another day's combat was necessary to settle the issue but it would involve only a portion of Johnston's army, without Johnston himself. Having received a disabling wound from a shell fragment, the hero of Manassas was sent to the rear for hospitalization. This was unfortunate for his army as his temporary successor, Gustavus Smith, proved unable to carry the burden of command. On June 1 Smith presided over an unassertive advance by Longstreet that accomplished little.

Early that afternoon, Smith was replaced by Robert E. Lee, who had happily left his desk job in the capital. Viewing the battle as a lost cause, Lee withdrew the army to its original positions outside Richmond. The siege of the Confederate capital was still on, but the besiegers had been roughly handled. The memory of the pounding ensured that McClellan would move more cautiously (if that were possible) in the future. Lee believed that, in due time, he might take advantage of that caution.[1]

As a result of his questionable performance on the 1st, Smith was relieved of his command; he never again served the Army of Northern Virginia. Neither would Johnston, who after recuperating from his wound was given a command in the western theater.

When Smith departed the army, Lee took the opportunity to reorganize. Ten days after Seven Pines, he sent Law's brigade (Whiting again in command), including the 6th North Carolina, along with the brigade of J. B. Hood, to reinforce Jackson, who was still wreaking havoc in the Valley. The rest of Smith's old command, four brigades, remained in the Richmond area; it would be assigned a new commander as soon as Lee found the man for the job.[2]

Pender did not accompany his regiment to the Shenandoah to serve under Jackson—a fortunate thing, for he would come to dislike Stonewall for several reasons, one being his dictatorial and distrustful attitude toward his subordinates. Instead, when it was confirmed that General Pettigrew was in enemy hands and likely to remain there for awhile, Lee appointed Pender a brigadier general to rank from June 3 and assigned him to the captive officer's command. As one of Pettigrew's (now Pender's) aides, Lieutenant Louis G. Young, noted, Pender's appointment was a temporary one, to continue in effect until Pettigrew was released from captivity, at which time, presumably, Pender would be shifted to another command. In fact, Pender's predecessor never returned to his brigade; upon his release from prison, he was the one who was reassigned.[3]

Pettigrew, although not a professional soldier, was a man of character and accomplishment who, like Charles Fisher, had won the respect and admiration of his men through inherent leadership. Pender therefore doubted that he would be warmly received by Pettigrew's troops. Although he left no account of his state of mind when taking over the brigade, he must have felt some trepidation. Still, he would have reminded himself that he had succeeded a popular commander before, and with success. There was no reason he could not do as good a job the second time out.

First impressions often last, and Pender failed to make a good impression on some of the officers he met when he reported to the headquarters of his new command on June 2. Perhaps to mask his nervousness, he assumed a bluff, even curt, manner from the outset. His new subordinates did not respond warmly, even when Pender announced that he "wished to pay the compliment" to their former commander "of keeping his staff as he [Pettigrew] left it." Lieutenant John W. Hinsdale, adjutant general of the brigade, thought Pender "the coldest looking man I ever saw," and he did not care for the officious way in which his new superior began to order him about.[4]

Hinsdale was not the only staff officer put off by the "cold and unfeeling" nature that even Pender sometimes accused himself of harboring. A second aide quickly expressed himself (in private, of course) as "a good deal disgusted" with Pender's brusque manner, for which Hinsdale did not blame him. Within two weeks of Pender's coming, the brigade's quartermaster had become so disenchanted with his new boss ("in fact," Hinsdale noted, "he hates him") that he resigned his position, vowing to serve under no one except the kindly Pettigrew. Yet another aide came to consider Pender "an unmannerly dog," while Hinsdale himself quit the staff after calling Pender "the most perfect resemblance of an iceberg in the shape of a man that I ever knew."[5]

In fairness to Pender, not every member of the headquarters staff came to dislike him. Some ascribed his off-putting behavior to his newness in command; a few professed to see in him great potential. Soon after Pender took command, Lieutenant Young also considered requesting a reassignment. Afterward he was glad he had not, for by remaining at Pender's side he gained what he later called "a valuable experience out of which was born a friendship, the memory of which is very dear to me." Other staff members, including the brigade's ordnance officer, Lieutenant George H. Mills, believed that Pender's coming was a boon to the brigade, which had been roughly handled at Seven Pines but which, thanks to his gifts as a disciplinarian and organizer, rounded "into good shape" in quick time.[6]

If he aggravated some of his staff, Pender made a better initial impression on the line officers, noncommissioned officers, and private soldiers of his brigade. Originally the command comprised two regiments of North Carolina Troops—the 22nd and 34th—plus two independent battalions, the 2nd Arkansas and 22nd Virginia. Three of these units were battle-hardened, but the 34th had a preponderance of raw recruits whom Pender would have to handle carefully if he wished them to become savvy veterans.

Later in the month, the brigade experienced gains and losses as Lee's Army of Northern Virginia underwent a reorganization, one object of which was to strengthen the state identity of each of its brigades. On June 7, the veteran 16th North Carolina Troops joined the brigade, and one week later, the green 38th North Carolina was assigned to it as well. Before month's end the battalion of Virginia infantry was transferred out of the command, leaving Pender four regiments of North Carolinians and a single out-of-state battalion.[7]

After making himself known to the officers through private interviews and to the rank-and-file via parade-ground speeches, Pender put everyone in motion on the drill-field and closely observed the results. He was heartened, if not surprised, to find the veteran regiments proficient at virtually every evolution and formation. He was concerned only with the small size of some of their companies, the result of camp illnesses and battle casualties. These losses had dropped brigade strength to 2,400 effectives, about half the number it ought to have fielded.[8]

In contrast to the thin and proficient veteran regiments, the rookie outfits looked huge but displayed little polish at drill. Still, their energy and enthusiasm made Pender look forward to reviewing their progress once they had a battle or two under their belts. He was further pleased when he learned that the officers of his old 13th North Carolina had initiated efforts to secure a transfer from Jackson's command to Pender's. Although it took four months for the move to be made, the addition of the 13th not only returned Pender to the company of familiar faces but deepened the experience base of the brigade, making it one of the most dependable components of the army.[9]

From his first days in command, Pender ensured not only that his units were drilled early and often but that they did so in close coordination. His concept of drilling by brigade rather than by regiment or battalion appears to have broken new ground. According to a member of his staff, "other Brigadiers asked him why he did it, and he gave such reasons that they began to follow his example. " The basic reason was that the method produced dramatic results. The staffer noted that "it brought his regiments into close communication with each other ... and inspired a confidence and a[n] esprit de corps that made his Brigade a unit in action, easily handled, each regiment relying implicitly on the others, and having unbounded confidence in their General."[10]

If Pender was pleased with what he observed on the field of practice, he was delighted by his divisional affiliation and his immediate superior. On June 11, the three brigades of Whiting's command that had not accompanied their leader to the Valley were assigned to Major General Ambrose Powell Hill. Hill had assimilated the units into a command he proudly dubbed the "Light Division." The name, which connoted speed and agility, had antecedents in European military history. Recent namesakes included the Napoleonic Light Division and the Light Division of the British army, which had fought in the Crimean War.[11]

Hill was a commander worth serving under. A West Pointer who had graduated seven years in front of Pender, the redhaired Virginian was a veteran of the Mexican and Seminole Wars and had served in western Virginia and at Manassas. He had made an exemplary record in brigade command before moving up to his new position. A highly talented drillmaster and tactician, he was occasionally slowed by a chronic urological complaint, but when in good health he could be counted on to attack and defend to the utmost of his energy.

From their first meeting, Pender and Hill hit it off. They shared many qualities, including coolheadedness under fire, a sometimes-brittle pride, and a high regard for discipline, dignity, and decorum. Their differences were mostly of personality. While Pender felt it necessary to maintain a grave demeanor both on and off the battlefield, A. P. Hill was more open, affable, and volatile. In later years one who knew him opined that of all the Confederate field leaders, Hill "was the most genial and lovable in his disposition." Pender was never described that way, but Hill and he quickly forged a working relationship that would redound to the benefit of both, and quickly.[12]

* * *

Pender understood that Johnston's offensive of May 31 had caught the Yankees off-balance but had neither crippled them nor lifted the siege of Richmond. Given McClellan's strength, perhaps neither was possible. The prospect must have given Pender pause, but he spoke of it bravely to Fanny. A few days after taking over his brigade, he answered a question she had posed to him: "Darling, you ask my opinion of our prospects. They are in some adversity now, but I do not and cannot believe they can ever conquer us. Let them take Richmond, what then; we can still fight and will fight. Let them take every large town and still we are not conquered. Did not the English have all the towns in the Revolution, and did [not] our fathers fight on until the end was gained? … No, my dear wife, never despair; we men will never give up…. Richmond has not been taken yet and before it is they will have to fight many a battle and desperate ones too."[13]

Behind the brave words, Pender must have sensed that the Confederacy could not afford the loss of its capital for fear of the political fallout. Undoubtedly he hoped that his army would launch a sortie to break the siege before McClellan clamped a stranglehold on the city. Robert E. Lee was of the same mind. Thus, as June wore on, the Army of Northern Virginia (as it was now called) underwent a slow but gradual shift from static defense to mobile offense.

The change was noticeable. In mid-month Pender was hard at work strengthening the works his brigade occupied five miles from the city limits. On one occasion—responding to an order from Hill to strengthen his left flank against an anticipated attack—his penchant for order and exactitude lowered his standing still further in the eyes of Lieutenant Hinsdale. The staff officer watched as Pender had his men cut a row of rifle pits in a straight line parallel to the Chickahominy River, "to make them look pretty I suppose." In so doing, the brigadier created what his adjutant considered a dangerous salient. Hinsdale was also surprised when Pender refused to expose his men to enemy fire by having them cut down a stand of trees, which "alone could make the rifle pits effective." When Hinsdale brought the matter to his superior's attention, Pender gave a curt reply. "From that time," Hinsdale wrote, "I took up the idea that he was a conceited fool…."[14]

Within a week of Pender's supposed exercise in folly, Lee was making preparations to sally forth and smite the foe. Since he was not quite ready to strike, he granted Pender a brief leave in Richmond, one object of which was to help Fanny's older brother secure a position in the army. He had already been trying to attach to his staff Lieutenant Jake Shepperd, who for the past year had been serving as a line officer in the 4th North Carolina. Now he attempted to gain the release of Jake's brother Frank from the Confederate Navy so that he too might join Pender's headquarters family. In this effort, however, he was unsuccessful. In a conference at the Navy Department, Secretary Stephen Mallory declared Frank Shepperd too capable an officer to be wasted on army service. Had Frank been inattentive to his duties, however, Mallory "would have been glad to have got rid of him."[15]

When writing Fanny of his failed errand, Pender appended neither news nor rumors of a forward movement. Yet one was very much in the offing. By the last week in June, McClellan had repositioned his army astride the Chickahominy but without reducing its vulnerability. Now all but one of his corps were situated below the river. The Valley campaign having ended, Stonewall Jackson and his men were en route to Richmond and General Irvin McDowell's corps, now idling at Fredericksburg, was again available to the Army of the Potomac. Major General Fitz John Porter's Fifth Army Corps held an isolated position north of the stream to form a link with McDowell. Porter's defensive line ran from a point northeast of the Richmond suburb of Mechanicsville, south and east toward Gaines's Mill. On a recent raid, J. E. B. Stuart had reconnoitered the position and found it ripe for assault. After conferring with Pender's classmate, Robert E. Lee agreed.[16]

Lee planned a strike against Porter's upper flank in hopes of rolling up his line toward the Chickahominy. If successful, the assault would block McDowell's advance and forestall further siege operations. Porter's opponents would be the divisions of Longstreet, D. H. Hill, and A. P. Hill—a total of nearly 48,000 men—to which the newly arrived Jackson would add 18,500 in time for the offensive. While the four divisions lashed out, the troops of Magruder and Huger, despite being handily outnumbered, would threaten, and thus hold the attention of, McClellan's main body south of the river. The operation seemed a risky undertaking, for success hinged on an unusually high number of variables. Yet the Confederate leader saw it as his best—perhaps his only—chance to prevent the slow, painful death of an army and a city.[17]

While Pender was not privy to the details of Lee's strategy, he was aware that the army was preparing to advance and perhaps attack. On June 24, A. P. Hill had his brigades stand ready to move east, at a moment's notice, toward Meadow Bridge on the Chickahominy. Before he got the order to move out, Pender sat down to pen a letter to Fanny. Instead of dwelling on the coming fight, he wrote of family matters, including the recent death from scarlet fever of Robert Pender's wife, and the serious illness of brother David, who had left the 13th North Carolina on sick leave. Pender "shudder[ed] ... to think of the consequences" that awaited the surviving spouses and children.[18]

In contrast to such tragic news, the general reported himself in good health. So too was his brigade, which now consisted of 2,700 effectives. He spoke of the army's growing confidence in General Lee, and in the Lord: "It seems to me that we can with the favor of God expect a most decided victory." And told Fanny she should "not feel uneasy if you do not hear from [me] for several days." He suspected he would be rather busy in the interim.[19]

*   *   *

At 5:30 on the afternoon of Wednesday, June 25, the tension along the defense lines was broken with the receipt of orders to start marching. Pender quickly relayed the word to his senior subordinates. When it began to move, just after dark, the brigade went forward with the 34th North Carolina at the head of the column, followed by the 22nd, the battalion of Arkansas infantry, then the 16th and 38th North Carolina, with Captain R. Snowden Andrews's Maryland battery, drawn from the division's artillery battalion, bringing up the rear.

After a couple of hours on the road, the brigade halted in a woods along the Meadow Bridge Road. The men were permitted to fall out and bivouac. While waiting for the order to resume the advance—expected to come at about 4:00 A.M.—Pender called up his regimental commanders. According to William J. Hoke, colonel of the 38th Troops, Pender informed everyone "that we would be in a fight soon, & that he expected every one to do his duty; the officers & men were [to be] informed that if this battle was lost Richmond would fall...." Hoke believed the speech had a good effect on everyone assembled; when it ended, "all seemed ready to do their duty."[20]

Pender had everyone ready to march by 4:00, but the word to move out did not arrive. Officers and men waited quietly in the morning darkness for musketry or artillery to start echoing from Meadow Bridge, but the sounds of fighting did not reach their ears until the sun was far above the horizon. This time the delay was due not to an acoustic shadow, but to Stonewall Jackson. The troops from the Valley were to have opened the attack at daylight by charging the Federal right and rear near Mechanicsville. Jackson was to have signaled his approach to the far left of A. P. Hill's line, the brigade of Brigadier General Lawrence O'Bryan Branch. But Jackson, through confusion and tardiness that he never attempted to explain, was not in position to attack until midafternoon, and when he was, Branch, just as inexplicably, failed to alert Hill. The result was a strategic foul-up unhappily reminiscent of the early going on May 31.

Jackson's error of commission and Branch's of omission drove the impetuous Hill into unilateral action. Without taking time to inform Robert E. Lee, he advanced his division to the bridge. First to cross the span, just short of 4:00 P.M., was the brigade of Brigadier General Charles W. Field, followed by the brigades of Brigadier Generals Joseph Reid Anderson, James Jay Archer, Pender, and Maxcy Gregg. Field's men quickly engaged Union skirmishers on the far left of the Fifth Corps and pressed them back upon Mechanicsville. Behind Field, Anderson and Archer kept on the winding road that led from the bridge to the village, while Pender and Gregg marched directly east, across open fields, toward Field's rear.

Soon after it left the bridge road, Pender's column came under a shelling by Union batteries hidden in woods north of Mechanicsville. In textbook fashion, Pender ordered up a section of Andrews's battery. When the two pieces opened, he moved east, his main body sheltered behind a strong skirmish line. His artillery support and the determined pace of his advance persuaded the enemy gunners to limber up and withdraw.

En route to the enemy's position, Pender suddenly realized that he was missing almost one-quarter of his strength. Relying on the geographic knowledge of a local guide, he had placed his left regiment, Colonel John S. McElroy's 16th North Carolina, on a road that should have brought it in on the flank of the rest of the brigade. Instead, the 16th was shunted well to the north beyond Pender's sight and reach. With his remaining regiments and single battalion, the brigadier continued to advance until a courier from Hill ordered him to close up on Field's brigade. Field was then engaging the main body of the Fifth Corps, the Pennsylvania Reserves of Major General George A. McCall, dug in behind Beaver Dam Creek.[21]

Pender attempted to conform his movements to Field's, but because the latter moved in such a manner as to expose his right flank to enemy fire, Pender's own right came under a barrage from cannons guarding a line of heavily occupied rifle pits. Leaving Colonel James Conner's 22nd North Carolina and Major W. N. Bronaugh's 2nd Arkansas Battalion to press the center of the enemy line in concert with Field, Pender rode off to deal with the threat to his right. Without waiting for an order from Hill, he obliqued the two regiments on his right—the 34th and 38th—until they were aiming for the Union left, opposite Ellerson's Mill on Beaver Dam Creek.

Pender's movement connoted enterprise, but it hinged on luck that was not granted him. First, his troops were heading for an impassable barrier, a wide and tall abatis of sharpened stakes, behind which thousands of sharp-shooters lay in wait. Second, the Pennsylvanians detected the advance when Pender's men were 200 yards from the cannons. They swung the guns about and opened at murderous range, bowling over rows of North Carolinians with shell and canister.

The lay of the land was such that cover was hard to come by, and so Pender withdrew the 38th before it could be annihilated. In his after-action report—the first he penned as a general officer—he took pains to note that despite the shelling, Colonel Hoke's pea-green regiment had "advanced bold-ly" to within 100 yards of the abatis and had "maintained its ground" until recalled. Pender was less complimentary of the other, equally inexperienced outfit he had thrown at the Yankee defenses. Under the wayward leadership of Colonel Richard H. Riddick, the 34th North Carolina had veered off-course, failing not only to strike the guns but to support Hoke's men against the can-nonade.[22]

When the bloodied 38th withdrew and the unharmed 34th made its roundabout way to the rear, Pender held his main body out of cannon-range. Later, when the shelling slackened, he sent the 34th to the far right, "to make as much diversion as possible in that direction." The results, however, were negligible.[23]

At this point Pender's men were spelled by Brigadier General Roswell S. Ripley's brigade, the lead element of D. H. Hill's division, which had followed A. P. Hill across Meadow Bridge. Ripley was on the scene because Pender had personally importuned Harvey Hill for two regiments to help him turn the Union flank, but one brigade was all that Hill could spare. Ripley's men advanced resolutely and hopefully over much the same ground as the 38th North Carolina had crossed to its regret.

In doing so, the newcomers wandered farther to the left than both Pender and A. P. Hill thought prudent. The result was predictable. Pender, who had been slightly injured when his horse was killed by shrapnel, again advanced the 34th, this time to cover Ripley's left, to no avail. The relief brigade took heavier casualties than the units that had gone before and gained no more ground. Ripley, in fact, got only as far as the mill-race at Ellerson's before his advance bogged down at about 9:00 P.M. His men hung on at the mill, mak-ing ineffective attempts to cross the stream. All Ripley could do was to team with Pender to safeguard the vulnerable right flank until their commands were relieved early on June 27.[24]

*   *   *

The day just ended loomed like a nightmare in the minds of those who had survived it. The fighting had been so savage and yet so confused that a lieutenant in the 22nd North Carolina gave up all hope of explaining it in a letter to his family. The attackers had fought stubbornly, valiantly, but they had not achieved tactical success for Robert E. Lee. In fact, as Douglas Southall Freeman would observe, Lee's once-promising offensive had ended as a "ghastly failure." Up and down the line, including the front of the Light Division, Confederates had failed to dislodge Yankees from the positions behind Beaver Dam Creek. Those positions had turned out to be far stronger than anyone in gray had expected. Later D. H. Hill laid the blame on inadequate reconnaissance. No one, he noted, had known the nature or the complexity of the Union defenses until it was too late.[25]

Despite their repulse, the Southerners had gained a great deal in the strategic sense. On June 25, McClellan had launched a limited offensive on the south side of the Chickahominy that had run aground against heavy resistance. Now his isolated right flank had absorbed a blow, while other Confederates had put up a fight south of the river. Although the attack at Mechanicsville had been tossed back with great loss to the South (1,500 Rebel casualties as against fewer than 400 in the Fifth Corps), McClellan began to fret that he was outnumbered and outpositioned on both sides of the river.

He reacted—as Lee had hoped—impulsively, precipitately. On the evening of the 26th he ordered Porter to fall back to prepared positions at Gaines's Mill, near the bridges that his corps could use to join the rest of the army. Thus began a withdrawal that, over the next week, carried the Army of the Potomac almost 20 miles from the city it had been ready to take by assault or investment.[26]

Considering the drubbing the Yankees had administered on June 26, Pender must have been surprised by their retreat. In the brief respite granted him before a pursuit was put in motion, he took stock of his situation. His command had suffered almost 200 casualties, three-quarters of them in the ranks of the 38th during its unequal duel with Yankee cannons. Three of the losses had come in the upper ranks of the brigade: Major Bronaugh of the 2nd Arkansas had been killed, Colonel Hoke of the 38th North Carolina had been wounded, and Colonel Conner of the 22nd had been disabled by a leg wound. Two staff officers had also become *hors de combat*, Lieutenant Young having an ear lacerated by a shell fragment and Lieutenant Colonel William

J. Green, the only volunteer aide de camp on the headquarters staff, having been shot through the heart while carrying messages to various portions of Pender's line. Pender himself had barely escaped injury when blown out of the saddle. In sum, his command had experienced a bloodletting, with worse likely to come.[27]

Pender did not know how to gauge his own performance in the fight just ended. He had erred at the outset, as he had at Seven Pines, this time by losing control of a regiment. The 16th had ended up on D. H. Hill's part of the field, where the division leader had appropriated it for his own use—with unhappy results. At Hill's order, Colonel McElroy had gone forward to "feel the enemy," who turned out to be in overwhelming force. In consequence, the 16th had been, in the words of Lieutenant Young, "knocked… to pieces."[28]

Pender had also fought most of the day without the 22nd North Carolina and the 2nd Arkansas Battalion, which had gone to the support of General Field. Assuming effective control of both units, Field had placed them in a dense woods where Yankees surrounded and scattered them. When their leader fell, the 2nd Arkansas had disintegrated. At battle's end, only 30 members of the battalion remained with the brigade.[29]

Pender could take credit for what he had accomplished with the regiments that remained with him throughout the fight. They had firmly supported not only Field's brigade but Ripley's as well. The 38th North Carolina had made a gallant effort against impossible odds. And Pender's combativeness, displayed in his repeated efforts against the abatis and rifle pits near Ellerson's Mill, to the extent of seeking help from other commands, won the admiration of many onlookers, including his superiors.

Still, Pender was upset by the things that had gone awry, and he was appalled by the slaughter on his part of the field. Mulling over these concerns, the next morning he put an unusual question to Louis Young. "He asked me to tell him candidly," the aide recalled, "if I thought he was fit to command the Brigade." Young, who the previous day had heatedly but unsuccessfully advised his commander against charging cannons, had a basis for replying in the negative. Nevertheless, considering Pender's overall performance, the staff officer decided that he was fit to command and told him so. The brigadier looked immensely relieved. Later Young mused that "if I had said *no* I believe in his t[h]en frame of mind he would have resigned his commission."[30]

*   *   *

On the bright, warm morning of June 27, A. P. Hill prepared, of necessity, to resume the assault on Beaver Dam Creek. When Pender and the other brigade leaders got the word, they visualized another frontal assault on the Yankee position and a second, perhaps a bloodier, repulse. They knew, however, that although he had been late in reaching the field, Stonewall Jackson was now in position on the right rear of Porter's Federals. After a hasty conference, the other commanders agreed that Pender should advise General Hill to withhold an assault until Jackson could strike from his more advantageous position. It was possible Stonewall would uproot the Union line with little or no assistance from Hill.

Pender sent Lieutenant Young, by now his most trusted aide, to run the errand. First, however, he escorted the aide on a reconnaissance of the ground between Jackson and the enemy. Then Young galloped back to Mechanicsville, where he found Hill and General Longstreet, the senior division commander, poring over a map. Young broached his errand to Hill, who deferred a reply till Longstreet spoke. With a look of extreme aggravation, Longstreet told the aide: "Go back to those Generals and tell them, that they will not succeed unless they try, that the attack must be made as directed...."[31]

Rather sheepishly, Young carried the message back to Pender, who "made no comment, but became very serious" at the thought of renewing the assault. As it turned out, however, there had been no reason to contact Hill or Longstreet. When Pender probed the enemy line in cooperation with Gregg's brigade, late that morning, he encountered no cannon-fire, only scattered volleys of musketry. Moving closer, he found that only a rear guard remained in position behind the millrace. The remaining Federals, realizing that their safety had been compromised by Jackson's presence toward their rear, had decamped for points south and east.[32]

Some of Gregg's men crossed the creek and flanked the rear guard into retreat. The remainder of their brigade then forded near the millrace. They were followed, at about 2:00 P.M., by Pender's advance. Beyond the stream everyone hastened after the fugitives by way of the River Road which paralleled the Chickahominy. In rear of Pender came Andrews's battery, the balance of the Light Division, and then Longstreet's troops. Meanwhile, D. H. Hill's soldiers were advancing farther north along the Old Church Road. D. H. Hill planned to swing south and join his comrades once the Federals had been brought to bay.

A little before 2:30, skirmishers from Gregg's and Pender's brigades found

Porter's troops holding a formidable-looking line of works, semicircular in shape, on the far side of three natural obstacles: a dense woods, Powhite Creek, and Boatswain's Swamp. Trees had been felled to add strength to the position, while the muzzles of cannons pointed toward the approaching Rebels. It looked like the Federals were at least as well situated as the previous day. To capture their position would cost an attacker severely.[33]

Undaunted by the odds, A. P. Hill prepared to go forward. As soon as Longstreet arrived to support it, part of the Light Division swept forward, its men keening the tremulous, nerve-tingling cry already known as the Rebel Yell. At first, only the brigades of Branch, Gregg, and Anderson were engaged, Pender's men being held in reserve to the left and rear along the Cold Harbor Road. The respite enabled Pender's command to reunite. Having miscon-strued Pender's instructions, Colonel Riddick had moved to the Cold Harbor vicinity well in advance of the rest of the brigade. His errant march earned the colonel another black mark in Pender's mental ledger. Riddick, whom some in the brigade considered a tough and brave fighter, would fall wounded in the day's fight, but his loss would not depress his superior. Pender considered the regiment's executive officer, Lieutenant Colonel R. H. Gray, to be as courageous as his superior and more levelheaded.

When Porter's marksmen and batteries began to tear holes in the front ranks of the Light Division, Pender's brigade was hurled into the fight. It moved out under the watchful eye of Robert E. Lee, who had ridden up the Cold Harbor Road to observe the fighting at close range. As he led them for-ward, Pender shouted to his men: "The eyes of your chieftain are upon you!"[34]

Pender guided the brigade over boggy ground, through an open interval between Anderson's troops on the south and Gregg's to the north, and into a woodlot on the right side of the Cold Harbor Road. Once among the trees, Pender reported, "we were soon hotly engaged, and drove the enemy slowly before us for about 250 yards." At that point resistance stiffened and the North Carolinians took casualties. Still, McElroy's 16th and Gray's 22nd man-aged to plow through the blue line until they gained the crest of the plateau on which Porter's defenses rested.[35]

By now Pender, having studied at short range the obstacles he faced, had sent Lieutenant Young to the rear to scare up reinforcements. After several minutes the staff officer returned at the head of one of General Branch's regi-ments. But the 37th North Carolina did not arrive in time to secure McElroy's and Gray's hold on the crest. Union supports rushed up, flanking and staggering both regiments. Many of Gregg's troops, on the division's left, had already fallen back, forcing Pender, who had been slightly wounded in the right arm, to withdraw and regroup his command. He tried to lead it into the fight yet again, only to find his path blocked by hundreds, if not thousands, of bluecoats. In his report he explained that "my men were rallied and pushed forward again, but did not advance far before they fell back, and I think I do but justice to my men to say that they did not commence it.... My men here fought nobly, and maintained their ground with great stubbornness."[36]

The abortive counterattack effectively ended the brigade's participation in the fighting around Gaines's Mill. But even as Pender's bullet-riddled companies passed to the rear, other forces were keeping pressure on all sectors of the Union line. Late in the afternoon, Hood's brigade of Whiting's division and troops from Longstreet's command, including the brigade of Brigadier General George E. Pickett, broke through in a sector that had been weakened by the hammering of the Light Division. When other gaps appeared in the line, it cracked and collapsed, sending Porter's survivors racing for Grapevine Bridge over the Chickahominy. Pockets of stubborn resistance and the darkness of night prevented the Army of Northern Virginia from cutting off the retreat and turning defeat into disaster.[37]

*   *   *

The following day, June 28, was a day of rest and recuperation for the Light Division, as also for much of Lee's army. Pender, who now wore his injured arm in a sling, was truly grateful. As best he could, he patched up the fissures in his ranks, finding capable replacements for the field officers whose services he had lost over the preceding two days.

Before day's end, it had become clear not only that the Fifth Corps, but the Union's entire Army of the Potomac, was fleeing from the gates of Richmond. Lee intended to push that army as far as possible from the capital and keep it there. On the morning of the 29th, Robert E. Lee sent his advance echelon over the river in pursuit of the more numerous but less resolute enemy. Longstreet's command, followed by the Light Division, crossed at New Bridge, a time-consuming operation. Meanwhile, Jackson, D. H. Hill, and Whiting crossed four miles downstream upon recently burned and more recently repaired bridges. Magruder, Huger, and the other commands south of the river pressed eastward in hopes of helping cut off McClellan's retreat.

By the time Pender's brigade reached the far shore and marched down along it, it was late afternoon; contact with the Yankees would have to wait till tomorrow. Given the heat of the day; the lack of potable water along the route, and the clouds of dust through which everyone passed, Pender was ready to call it a day. That evening he and his staff took their supper in the home of a farmer and spent the night on the floor of the house. The makeshift bed would have felt hard to a waking man, wrote Lieutenant Hinsdale, "but soft to a sleepy soldier."[38]

If June 29 was hot, the next day was torrid. Under a merciless sun, dozens of men fell along the roadside, gasping for breath and water. Undeterred, Longstreet and A. P. Hill, accompanied by Lee, kept moving at a steady pace down the Long Bridge Road. As the troops crossed the tracks of the Richmond & York River Railroad and approached White Oak Swamp, the rear of one of McClellan's columns came into view in the late afternoon light. Lee ordered an immediate attack, and Longstreet's men sprang forward.

Just as at Mechanicsville and Gaines's Mill, the attackers found their way strewn with breastworks, well protected by artillery. The guns brought Longstreet's advance to an abrupt halt. For a time Hill's people remained in the rear in the role of spectators while the fighting ebbed and flowed in front of them. Not long after Pender's men had formed in column of regiments, artillery rounds screamed in their direction. "We had hardly taken our places," wrote Hinsdale, who stood next to his colonel, "when a 12 pound shell struck in front of us—we could hear it coming a long time, and ricocheted, knocking up the dirt just in front of us. Then it struck, passing between us, we were three feet apart, Gen. Pender & I., and cutting off the head of a captain in the 16th N. C. who stood just behind us."[39]

After 30 minutes of standing fire, unable to fight back, Longstreet, the senior commander on the scene, directed Hill to support his division. Gregg's brigade was the first unit to answer the call, followed by those of Branch, Field, and Pender. When Pender's turn came, he advanced in rear of Brigadier General Joseph B. Kershaw's brigade of Longstreet's division until he was within striking distance of the Union center. In his report of the engagement, Pender claimed that he penetrated as far as the junction of the Darbytown and Long Bridge Roads, but he was in error, as that site lay well behind the enemy line. He appears to have halted well to the west of the intersection, in rear of Field's brigade.[40]

On the verge of closing with the enemy, Pender was astonished to see a blue regiment cross his front, from right to left, apparently oblivious to his presence. Thankful for large favors, his troops poured volley after volley into the enemy flank at a range of under 100 yards (30, according to Hindsdale). The fusillade scattered the Yankees "in every direction." When they fled, they uncovered an abandoned battery of rifled cannons, a prize of great value to infantrymen. Pender acted quickly, deploying in such a way as to foil enemy efforts to retake the guns and to outflank the North Carolinians.

After securing the threatened sector with a detachment of the brigade, Pender "pushed forward [with] the rest well into the woods." The action would come to characterize him—while another commander would have been content to shore up his line and block a flanking movement, Pender went over to the offensive, rapidly and aggressively.[41]

On this occasion, however, perhaps he should have been more prudent. As soon as they entered the woods his men, whose cartridge boxes had not been replenished since Mechanicsville, began to run low on ammunition. Eventually Pender had to pull the brigade back to the edge of the trees, though not out of the fray. En route to the rear, his regiments were fired on by a battery. Instead of continuing his retrograde, Pender turned the rear of his command about and charged the guns before they could fire another round. Wide-eyed artillerists fled for their lives.

With darkness descending, Pender finally retired to more defensible ground on the crest of a ridge. Even then he was not done fighting. Happening upon two of Field's regiments that had become separated from their command, Pender deployed one to bolster his new line and led the other forward to threaten the now-retreating enemy. The eleventh-hour drive accomplished little, however, for the Northerners abandoned the field so quickly they left behind their dead and many of their wounded. The battle of White Oak Swamp (or Glendale, or Frayser's Farm) was over.[42]

* * *

Pender would receive much credit for the success Hill's division achieved in the multi-named fight. That success had contributed materially to forcing the Yankees to flee south to Malvern Hill, a commanding eminence on the north side of the James River. There McClellan would be beyond striking range of the Confederate capital. Richmond, which a week ago had appeared on the verge of capture, had been saved, but at enormous cost—more than 30,000 Confederate and some 25,000 Union casualties.

No one was more gratified by the Army of the Potomac's withdrawal than

Jefferson Davis, who once again left his office in the city to stand with his nation's troops on the firing lines. Late in the afternoon of the 30th, as he had one month before, the Confederate president made his way to Pender's side, where he congratulated the brigadier on his recent performances. On this occasion, noticing the sling that supported Pender's arm, Davis was "so gracious" as to inquire about the severity of the wound and the progress of Pender's recuperation.[43]

While the majority of the army pushed south next day, Pender and his command spent the first half of July 1 resting on the hard earth. Not until 2:00 P.M. was the brigade ordered into line and sent south. Throughout the journey, the boom of cannons could be heard from the direction in which Pender was heading. Most of his soldiers anticipated another battle, but fortunately, they were not prescient. Officers of the divisional staff escorted them almost two miles from the scene of the previous day's fighting, but halted them short of Malvern Hill. Then, after waiting in line for some time, they countermarched for about 500 yards and halted again. By now everyone, including Pender, was confused and frustrated. By now, too, evening was approaching and it was too late to commit the brigade to the fighting farther south.[44]

Thus Pender's command was not repaid for its exemplary performance on the 30th by being thrown into the cauldron of death one day later. The fighting at Malvern Hill, last of the so-called Seven Days' Battles, was the outcome of Robert E. Lee's mistaken attempt to prod an already-retreating army into full flight. It culminated in three hours of suicidal assaults against an impregnable position. Union sharpshooters posted on the slopes of the hill blew the attackers—portions of D. H. Hill's, Magruder's, and Huger's divisions—to pieces. Those not felled by bullets were blasted by more than 100 cannons parked hub-to-hub at the summit. By day's end, more than 5,300 Confederates had been killed or wounded without gaining any advantage over their enemy. When Pender learned the scope of the carnage, and the futility of it all, he considered himself and his men truly fortunate to have been kept out of it.[45]

Soon, in fact, he was out of the war itself—temporarily. A few days after McClellan's army withdrew from Malvern Hill to Harrison's Landing on the James, Pender took leave of the army and went home to North Carolina. There he would recuperate from his wound while seeing Fanny and the children for the first time in more than four months. By any standard of measurement, he had earned a rest.[46]

Chapter Seven

"I Flatter Myself I Did Good Service"

The time Pender spent in Good Spring helped heal not only his injured arm but also his frame of mind. The Seven Days' Battles had taken a terrible toll of his brigade—more than 850 casualties, nearly one-third of the command's pre-campaign strength. The loss rate troubled their leader a great deal, especially when he considered that the errors he made at Seven Pines and Mechanicsville may have accounted for some of them. Beyond his concern for the men, Pender was worn down physically, having long snatched at sleep wherever he could find it. He had slept on hard earth, on bare floors, and, on the evening following the slaughter at Malvern Hill, on a pile of newly cut wheat. Thus the respite he enjoyed at the home of his in-laws, where he could sleep in a real bed, was a tonic. In the bosom of his family, the war became a faint echo. He knew he had not experienced "such perfect content[ment]" in a long time.[1]

Which made it all the harder to break away at the end of 20 days and return to the seat of war. "There is no rest for a poor soldier," he lamented. Soon he was kissing his wife and babies good-bye and boarding the train at Salem. By 11:00 A.M. on July 29 he had reached Richmond, where the buzz of war could not be drowned out by the most determined exercise of will.[2]

Although he was back in the capital, his brigade was not. It had left for points west the previous evening under the supervision of General Archer. Throughout Pender's absence from the front, McClellan's shot-torn army had remained at Harrison's Landing, where it showed no signs of threatening either General Lee or the seat of his nation's government. Soon, however, Lee had a second threat—a second Union army—to contend with. In the wake of the Valley campaign, the War Office in Washington had unified the three major forces that had failed to run down Jackson's "foot cavalry." The result was the Army of Virginia, commanded by an officer heretofore unknown in the eastern theater but who had been successful in the west, Major General John Pope. The missions assigned Pope's army included cooperating with McClellan to defeat Lee and striking toward Gordonsville, terminus of the Virginia Central Railroad, there to break the primary link between Richmond and the Shenandoah. While Pender lolled in North Carolina, Pope had begun to move on the rail junction at the head of 50,000 men. He expected to be reinforced with troops sent him from the Peninsula.[3]

The threat to Confederate communications was severe and had to be neutralized before disaster struck. Thus, on July 13, Lee sent the left wing of his army, two infantry divisions and some cavalry under Jackson, to halt Pope short of the railroad. For a time A. P. Hill's division remained with the right wing, opposing the Yankees at Harrison's Landing, but then Hill and Longstreet became embroiled in a controversy stemming from newspaper accounts of their roles at White Oak Swamp. The heated dispute that resulted took dangerous turns when the jealous Longstreet arrested Hill and the prickly Hill challenged Longstreet to a duel. Lee intervened to patch things up, at least temporarily, but by late July the two men remained on icy terms. When Jackson requested reinforcements in order to subdue Pope, Lee on July 27 sent the Light Division to Gordonsville, thus avoiding further squabbling on the Peninsula. And so Pender had arrived too late to accompany his command west. He was just in time, however, to accompany Hill, who had been released from arrest only after the Light Division departed.[4]

Leaving Richmond on the evening of July 30, the generals rode together all the way to Gordonsville, a 10-hour trip. Upon stepping down from the train, Pender spied a familiar face, Fanny's older brother, Hamilton Shepperd, an officer in Jackson's division, who inquired about events at the home his brother-in-law had just visited. As Pender wrote his wife, having gone without a furlough for months, "Ham" wondered how Fanny "managed to get me home." Obviously, Ham lacked the connections a general officer had at his disposal. Pender also sent Fanny news about her oldest brother, William ("Willy"), who had followed Ham's lead by joining Jackson's command and whom Pender saw frequently during his time at Gordonsville.[5]

After a long chat with Ham, Pender rode a borrowed horse to the campsite of his brigade. As he trotted along, he was struck by the number of tents that stretched into the distance in every direction. "We have quite a force here," he told Fanny, "and unless Pope should be or has been reinforced we will probably be too much for him." Upon reaching his destination, he was greeted warmly not only by his line officers but by a couple of new staff members, Captain S. S. Kirkland, successor to Lieutenant Mills as brigade ordnance officer, and Captain Samuel A. Ashe, an Edgecombe County acquaintance who had replaced the disgruntled Hinsdale as brigade adjutant. Welcoming gestures attended to, Pender inspected the enlisted men in their quarters and on the parade-ground. He did not like what he saw.[6]

Every unit had shrunk. The ranks of his four regiments looked terribly thin, principally the result of the carnage on the Peninsula. But he was especially alarmed when he learned that not every gap was the result of wounds or disease. On the journey from Richmond several men had slipped away from their units; none had returned. The problem of desertion was destined to plague Pender's command, and in fact virtually every brigade in the Army of Northern Virginia, for the rest of the war. As the fighting dragged on and individual victories failed to produce final triumph, growing numbers of men—especially those of whom Pender had spoken so feelingly at Bristoe Station, with starving families at home—quit the army for good. In the months to come Pender would publicize his condemnation of desertion to subordinates and superiors, as well as to editors and politicians on the state and national levels—but to no avail.[7]

At Gordonsville he had little time to deal with the matter—little time for much of anything beyond drilling the men and filling some officer vacancies with veteran non-coms. Within a week of his arrival from Richmond he was writing Fanny that "we are now ready loaded up to move, but where to is not for those of my low rank to know.…" Orders to stand ready to march had come the previous day without so much as a hint of direction or destination. This was typical of his commander, Pender had learned: "None of Jackson's old officers ever try to divine his movements."[8]

Those who were familiar with their commander's foibles included Charles S. Winder, who commanded the division once led by Stonewall himself. At Gordonsville, Pender fraternized as often as possible with the Maryland-born brigadier, with whom he had shared garrison duty in the Northwest. Captain Ashe, who also dined as Winder's guest, recorded one conversation during which their host regaled Pender and him with an account of Jackson's Valley operations: "He thought Jackson eccentric almost to the point of aberation [sic] of mind, yet a genius in war."[9]

Pender shared only some of these sentiments. For all he knew, Jackson might be the second coming of Napoleon, but having been influenced by the assessments of other subordinates less well disposed toward the general, Pender thought of Stonewall as a peculiar, querulous man who could be insensitive to the physical and moral needs of his troops. Pender was not happy that the Light Division had come under the control of the hero of the Shenandoah.

Of course, to harbor such critical thoughts—even if he kept it to himself—suggested that Pender was backsliding again in his religion. It was only one of several lapses of faith of which he considered himself guilty. That realization was especially painful now that he appeared to stand on the verge of another campaign. "Oh how I do wish I could be a Christian," he exclaimed to his wife. "I feel now how far I am from what I would believe myself [to be] and what we should be, particularly one who has taken such solemn vows as I have." He had attended church in Gordonsville on Sunday, August 3—the service had been conducted by the chaplain of the 13th North Carolina, Reverend Stuart—but the experience had not soothed him; in fact, he had come away from it fearful he was beyond redemption. Now he asked Fanny to pray for him, that he might not go into a fight with his back turned to the Lord.[10]

*   *   *

By August 7, the advance element of Pope's army had reached Culpeper Court House, 20-some miles north of Gordonsville and half that distance above Cedar Mountain. That day Jackson started north to engage the enemy, hoping to overwhelm the only troops then around Culpeper—the Second Army Corps, almost 9,000 strong, under Major General Nathaniel P. Banks, former speaker of the U.S. House of Representatives. If Banks were beaten, Stonewall could strike and defeat the rest of Pope's army in detail.

By the evening of the 8th, following a rather confused movement north, the result of a change in the marching order that Jackson had failed to communicate to Hill, the Light Division had gone into bivouac one mile north of Orange Court House. The next morning the three divisions under Jackson forded the Rapidan and by midmorning had closed up at the foot of Cedar Mountain. Jackson's leading division, Major General Richard S. Ewell's, had already begun sparring with Union cavalry northwest of Cedar Mountain. Reinforced by Jackson's main body, including Winder's division, Ewell began to angle toward Banks's left flank. The Yankee infantry had advanced to Cedar Mountain, looking for a fight.[11]

For some hours the fighting raged inconclusively as both sides jockeyed for position; during this period the Light Division closed up in Jackson's rear. As soon as he reached the field, Pender began to look for an opportunity to commit his brigade, which stood fourth in line behind Jackson. Captain Ashe accompanied his general as Pender rode along the rear of the battleline. The adjutant recalled that "I had been advised to keep a good lookout on General Pender himself, and try to protect him, for his intrepidity was such that ... he might expose himself unnecessarily. This caution led me to observe him with more particularity than I would otherwise have done. I was struck by his coolness, the entire absence of excitement or emotion. At that period there were none in the Army who could be called veterans, for as yet, neither officers nor men had become ... hardened by experience ..." And yet Pender appeared to have already made the transition.[12]

Just before the Light Division was committed to the battle, Ashe was able to contrast Pender's demeanor with that of a colleague. General Archer, commander of the brigade immediately in front of Pender's, suddenly rode up while Pender sat his horse at the edge of a wheatfield and asked: "Pender, do you curse in times like this?" Ashe saw Pender smile as he replied that he never did. "Well I know it is wrong," Archer exclaimed, "but I['ll] be damned if I can help it!"[13]

As the anecdote illustrates, Pender had greatly reduced his vocabulary of four-letter words, and he disliked to hear others use them. At about this same time, Colonel R. H. Brewer, who had served with Pender in the 1st Dragoons, joined the brigade staff as a volunteer aide-de-camp, taking the place of Colonel Green. "He is a very nice fellow," Pender wrote of Brewer, "and a great acquisition. His only objection, he swears so much … I could not help remonstrating with him about it when he came." It is not known whether Pender "remonstrated" with Archer on the same subject. For whatever reason—perhaps it was only a case of clashing personalities—Archer became decidedly cool toward his fellow brigadier over the next four months.[14]

The fighting near Cedar Mountain continued to be as hot as the sun on this midsummer's day, but it heated up even more as the afternoon drew to a close. At about 6:00 P.M., a large body of Banks's infantry fell upon the Confederate left flank, threatening to roll up Jackson's line. Jackson threw in the Light Division, hoping to restore order. In front was the brigade formerly led by Joseph Anderson and now by Colonel Edward L. Thomas; farther to the rear marched the men of Branch, Archer, and Pender.

Although they entered the fight enthusiastically, Thomas and Branch moved too far to the right to stop the flank drive. That left the task to Archer and Pender, whose commands advanced roughly side-by-side, Pender on the left, beyond the road leading north to Culpeper. Archer's troops went straight ahead through the wheat, while Pender wisely obliqued toward Archer's flank, thus presenting a thinner front to the enemy. The difference in their formations was reflected in the disparity in their casualties. Before fully engaged with the enemy, Archer lost more than 100 men killed or wounded, Pender fewer than 20. In proportion to the numbers engaged, however, the difference was not so great. Archer committed his entire brigade, four regiments from Tennessee and Georgia plus an Alabama battalion, while only three of Pender's regiments participated. He had left the 22nd North Carolina to guard his left rear, a move that kept a force of Yankee cavalry from interfering with the attack.[15]

Pender's and Archer's men eventually became mixed up in the wheat and the woods beyond, making individual achievements hard to identify. Even so, there was little doubt that Pender, not his colleague, landed the decisive blow of the battle. Pender's hard-driving counterattack "changed the aspect at once," admitted one of Archer's Tennesseans, who recalled that the enemy "hesitated a moment, then broke and fled in confusion from the field." As

Pender himself noted, his men broke through the enemy with unexpected ease, "repulsing him with heavy loss in almost the first round." Demoralized by their broken formation, Banks's people withdrew, leaving the field in the hands of the victors.[16]

*   *   *

Pender took great satisfaction in his men's success at Cedar Mountain. For their commander it was, by any measure, a landmark battle, one that showcased his talents and suggested his fitness for higher command. The only aspect of the fight that did not please him was Jackson's lengthy casualty list, which included the mortal wounding of Charles Winder.

After Pender and Archer had chased the Federals to the far side of Cedar Run, orders reached them to halt and regroup. This Pender did, holding the ground he had taken "until late," then passing over to the Culpeper Road, where he made a brief effort at pursuit. But the Yankees were gone from the field, except for the human and inanimate debris they left behind. Although the enemy had given some of Jackson's men a rough time, Pender considered their resistance to his advance pitifully weak. Five days after the fight he wrote Fanny that "the specimen of fighting shown us the other day by the Yankees does not compare to that of the rascals around Richmond. In fact, Pope's men did not fight at all."[17]

The overstatement may have reflected the scorn with which he and every other Confederate had come to regard the opposing commander. During his brief tenure, Pope had issued inflammatory and highly publicized addresses to his troops. In these he had stressed his expectation that, as soon as he caught up to it, he would smash Lee's army or capture it whole. Throughout the South, Pope had become the symbol of the pompous, insolent Yankee, the one general every self-respecting Rebel would love to whip.

Everyone realized, of course, that so far less than a quarter of Pope's command had been defeated. A sense of urgency underscored the necessity of beating the entire Army of Virginia. Two days before Cedar Mountain, McClellan's army had begun to depart the Peninsula, by transport, for the lower Potomac. It was bound for Pope's department, where Union forces just up from North Carolina were also expected to arrive. Lee realized that he must throw his army at Pope—if possible, crushing him between Jackson's and Longstreet's wings—before the reinforcements rendered this outcome impossible.[18]

Thus, on August 13, Lee started Longstreet's infantry and Stuart's horsemen to Gordonsville, where he himself arrived two days later to take charge of operations. There he was reunited not only with the troops he had just sent west but also with Jackson. Concerned that Pope might attack with his full force, Stonewall had slipped back across the Rapidan. Pender did not like the idea of retreating, especially in the wake of a successful battle, but he tried to remain philosophical. "Pope seems to be satisfied for the present with having caused Jackson to fall back," he informed the folks at Good Spring, "but let him wait a little while.... He will take to thinking about lines of retreat yet ...."[19]

Lee's initial intent was to bring Pope to battle with the Rappahannock River at his back holding him in place until his army could be destroyed. The rub was that Pope had gotten wind of his opponent's intentions; he retreated across the Rappahannock on the evening of August 19. While frustrating, the maneuver only committed Lee, more than ever, to the goal of catching and throttling his opponent.

Fearing that delay would kill his plans, Lee sent both Jackson and Longstreet across the Rapidan. By August 21 Pender's brigade was marching with the rest of Hill's corps to the Rappahannock line. Careful not to reveal his advance to a segment of Pope's army encamped near Beverly Ford, the following day Jackson veered eastward across the Hazel River, a Rappahannock tributary, near Wellford's Mill.[20]

Left behind on the south side of the river was the Light Division. On the 24th Pender observed from a distance what he called "the most terrible artillery duel" in his experience, as Hill's guns exchanged shells with Pope's across the river. "It lasted from 11 A.M. till night with slight intermissions. I can form no idea of what we are to do but suppose [we are] to advance. Pope has been running from us but seems determined to make a stand behind this river."[21]

He was right on both counts. Pope was holding his ground above the river 20-some miles from his nearest reinforcements at Fredericksburg. And Lee, determined to prevent those supports from reaching Pope, was continuing to advance against the Army of Virginia. A confrontation was inevitable and not far off.

*   *   *

On the march from Cedar Mountain to the Rappahannock, a pair of incidents, similar in nature, combined to illustrate two of Pender's most enduring traits, his quickness to take offense at slights real and imagined, and his readiness to defend his honor. Although his religion regarded pride as a sin, it was one vice whose hold the Christian warrior never broke.

The first incident had its origin in the fighting of August 9, when a captain in Pender's brigade picked up a rumor that impugned the courage of a certain general officer. Captain Ashe of Pender's staff, who related the story after the war, never revealed the identity of either man involved, but internal evidence suggests that the general was Pender's fellow North Carolinian, Lawrence Branch.

After the battle the falsehood came to Branch's ears. Two weeks later, while the Light Division was on the march from Cedar Mountain to Manassas, Branch summoned the captain to his headquarters tent. Pender, through whom Branch issued the summons, received the impression that it was a dinner invitation. His indirect involvement made him see himself as a party to what followed. He was shocked when the captain returned from the general's tent to complain that, instead of feeding him, Branch, "full of indignation at what had taken place … abused [him] … severely and told him that his sword ought to be broken." This was a mortal affront to any self-respecting Confederate officer, but, fearing the wrath of high station should he protest, the captain left Branch's tent without reply.

When Pender learned of the confrontation, he did not sympathize with the captain. Instead, he berated him for failing to show "the spirit" Pender "required of his officers" and informed him "that he had no further use for him in the Brigade, and that he [should] go home." Pender's reaction stemmed from his belief that the captain had not sufficiently resented the insult dealt him. The man ought to have protected his honor by challenging his detractor to a duel.

But Pender was not through. As if the insult had been directed at him, he addressed a letter to Branch, detailing the captain's complaint and demanding an apology to both of them. Captain Ashe observed that "the result of the correspondence was an agreement between these Generals that when peace should come and the country no longer have need of their services on the battlefield," Branch would give his colleague the satisfaction he sought. Ashe, himself a gentleman, praised Pender's role in the incident, which displayed the brigadier's "spirit and unconquerable devotion to honor."[22]

The second incident occurred "not long after" the first. In telling it, Ashe again omitted the names of the principals. During a night march, a member of Pender's staff "unwittingly gave some provocation" to an officer in a

Virginia regiment. The officer then identified himself as a colonel and gave the aide a vicious dressing-down. Afterward the aide decided that his honor had been violated and wondered if he ought to demand satisfaction. To help him reach a decision, he consulted not Pender but General Archer, who knew the colonel well. At Archer's suggestion, the staff officer demanded that the colonel meet him shortly on the field of honor.

Before the colonel could reply, Pender learned of the affair and asked the aide for details. When the man recounted how the colonel had verbally thrashed him, Pender exclaimed: "Why didn't you strike him?" Taken aback, the aide explained that his detractor's rank had intimidated him. "With great warmth and vigor," his commander replied, "Why, sir, you should strike any man who insults you—even General[s]...."

This incident blew over when the colonel, although a noted duelist, apologized to the captain for the abuse he had heaped on him. Whether in the future the aggrieved party heeded his boss' advice is unknown. For his part, Pender never revised his belief that if self-respect was to be maintained, insults to honor required an immediate, and if necessary, a violent response.[23]

*   *   *

Unwilling to concede defeat when Pope recrossed the Rappahannock, Lee decided to send Jackson around the Union right against Pope's line of supply, the Orange & Alexandria, in the vicinity of Manassas Junction. On August 25, as Longstreet took on the task of holding the Federals' attention, Jackson pushed across Hedgeman River, another Rappahannock tributary, at Henson's Mill. Then he moved to interpose between Pope's army and points north, including Washington. Undoubtedly, Pender was in high spirits this day as he moved his men at a rapid clip through the village of Orleans and into the equally small town of Salem, where they camped for the evening in the shadow of the Bull Run Mountains.[24]

Early on August 26 Jackson's column debouched from the mountain range at Thoroughfare Gap, trudged through Gainesville, and at sunset closed up on the O & A depot of Bristoe Station, former campground of the 6th North Carolina. By the time he bivouacked for the night, Pender had spied another familiar sight: J. E. B. Stuart, now a major general, commanding the division of cavalry that had overtaken Jackson's column with orders to screen its march and protect its right flank.[25]

After capturing a couple of supply trains at Bristoe and appropriating supplies earmarked for Pope's army, Jackson learned that seven miles up the tracks at Manassas Junction "stores of great value" had been stockpiled. These, too, Stonewall determined to deny to Pope. Stuart, with his horsemen and 500 foot soldiers, was sent that night to secure the supply depot, while Jackson headed there next morning with more than two-thirds of his force, including the Light Division. Upon arriving, the famished, poorly clothed Confederates descended upon two trains filled with an incredible variety of foodstuffs and materiel. The captors appropriated everything from barrels of salted beef and pickled herring to uniforms, rifles, ammunition, and caches of letters written by Pope's men to correspondents who would never receive them.[26]

It is not known to what extent Pender's troops helped themselves to Pope's commissary, but their time at Manassas was not solely deviated to spoils. In the middle distance, a hidden battery suddenly opened fire on the looters, causing Pender and his men to spend an hour or more "lying under cover from the occasional shots from the enemy's artillery." It took time for the nearest Confederates, Branch's and Archer's, to silence the gunners and disperse some Pennsylvania cavalry who had supported the battery.[27]

Eventually, Pender was called on to support Branch and Archer. As he moved to do so, his attention was directed northward to the railroad bridge over Bull Run. Above the span he spied a large body of oncoming Federals that turned out to be a brigade of New Jersey infantry. Having heard the commotion at Manassas, the Jerseymen intended to evict from their army's supply depot what they thought was a small body of raiders.

Branch's marksmen, backed by two batteries, opened fire with minie balls and canister. The result was chaos in the Union ranks, most of whose men fled up the tracks in wild disorder. They left behind 200 dead, including their commander, Brigadier General George W. Taylor, along with wounded men and others gathered up as prisoners.[28]

Taylor's subordinates re-formed the fugitives on the north side of Bull Run, placed them behind cover, and united them with two Ohio regiments coming down from the north. The combined force swept the approach to the stream with musketry. Branch and Archer accepted the challenge and moved forward. Pender covered the right flank of both while also endeavoring to capture the bridge and chase the Federals away. His skirmishers made contact with the enemy just below the bridge and a standoff ensued, both sides hunkering down and sending hundreds of missiles across the stream.

The impasse was broken when an impatient Pender threw two of his regiments across the water to threaten the Union line. He was about to lead them in a flank assault when Field's brigade appeared in his rear and its commander called a quick conference. The decision the generals reached prompted Pender to recall his troops from the far side, then lead them, in single file, farther downstream. He intended to force another crossing, this time aiming for the enemy's rear.

But he did not get that far. Upon reaching the opposite shore—the first man in the brigade to do so—Pender discovered that the Federals had already withdrawn; Stuart's horsemen were soon on their tail, harassing their retreat. The result suggested that Pender had worked long and hard for nothing. Yet he had chased off the enemy while giving yet another public display of his combativeness and resourcefulness. After wrecking the railroad bridge, he and his men turned back to Manassas.[29]

In the small hours of August 28, the Light Division departed what remained of Pope's supply base, heading north to Centreville, on the northeastern edge of the Bull Run battlefield. The movements of Pender's men were bathed in the lurid glow of burning freight cars and warehouses. By heading north, Jackson indicated that his scattered elements should unite on the very ground where he had won his nickname. There, it was hoped, they would soon be joined by Lee and the rest of the army. By now Longstreet had broken off his holding action below the Rappahannock and was moving north via the same route beyond the Bull Run Mountains that Stonewall had taken two days before.

Lee hoped to unite Longstreet and Jackson before Pope could purposely or inadvertently intervene. The opportunity appeared to pass when Pope, aware that Jackson had gotten in his army's rear, sent his main body into the Gainesville-Warrenton area. Thus the Federals interposed between Jackson and Longstreet's destination, Thoroughfare Gap, thereby threatening both wings with piecemeal destruction. Pope may not have been much of a gentleman but he thought of himself as a tactician and a fighter, and he seemed determined to prove both points.[30]

Jackson reacted to this unexpected turn of events by deciding to place his troops atop high ground along the Warrenton-Alexandria Pike near the village of Groveton. Because he failed to give Hill critical information, however, the Light Division was almost too late to join him in opposing a Union column that moved through the Groveton area late on the afternoon of the 28th. As it was, beyond some "little artillery practice," Hill and Pender saw no involvement in the desperate clash that resulted and that ended with a Union withdrawal at about 9:00 P.M.[31]

The next morning Pender and his comrades saw that Jackson's wing was facing a reinforced enemy line—Pope was on the scene with his entire army. Though heavily outnumbered, Jackson prepared to meet the Yankees in battle, his men holding the woods and plains west of Groveton, beyond the cut of an unfinished railroad. The Light Division was on Jackson's left, facing that part of the enemy line to which Pope had shifted most of his weight. Pender's brigade was in the second of Hill's lines of battle, with Archer's and Branch's brigades on its left and Thomas's in front. Although his position relegated Pender to a reserve role, he suspected that the fighting would prove fluid enough that his men would all be needed soon enough at the front.[32]

As on earlier occasions when battle neared, his instincts were sound. The ball opened at about 10:00 A.M. with Pope sending waves of attack first against Jackson's right flank and then against his center. For five hours fighting gyrated back and forth across farm fields and open ground and through pockets of woods whose trees were blasted to fragments by cannons on both sides.

The outgunned Confederates held on stubbornly under the pounding, prompting Pope, at about 3:00, to concentrate against the Rebel left. With sudden impact, New Englanders and Pennsylvanians from the brigade of Brigadier General Cuvier Grover, part of Major General Joseph Hooker's division, smashed into Thomas's Georgia brigade, in front of Pender's right flank. Dazed by the blow, many Georgians fell back. Soon hundreds of shouting Yankees were making for a widening gap between Thomas's left and the right of Gregg's brigade of South Carolinians.[33]

Two events saved the day for the Light Division. First, Thomas and Gregg each rushed up a regiment to plug the hole, at least temporarily. The second and more momentous event was that Pender took it upon himself to repair the breach. "It seeming to me to be the time to go to his assistance," he led his regiments to the place where Thomas's exhausted, ammunition-poor troops appeared on the verge of collapse. Supported by a portion of Brigadier General Jubal A. Early's brigade, Pender's fresh troops slammed into Grover's men and gradually forced them back through a woods southeast of the contested ground.[34]

Pender's assault had been a defensive success, but he wished to achieve more. His apparent intent was to push Grover well to the south, past the railroad cut, where he would pose no further threat to the Light Division. But as

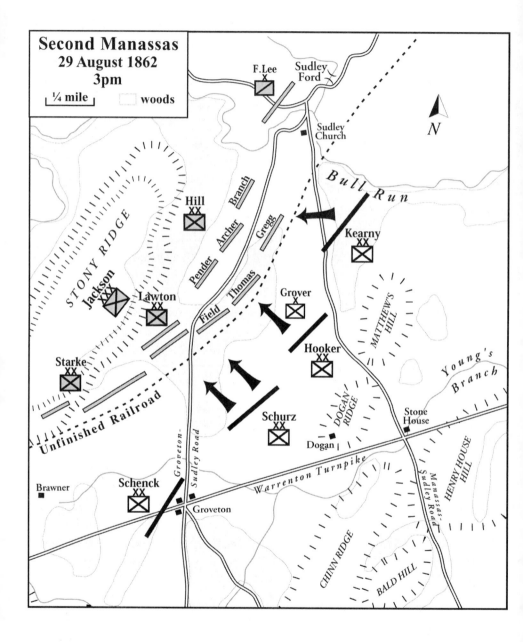

Second Manassas
29 August 1862
3pm

¼ mile   woods

F. Lee
Sudley
Ford

Sudley
Church

Bull Run

Branch

Hill

STONY RIDGE

Archer

Gregg

Kearny

MATTHEW'S
HILL

Pender

Jackson

Lawton

Field

Thomas

Grover

Hooker

Young's
Branch

Starke

DOGAN
RIDGE

Stone
House

Unfinished Railroad

Schurz

Dogan

HENRY HOUSE
HILL

Brawner

Schenck

Groveton

Warrenton Turnpike

Manassas-
Sudley Road

Groveton-
Sudley Road

CHINN RIDGE

BALD HILL

N

he started across a field toward a Union artillery position, Pender found that Early was no longer advancing on his flank. Offered an easy target, the gunners pounded Pender's men with impunity. Pender went down when a shell fragment plowed a furrow across the top of his skull, shearing off a clump of hair. He scrambled to his feet and with blood streaming down his face tried to rally his now-disorganized ranks. When he saw the futility of it, he ordered everyone back to the starting point of the attack. Although Pender would describe his second battle wound as a scratch, at least one of his biographers speculates that he would have been killed had it not been for a woolen headpiece he was wearing under his kepi.[35]

After its withdrawal, Pender's command was relieved by Archer's brigade. Placed in the rear, it saw little additional involvement in the day's fighting. It had earned its rest, as had the bulk of the Light Division, whose men, throughout the day, had repulsed assault after assault by troops double or triple their number. The result of the day's fighting was that when the sun set, Pope's line had been shoved well beyond the railroad embankment, which now ran between the lines. For his role in the outcome, Pender was warmly commended by A. P. Hill.[36]

*   *   *

Pender's brigade was again engaged, to its great credit, when Pope, refusing to relinquish his dream of annihilating Jackson, remained in position to make a second attempt. The decision was one of the worst of the Westerner's career. By the morning of the 30th, even before Pope renewed his attacks, the odds had shifted dramatically. Beginning the previous morning, Lee, with elements of Longstreet's command, had reached the field of battle on Jackson's right. Now Pope was facing twice the number that had been arrayed against him on August 29. Incredibly, he had no inkling of the fact. He would pay dearly for his ignorance.[37]

When the fight resumed early the next morning, Pender's command was stationed on the far left of Jackson's line. As on the previous day, Pope concentrated against Jackson's right, then expanded his drive toward his center. All the while, Longstreet lay in wait for an opportune time to strike. When Jackson's right came under so much pressure it seemed ready to give way, the Light Division was rushed to its rescue. Pender led his men across the railroad embankment into the area he had charged over and then withdrawn across the day before.

On August 30, unlike the day before, he had little trouble reaching the enemy's line, which broke almost at first contact. Pope's legions had advanced obliquely toward Jackson's right, a maneuver that bought their left directly opposite Longstreet's front. In so doing the Union leader copied, on a much larger scale, the mistake that the unidentified Yankee regiment had made at Gaines's Mill when it marched across Pender's front. Keening the Rebel Yell, Longstreet's soldiers charged the open flank and smashed it flat. In a matter of minutes, Pope's left was a bloody, mangled fragment and its pieces were flying everywhere.

As Longstreet's men continued to pour onto the battlefield, panic communicated itself along the Union line and troops gave way at all points. After a flawed effort to stanch the gray tide on Henry House Hill, a landmark in what was now known as the battle of First Manassas, Pope turned his beaten army about and headed for the Washington defenses. A retreat reminiscent of July 21, 1861, was soon in progress.[38]

Pender had a hand in helping his enemy along. When Longstreet struck, his brigade had pushed beyond the railroad cut and up against an overwhelming array of infantry and artillery, from which he properly withdrew. After Pope's ranks dissolved, Pender's troops were sent forward again, this time in concert with Archer, Thomas, and part of Brigadier General William B. Taliaferro's (formerly Winder's) division. As Pender reported, he and his colleagues "advanced steadily, driving the enemy from the field through the woods." The movement continued until darkness halted it.[39]

In the haste to bag prisoners and cannons, the various Confederate commands became intermingled. Pender informed Fanny about this part of the action: "I commanded three Brigades and parts of two others. I presumed to direct and the officers seemed very willing to have someone who would take the responsibility. My [enlarged] command took several pieces of Art[illery], my brigade taking two." He appended a typical bit of understatement: "I flatter myself I did good service."[40]

In fact, the battle of Second Manassas had been a splendid victory for the Confederacy, and the service that Pender and his brigade had rendered—as he must have known—had been truly outstanding. Although many had contributed to success on both days of battle, at the critical moment none had contributed more than he.

Chapter Eight

SIEGE AND SLAUGHTER

On September 7, Pender wrote to Fanny from Frederick City, 40 miles west of Baltimore, asking "are you not surprised to find us in M[ary-lan]d? We crossed [the Potomac River] day before yesterday and now have possession of this part of the State. Our Cavalry are hovering around Washington and it is said they have gone into Penn[sylvania]. Gen Lee is in good earnest and the Yankees are terribly frightened."[1]

It had been a hectic week since the great triumph on the plains of Manassas. Pender's army had spent the following day, August 31, rounding up its many prisoners and caring for its many wounded, which included Fanny's brothers, Ham and Willy (neither had been seriously injured). Other troops pursued the enemy, overtaking Pope's rear guard the following day at Chantilly, north of Centreville. In the sharp fighting that resulted, another 1,300 Federals and 800 Confederates had been rendered *hors de combat* to little obvious purpose. Although slowed and battered, Pope's army continued its withdrawal, which ended successfully in the Washington suburbs. Pender had "but little to say" of the contest at Chantilly, admitting that "none of us seemed anxious for the fight or did ourselves much credit," although they had killed two of Pope's more capable generals, Philip Kearny and Isaac I. Stevens.[2]

Shortly after the rear-guard action, Robert E. Lee—certain that Pope would not retake the field for weeks to come—decided to implement a plan whose possibilities had long intrigued him. Predating Pender's recruiting efforts in its largest city, Maryland had been considered a bastion of secessionist sentiment, to the point that it was represented by a star in the Confederate flag. Now Lee would test the depth of that sentiment by leading his army into the state's western reaches. The move would enable him to recruit for his army and to supply it with rations, forage, and materiel drawn from a region that had not been ravaged by campaigning. By so moving Lee would also lure the enemy after him, thus relieving Virginia from a plague of blue-clad locusts.[3]

On September 3, Lee acted on his decision by moving his troops toward the Potomac crossings near Leesburg. The following day he passed over the river at the local fords. His route of march led north through Poolesville to Frederick, which his advance guard, part of Jackson's wing, entered on the 6th. Contrary to Pender's belief, Stuart's cavalry escorted the main army all the way, although a month hence it would indeed raid south-central Pennsylvania, wrecking communications and ransacking government warehouses west of a town named Gettysburg.[4]

As Lee and Pender both anticipated, the invasion did not go uncontested. The day Pender wrote home from Frederick, an enlarged Army of the Potomac, which had absorbed Pope's survivors, left Washington in slow but steady pursuit. George McClellan rode at its head, Pope having been relieved from command. Behind Little Mac marched more than 85,000 effectives; 72,000 other troops had been left behind, under Nathaniel Banks, to man the Washington defenses. Lee's army, minus many of the 9,000 casualties it had taken on the bloody road from Cedar Mountain to Chantilly, comprised less than half the number at McClellan's disposal.

But the Army of Northern Virginia enjoyed intangible advantages that its opponent lacked, foremost of which was a corporate self-confidence born of a year-long series of tactical and strategic victories. Typical was the reaction of a surgeon in Branch's brigade as he set foot on Maryland soil: "The people are mostly glad to see us—& hail us as deliverers. We have certainly made a tour of conquest, the most remarkable of history. Our troops are enthusiastic, & under Lee and Jackson invincible."[5]

Brigadier General Pender shared the prevailing view that whatever the army's leader attempted would be accomplished, no matter the obstacles he faced. Anything was possible, and anywhere was within reach. Pender half jokingly suggested that Fanny "need not be surprised to hear of our being in Philadelphia in less than ten days. Md. is rising, we have a victorious army, and no troops in our front. Gen. Lee has shown great Generalship and the greatest boldness." He was already convinced of the invasion's success, boasting that "there never was such a campaign, not even by Napoleon."[6]

Pender's views of General Jackson remained far less laudatory, especially at present. On the morning of September 4, while marching inland from the Potomac, General Hill had displeased his wing commander by not obeying Jackson's marching orders with the alacrity and exactitude that Stonewall demanded. Later in the day the generals had quarreled when Jackson issued orders to one of Hill's brigades without the latter's knowledge or consent. The upshot was that Hill had been placed under arrest for the second time in two months while General Branch took over the Light Division. Now Hill was accompanying the rear of the column on foot, feeling dejected, humiliated, and angry. Pender visited his superior whenever possible, commiserating with his situation and joining him in condemning Jackson's perversity.[7]

Another recent event that distressed Pender was the tendency of his men to straggle from the line of march and, once beyond the sight of their officers, loot and pillage. The practice was a terrible way to win the hearts and minds of the populace. Beyond that, he could not tolerate such a flagrant breach of discipline. On the day his brigade forded the Potomac, he called together his subordinates and enjoined them to keep "a firm hand on the men of their commands, and that he would hold them responsible for their conduct." Later, he wondered if he might have saved his breath. In later days he saw large groups of soldiers—perhaps his own, perhaps members of other commands— break ranks to "clean out a big orchard in half an hour.... such a filthy undisciplined set of villains I have never seen. They have lost all honor or decency, all sense of right or respect for property. I have had to strike many a one with my sabre." Anticipating trouble when the brigade reached Frederick, he saw to it his regiments camped well beyond the town limits.[8]

The three-day stopover did not prevent Pender himself from visiting the town and doing some shopping. The experience made him feel almost like a civilian. On September 8 he picked up "some little articles" for Fanny and the children, "but it has been so long since I shopped that I fear the whole thing will prove a failure except the handkerchiefs," which cost the princely sum of two dollars apiece in Confederate bills. It seemed an exorbitant amount, but he was willing to buy whatever he thought would please his family, providing it "would not make much bulk" on the march. In the event he stayed in Frederick for some time, he asked Fanny to send him a list of her needs.[9]

But his request was in vain, for he left Frederick in a hurry on the 10th. The previous day, Lee had sent to his lieutenants copies of Special Orders No. 191, a blueprint for the coming campaign. The orders called on Jackson's troops, supported by three of Longstreet's divisions, to march southwestward through the mountains to capture the Union garrison at strategic Harpers Ferry, which was vulnerable to attack from atop the mountains that surrounded it. While Jackson neutralized that communications center where the Potomac and Shenandoah Rivers met, Lee, with the remainder of Longstreet's command, would move north and west toward Hagerstown, close to the Pennsylvania line. There or thereabouts Jackson would join him once John Brown's old bailiwick had been captured. The last thing that Lee or any of his subordinates would have expected was that an errant copy of the orders would fall into enemy hands—which happened on the 13th when the Army of the Potomac camped outside Frederick on ground recently occupied by its adversary.[10]

Confidence would have buoyed up Pender and his comrades all the way to Harpers Ferry even if they knew McClellan had learned where they were going and why. By September 14, as Jackson arrived within striking distance of his objective, the left wing of the Army of the Potomac was marching to the garrison's relief. It was Jackson's good fortune that the rescue column was commanded by Major General William Buel Franklin, a slow-moving old Regular not known for boldness or initiative. Upon being challenged by a smaller Confederate force at Crampton's Gap in South Mountain, Franklin would move even more slowly than before, leaving Harpers Ferry at Jackson's mercy.[11]

The expeditionary commander wasted no time moving with 26,000 men on the town and the 11,000 troops that defended it. On September 10 Jackson led his own divisions through Turner's Gap in South Mountain, then to Boonsboro. From there he pushed northwestward, halting along the Potomac at Williamsport. On the 11th, while the other divisions assigned him for the mission moved on Harpers Ferry from the Maryland side, Jackson crossed the river with his organic force. That force again included A. P. Hill. Jackson had granted his subordinate's request to be restored to command of his division for the battle that lay ahead.[12]

On September 12, the attackers moved to surround Harpers Ferry. The three divisions borrowed from Longstreet occupied Maryland Heights and, across the Potomac, south and east of the garrison, equally strategic Loudoun Heights. At the same time, the Light Division and its comrades marched through Martinsburg, chasing its small garrison to the larger stronghold farther east. Arriving west of Harpers Ferry shortly before noon on the 13th, Jackson sent Hill's troops along the bank of the Shenandoah River and placed them in position on School House Ridge. There, immediately west of the main Union position on Bolivar Heights, the division faced the Union left flank.[13]

Once the Confederates hauled artillery onto these commanding slopes, Harpers Ferry was doomed. Believing the game already in their hands, Longstreet's men attacked soon after getting settled, but they found the enemy more combative than expected. Heavy but inconclusive skirmishing lasted through the day and into the night.

Jackson believed that his enemy had no alternative but to surrender. He expected that he need only tighten the screws a little and the garrison would be in his hands. Early on September 14 he moved to contract his siege lines, and A. P. Hill, wishing to demonstrate that his place was with his command, not in arrest, moved rapidly east.[14]

Pender was in the forefront of the advance, and not only as a brigade commander. When the Light Division neared a line of Yankee works, Hill demonstrated great confidence in his favorite brigade leader by assigning him command not only of his own brigade but also the commands of Archer and Field, the latter now commanded by Colonel J. M. Brockenbrough, with Thomas's brigade in close support. He instructed Pender to attack and capture "an eminence crowning the extreme left of the enemy's line, bare of all earthwork, the only obstacles being abatis of fallen timber." Bereft of artillery, the position was extremely vulnerable. Why Hill felt constrained to assign four brigades to take it, he never explained. Perhaps he was determined not to fail under the gaze of the superior who had jailed him.[15]

Placing his own command in the hands of Colonel Brewer, the staff officer with the sinful vocabulary, Pender went forward at the head of his enlarged command. After crossing the intervening ground under fire, his men swarmed over the position, capturing it within minutes. With this success, Hill observed, "the fate of Harper's Ferry was sealed."[16]

Still, it took time for the Yankees to realize or to admit the fact. Even after Pender's men took other objectives atop Bolivar Heights, the garrison refused to capitulate. Lee had hoped that Jackson would force its surrender on the 14th so that the wings of his army could quickly reunite. McClellan was moving toward him with uncharacteristic speed; this day, the Union advance guard was pushing through two gaps in the mountains, threatening to interpose between Jackson and Longstreet. Lee briefly considered retreating to Virginia, but when Jackson sent him assurances that the garrison would surrender next day the army chief agreed to remain in Maryland till Stonewall rejoined him.[17]

Early on September 15, Harpers Ferry absorbed a tremendous cannonade from every side. Pender, who had returned to brigade command, considered moving even farther up the mountain, but before he could start out white flags went up on Bolivar Heights. Unnerved by the barrage and no longer hopeful that McClellan would rescue him, the garrison commander, Colonel Dixon S. Miles of the regular army, had called it quits. Some historians would claim that Miles, a conservative Marylander who fell mortally wounded when a Rebel battery mistakenly opened on his surrender party, had orchestrated the capitulation through a secret allegiance to the Confederacy.[18]

Of this possibility Pender knew nothing. He attributed Jackson's victory, as he had so many past Confederate successes, to a lack of intestinal fortitude on the part of the foe. "If the enemy does not run before the fight," he told Fanny four days after the garrison fell, "they do when the fight commences."[19]

*   *   *

Pender declared that the Light Division had done the brunt of the fighting—in fact, the *only* fighting—on September 13 and 14. Apparently Jackson agreed, for he rewarded the command by assigning it the easy tasks of taking possession of the town and paroling its garrison. Meanwhile, the wing leader marched north with the rest of his command and the troops on loan from Longstreet.[20]

With speed borne of urgency, Jackson made for Sharpsburg, a quaint little village nestled between the Potomac and one of its tributaries, Antietam Creek. Lee had been passing through the town on the afternoon of the 15th when word of Jackson's success reached him. The knowledge that most of Jackson's and all of Longstreet's troops would soon be at his side prompted the army leader to face about. He would meet McClellan head-on by making a stand on the west side of the Antietam, with the Potomac at his back.

The result, beginning shortly after dawn on the 17th, was the bloodiest day of the war. Remaining on the defensive throughout, Lee repulsed a series of attacks up and down his line, first on the north flank, then in the center and, in early afternoon, against the lower end of his line. Throughout the fight, Lee received critical support from the troops that had captured Harpers Ferry. Most had reached the new battlefield the day before McClellan attacked.

The critical phase of the battle began at about 3:00 P.M., when troops on McClellan's left, part of Major General Ambrose E. Burnside's Ninth Corps, pushed across the creek via Rohrbach Bridge and made for Lee's lower flank. Under Burnside's pounding, the weary Confederates in that area began to waver and fall back. The flank, and perhaps Lee's entire line, appeared on the verge of destruction. At the critical moment, however, the Light Division— all but the one brigade that Hill had left at Harpers Ferry—reached the scene of desperate struggle.[21]

Lee had summoned Hill north at 6:30 that morning. A killing march had brought his troops to the place where they were most needed, when they were most needed. Upon arriving, Hill placed Pender's and Brockenbrough's brigades on the far right of his hastily formed line. Both quickly came under long-range musketry but saw little action. Farther north, however, the brigades of Branch, Archer, and Gregg made critical contributions to the battle, fending off thousands of Federals who had broken through Longstreet's line on their left. Their heroics came at a high cost in casualties including Branch, killed instantly by a sharpshooter's ball. Then, "with a yell of defiance," Archer counterattacked, driving the Yankees away, recapturing a battery they had taken, and effectively ending the battle.[22]

The casualty toll this day included nearly 14,000 Confederate casualties; some of Lee's more heavily engaged units had virtually gone out of existence. Throughout September 18, the armies remained stationary on their respective sides of the creek, Lee daring McClellan to reprise his offensive and McClellan vowing to make no such mistake. That evening, believing he could remain no longer between a river and a more numerous enemy, Lee recrossed the Potomac to Virginia.[23]

Lee's expectations for the invasion had not been fulfilled. For one thing, Maryland, especially its western reaches, had proven to be an inhospitable place. Pender left it gladly, without a backward glance. McClellan's repulse notwithstanding, he considered the army's foray north of the river a dismal failure. "Our Army," he told Fanny, "has shown itself incapable of invasion and we had better stick to the defensive." Since leaving Richmond six weeks ago, the army had undergone such a bloodletting that "the more we fight the less we like it." In a later letter he confirmed that his only regret about campaigning north of the Potomac "is that we ever crossed it in the first place." While the enemy "cannot drive us from any position we choose to take," it was easier for McClellan, when in his own territory, to gather enough reinforcements to "cause us to draw off...."[24]

Pender's gloomy mood dissipated, at least briefly, as a result of the fighting that took place two days after his army returned to the region for which it had been named. On the evening of the 19th, two brigades of the Fifth Corps, Army of the Potomac, forced a crossing at Shepherdstown (or Boteler's) Ford against light opposition and shoved Lee's rear guard south, capturing men and cannons. Next morning, when a larger segment of the Fifth Corps crossed at the ford, Jackson sent Early's and A. P. Hill's divisions to return the favor.

When Hill reached the scene at about 7:00, he found hundreds of Yankees wading through the water and dozens of others forming lines of battle on the near shore. Across the river no fewer than 70 cannons had been positioned to sweep the Rebel side. Without blinking an eye, Hill formed a line of battle with Pender's, Gregg's, and Thomas's brigades in front and those of Archer, Brockenbrough, and Colonel James H. Lane (formerly Branch's) farther to the rear.[25]

At the signal, everyone moved forward. "We did it," wrote Pender, "under the most terrible artillery fire I ever saw troops exposed to.... It was as hot a place as I wish to get in." Despite Hill's resolute advance, despite his artillery support, the Federals held their ground. Then they massed across Pender's path and even moved to threaten his left flank, a tactic thwarted by the timely intervention of Archer's Tennesseans, Georgians, and Alabamians. As the enemy drive faltered, Pender joined Archer in a general assault, now supported by Gregg. Their troops charged the enemy with rifles spitting, halting only long enough to reload and fire again.[26]

Forgetting Sharpsburg, Hill called the result "the most terrible slaughter that this war has yet witnessed." Even before Pender and Archer closed with the enemy, the Union line gave way, its men turning about, leaping into the water, and paddling to the far shore. Many did not make it. Hill claimed that when shooting ceased, "the broad surface of the Potomac was blue with the floating bodies of the foe. But few escaped to tell the tale...." The Confederate shore was free of the enemy except dead and wounded men and prisoners.[27]

Southern defeat had been avenged—Pender and Archer had made amends for the failings of "some of our miserable people [who] allowed the Yankees to cross." Reviewing the fight, Pender borrowed some of his superior's hyperbole by declaring it "the most brilliant thing of the war." He spoke with less exaggeration, however, when he added that "Hill's Division stands first in point of efficiency of any Division of this whole Army."[28]

*   *   *

Although McClellan would not mount a pursuit with his entire army for six weeks, Lee cleared the Potomac shore with dispatch. Aware that "the condition of our troops now demanded repose," he led his weary, grimy, bloodstained ranks to the northern edge of the Shenandoah Valley. He stopped first at Martinsburg and later headed south to Bunker Hill and Winchester. In the pasturelands that abounded in each of these areas, his regiments procured rations and forage, while taking some long-deferred rest.[29]

The army desperately needed a breather. It had been on the march for the better part of two months, and it had suffered terribly throughout that period. Writing Fanny from Martinsburg, Pender gloried in his command's reputation but worried about its ability to sustain it record in its present condition. Pender wrote that General Hill, who had not been returned to arrest, had told him "that I had the best discipline of any Brigade he had. But when I tell you that this Division has lost 9000 killed and wounded since we commenced the Richmond fight at Mechanicsville, you can see what our reputation has cost us. We started in that fight with 15,000, now we have 6,000, 9,000 disabled. My Brigade has lost between 12- and 1500." The arithmetic was so painful that at length he told Fanny, "let me cease to write about war and killing."[30]

He wrote home in a better frame of mind three days later, September 28, this time from Bunker Hill: "Our ranks are being filled by the returning of men from [the] hospital and those who have either broken down or willfully straggled." This was cheering news, but the mention of straggling launched him into a discussion of that too-prevalent practice, which he condemned with nearly as much vituperation as desertion. "This straggling," he railed, "is becoming … the curse of the Army and unless Congress pass[es] some law to stop it there is no telling where it will end. Men find it safer to get behind [the] lines than to fight. We will have to shoot them before it stops."[31]

Personal matters as well as military issues had the power to alarm him. By late September he was upset at not having gotten a letter from Fanny during the past four weeks, especially since her last had reported the ill health of their younger child. On the other hand, her silence told him that Dorsey had recovered from his "almost helpless condition"—had the boy taken a turn for the worse, the news surely would have reached him. Illness at home only deepened Pender's regret at his estrangement from his family, whom he hoped to see again before long. Although battles loomed in the future, "most of the fall in my opinion will be taken up [with] maneuvering." If the Yankees corresponded, he would probably be able to secure a furlough.[32]

In the meantime, he worked hard to recruit his brigade's strength and to prepare it for what lay ahead—if not maneuvering, then fighting. For the next eight weeks a part of the army continued to occupy the Shenandoah Valley, unwilling to leave this gorgeous sanctuary until the enemy demanded it. McClellan, however, showed no sign of doing that. Throughout October, he permitted Lee to gather up foodstuffs and forage for his army. Still, the Confederate leader knew that his sabbatical would not last forever. To make it difficult for his enemy to occupy the lower Shenandoah once he left it, Lee had several miles of Baltimore & Ohio track torn up west of Harpers Ferry.[33]

From the Shenandoah Valley, Lee also orchestrated long distance operations, including Stuart's October 9-13 raid on Chambersburg, Pennsylvania. The officer who at West Point had been dubbed "Beauty" conducted the mission with such speed and stealth that he easily outdistanced the improving but still inferior cavalry of the Army of the Potomac. Pender informed his wife that the Yankees "knew before he crossed the river that he was going and had plenty of time to make all their arrangements to get him as he returned [but] he was too quick and sharp for them…. They express great mortification at it. Beaut is after a Lieut. Generalcy."[34]

In a sense, October was more notable for events in other theaters of operations, news of which Pender closely followed from campsites at Bunker Hill and Summit Point. Although cheered by early, incomplete accounts of these campaigns, in the end he did not like what he heard. Early in the month, two Confederate commands unsuccessfully attacked Union strongholds in northern Mississippi, while the Rebel invasion of Kentucky ended when a third army was repulsed during heavy fighting outside Perryville. On the political front, the big event was Lincoln's issuance of a preliminary emancipation proclamation. While the decree freed no slaves immediately, it was to exert a major influence on the political orientation of the conflict. Pender left no record of his reaction to the policy, but one of its possibilities would have troubled him: that the armies of the South might some day be opposed by ex-slaves in blue.[35]

October also spawned events that had an agreeable impact on Pender and his family. In mid-month Fanny's brother Jake, whom her husband had been striving to attach to his staff for more than a year, reported for duty at Pender's headquarters. And on the 21st, Pender's old 13th North Carolina joined his brigade—another result of months of wire-pulling. The addition of the outfit commanded by Colonel Scales gave Pender five veteran regiments. At the risk of appearing greedy, he decided he would try to add his old 6th North Carolina as well. This effort, however, would prove unsuccessful.[36]

Other events in late October helped Pender maintain his spirits. The widely publicized activities of pro-peace Democrats (known as "Copperheads") in states including New York, Illinois, and Ohio gave him hope that the Confederacy might gain its political objectives off the battlefield, and swiftly. If during the fall elections the Copperheads could make inroads into Republican-dominated districts of those and other states, "I cannot but have some hope of peace this winter. It would of all things be more to my taste than anything else." He would not despair even if efforts to negotiate an end to the war took a bit longer to germinate. As he told Fanny, "if peace is made by spring we can then be together, and when I say if peace, etc., I only say what is fully believed... by [a] great many...." But he was doomed to disappointment in this matter, for while the Copperheads did pick up votes in the fall as well as in elections the following spring, and while they impeded mobilization and war administration in some states, they never mustered the power to impose a negotiated peace on the country.[37]

Yet another hope bloomed in Pender, if only briefly—the prospect of a promotion. Late in the month, by which time the Light Division had moved to a point six miles from Shepherdstown, where it was tearing up the B & O, General Hill suggested that Pender use whatever political influence he could gather to gain the major generalship that his tactical performances from Seven Pines to Shepherdstown Ford had earned him. Lee had decided to divide his army into corps to be commanded by Longstreet and Jackson, each with the rank of lieutenant general. The reorganization, intended to reduce the army's unwieldiness, required new major generals to command the divisions thus vacated.[38]

Hill promised to do all in his power to see Pender promoted. At month's end, he wrote the new secretary of war, George W. Randolph, on his subordinate's behalf. Meanwhile, Pender considered playing what contacts he had in Raleigh and Good Spring, perhaps even tapping his father-in-law's influence. This, however, was a delicate matter, for Pender had recently implied that Augustine Shepperd consorted too frequently with the pro-Union faction in North Carolina (while "one part of the family is being shot at and cuffed about on the head and knees, the other [is trying] to keep up the good feeling with the sympathizers of the cuffers"). In the end, nothing either Hill or his subordinate did gained Pender's advancement. The major generalships went, instead, to two officers who had Longstreet's favor, Hood and Pickett.[39]

Pender assuaged his disappointment by heading home to Fanny and the children, the result of a medical furlough. On October 29, as McClellan's army finally stirred itself to return to Virginia, Pender employed recurrent but mild episodes of rheumatism to wangle a leave. This his superiors freely granted to one who had become, in Pender's own words, "the most home sick man you ever saw." A few days later he was in Good Spring, where, at least for 20 days, he could leave behind his concerns over promotions, politics, and peace efforts.[40]

*   *   *

As when he had gone home after Malvern Hill, the Army of Northern Virginia did some heavy traveling in his absence. As soon as McClellan showed signs of leaving Maryland, that portion of Lee's army commanded by Longstreet marched to Culpeper Court House, where it arrived on November 3. Jackson's new corps remained in the Valley to block any Union advance in that quarter; it would not head south to join Lee and Longstreet until the closing days of the month.

Instead of challenging Jackson, McClellan headed south on the east side of the Blue Ridge, heading for Warrenton, about 18 miles northeast of Culpeper. He moved just as slowly and as cautiously as ever, although fully a month before Lincoln had warned him that a speedy pursuit was imperative. When Little Mac contented himself with attacking Confederate outposts such as those manned by the Light Division near Snicker's Gap in the Blue Ridge,

Lincoln lost the last of his patience. On November 7 he fired his army leader and replaced him with Ambrose Burnside.[41]

Under Burnside, the Army of the Potomac appeared to recapture its old agility and speed. Like his predecessor, the new commander saw Richmond, rather than Lee's troops, as his primary objective. He planned to move there after feinting toward Culpeper or Gordonsville. After Lee shifted position to block him, Burnside would head eastward to Falmouth, there to cross the bridgeless Rappahannock via pontoons to Fredericksburg. From there it would be a quick jaunt to the Rebel capital.

The plan sounded good, but Lincoln wondered if the new man was sharp enough to pull it off. The president was pleasantly surprised when Burnside got off to a flying start. His advance started down the Warrenton Pike on the 15th; five days later, nearly his entire army—no fewer than 116,683 officers and men, present for duty—held the heights overlooking Fredericksburg.[42]

When Pender returned from North Carolina on November 21, he learned that Lee and Longstreet had reached Fredericksburg two days before to confront Burnside. Although no one in Richmond knew its whereabouts, Jackson's corps had left the Valley for the Rappahannock line. For more than a week after his arrival, Pender lingered in the capital, at Adjutant General Cooper's suggestion, until he located his command. Not until December 2, amid snow flurries and falling temperatures, was Jackson ensconced at Fredericksburg following a forced march in wretched weather. That day Pender at last rejoined his command, which he found positioned south of the Richmond, Fredericksburg & Potomac Railroad tracks about three miles below the city. On the right of the Light Division, extending as far downriver as Hamilton's Crossing, the divisions of Jubal Early and D. H. Hill had camped (the latter had been transferred from Jackson's corps during the recent reorganization). Harvey Hill's troops constituted the far right of the army. In rear of the Light Division, William Taliaferro's command formed a corps reserve.

A gap intervened between Jackson's left flank and the right of Longstreet's line farther north. Longstreet's people occupied a perimeter that ran past Fredericksburg to the Rappahannock at Dr. Taylor's House. All told, the main line of the Army of Northern Virginia covered a distance of six and a half miles. Along its length, works of all types had been constructed and row upon row of cannons had been emplaced. To reach the line, an attacker would have to cross a wide and deep plain that was virtually bare of cover. Pender was right to regard his army's position as unassailable.[43]

Lee had been granted the time to perfect his defenses because the bridge materials Burnside required to force a crossing had been late in arriving from Washington. Unable or unwilling to revamp his strategy, for a week after Pender rejoined the army the Union leader did little but march his men back and forth along the Falmouth shore as if practicing for an assault. Pender viewed the maneuvering as a bluff.

But when Burnside's engineers began laying the errant pontoons on the morning of the 11th, Pender thought again. He watched intently as sharp-shooters holed up in the houses of evacuated Fredericksburg popped away at the bridge-builders, killing some of them. To complete the work, Burnside was forced to send over in pontoon boats enough troops to evict the Rebels in street-to-street combat. This took place, however, only after a mammoth artillery barrage had leveled a goodly portion of the city. Pender fumed at the "barbarity" of the cannonade, which he considered a violation of the basic rules of warfare.[44]

If Burnside had surprised Pender up to now, when the Yankees crossed the river in the wake of the street fighting, Pender was astonished. On December 3 he had written Fanny (who, he had recently learned, was again pregnant) that "one cannot imagine the degree of confidence and high spirits displayed by our men." The high morale was a function not only of past successes but of the great advantages of terrain and position the army enjoyed. Any attempt to seize the high ground on which Lee's troops were posted would be suici-dal.[45]

But Pender could only watch, mouth agape, as Burnside defied the mon-umental odds facing him. On the cold, foggy morning of December 13, hav-ing positioned on the Fredericksburg side what he considered to be enough artillery to support an advance, the Union leader sent wave after wave of attackers across the open ground against many points on the Confederate line. As Pender had anticipated, before the Yankees were well across the plain, can-nons blew gaping holes in their lines, crushing assault formations and piling up bodies. Then mobile artillery units, including some under Pender's direc-tion, ran forward to pour an oblique fire into the front and flank of the blue line.[46]

After the first wave broke and receded, others came on with almost mani-acal determination. Some advanced farther than their predecessors although

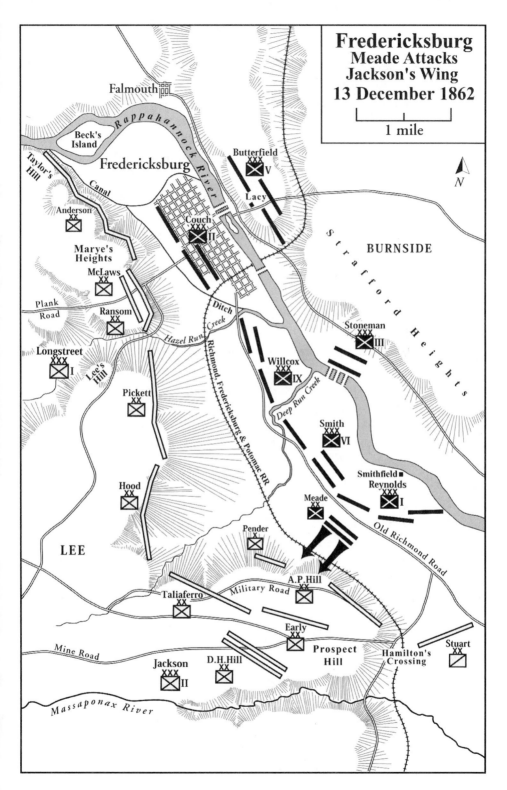

Fredericksburg
Meade Attacks
Jackson's Wing
13 December 1862

1 mile

N

Falmouth

Rappahannock River

Beck's
Island

Fredericksburg

Butterfield
XXX
V

Lacy

Taylor's
Hill

Canal

Anderson
XX

Marye's
Heights

McLaws
XX

Couch
XXX
II

BURNSIDE

Strafford Heights

Plank
Road

Ransom
XX

Ditch Creek

Hazel Run

Stoneman
XXX
III

Longstreet
XXX
I

Lee's
Hill

Willcox
XXX
IX

Richmond, Fredericksburg & Potomac RR

Deep Run Creek

Pickett
XX

Smith
XXX
VI

Smithfield ■

Reynolds
XXX
I

Hood
XX

Meade
XX

Old Richmond Road

LEE

Pender
X

A.P.Hill
XX

Taliaferro
XX

Military Road

Early
XX

Mine Road

Jackson
XXX
II

D.H.Hill
XX

Prospect
Hill

Hamilton's
Crossing

Stuart
XX

Massaponax River

— 153 —

in the end they too crumpled under a blizzard of balls and shells. By extraordinary effort, a few hundred Federals crossed the railroad tracks and penetrated a boggy gap between Lane's and Archer's positions, on Pender's right. The foothold that members of Major General George Gordon Meade's Fifth Corps division gained in that sector briefly threatened the stability of Jackson's flank, but a counterattack by other members of Hill's command and Early's division filled the breach and chased the Yankees away.

Although Pender's assistance was not needed to mend the break, the fight to do so resulted in the greatest personal tragedy of his career. Lieutenant Jacob Shepperd, only a few weeks into his stint on the brigade staff, was shot dead while trying to rally Lane's fugitives—a task he had taken upon himself, without orders. Pender would grieve over Jake for months—his wife for years to come.[47]

Pender's brother-in-law was not the only casualty this day in the ranks of his family. Although his sector was not nearly as hard-pressed as Lane's or Archer's, his brigade took its share of casualties from both musketry and artillery fire. At one point in the afternoon Pender was staggered by a minie ball that passed through his left forearm. When one of his subordinates expressed concern at the blood flowing down his sleeve, the general replied that the wound was trifling, no bones having been broken. Not everyone seemed relieved by the good news. Pender's relations with General Archer had deteriorated to the point that, when told of his colleague's wounding, Archer supposedly snapped: "I wish they had shot him in his damn head."[48]

Eventually, loss of blood forced Pender to the rear for medical attention, after passing command of the brigade to Alfred Scales. By then the one-sided battle was over on Jackson's front, so Pender missed nothing of consequence by quitting the front line. Yet Burnside's doomed effort was not over. He continued to hurl brigades at Longstreet's line until well after dark. By then his dead lay heaped on the battlefield like some ghastly sacrifice.

Chapter Nine

UNSURPASSED COURAGE
AND DETERMINATION

Only two of Pender's regiments, the 16th and 22nd North Carolina, had been heavily engaged at Fredericksburg, losing, respectively, 54 and 45 killed, wounded, and missing, of a total brigade loss of just under 170. This figure constituted the smallest loss of any brigade but one in the Light Division, confirming that the Federal attack on Jackson's line had been direct-ed south of Pender's position. And the effort expended on that part of the line paled in comparison to the furious desperation of Burnside's attacks on Longstreet's front and the blood that had been shed there. The losses testified that on December 13, the Army of the Potomac had suffered a defeat of cat-aclysmic proportions.[1]

Shocked by the horrors his strategy had wrought, Burnside tended to his casualties as best he could, then dragged what remained of his army across the river on the 14th and 15th. A few days later, convinced that not even a pig-headed general would attempt another crossing in the Rebel front, Lee placed his army—without moving it far from its positions during the battle—in winter quarters. Pender named his cluster of huts and tents "Camp Gregg," in honor of the South Carolinian, long a mainstay of the Light Division, who had died on the 15th of a wound received in the battle. William Gaston Lewis, who had attended Pender's wedding and was now a field officer in the 43rd North Carolina, made a brief visit to the camp, which he described as "a model of cleanliness, regularity, and good order," testimony to Pender's emphasis on discipline and formality in everything military.[2]

Although the camp was as clean as he could make it, Pender hoped to coax Fanny into a long stay with him by leasing a house for her a half mile from his headquarters. The place featured "a small attic room—with fireplace" and laundry services, though Fanny would have to take her meals at Camp Gregg. "You can judge," he told her, "as to bringing one of the children.... Rather than not see you I would say bring both, but if you could be satisfied to leave them it would be better for there is no telling how long before or when we may move. Turner would not be so much trouble to travel with as Dorsey. It may be possible to leave Turner in Edgecombe. But finally do as you please...."[3]

Fanny did come, without the children. She missed spending Christmas with her husband, who made merry at a feast served up by the divisional headquarters mess. She also missed seeing the old year out but was on hand to welcome the new. Her arrival coincided with a determined attempt at good cheer throughout the army, or at least within the officer corps. There certainly seemed to be grounds for celebrating the holiday season. On the home front, the Penders could look forward to the birth of their third child. On the military front, the fortunes of war—in the eastern theater, at least—had gone with the Confederacy. As a North Carolina surgeon put it, "to us the year draws to a glorious close,—to the enemy it has proven a cruel mockery."[4]

Fanny remained at Fredericksburg for almost two months, boosting her husband's morale amid the dull, numbing routine that set in once the Christmas festivities ended. Due to the weather, activity ceased on both sides of the Rappahannock save for roll call, picket duty, and a series of snowball fights, some of which attracted brigade-size opponents who fought according to textbook tactics. An officer in the 34th North Carolina noted in a letter to his sister that "the soldiers … enjoy themselves finely snowballing each other. Pender's brigade & Gregg's [now Brigadier General Samuel McGowan's] had a powerful time yesterday. Both parties held their ground. It imitates a battle as much as anything I ever saw…."[5]

But winter camp was not a time of fun and games; in fact, amusements were few at Camp Gregg. Although Fanny's presence served to take his mind off his own troubles, Pender was constantly reminded of the hardships his men endured throughout the cold weather season. They were not used to wintering in such a harsh climate as the Rappahannock country afforded. Not even stockaded tents and well-chinked cabins provided adequate resistance to frigid winds and plunging temperatures. The soldiers had so few bedclothes they had to share. "Often there was only one blanket for two men," one of Pender's officers recalled. Even that resort failed to prevent "much suffering" in the ranks. The result was a sick list that continued to lengthen despite Pender's best efforts, and a succession of funerals for the victims of respiratory diseases.[6]

Those who could escape the misery of duty at Camp Gregg did so by any expedient. Furloughs were eagerly sought; Pender was liberal in granting them consistent with the needs of the army. Some officers sought transfer to regiments that were going to be raised strictly for the defense of North Carolina. The surgeon of the 34th applied for a commission therein, noting that he served "in a Brigade & Div[ision] that is [sic] second to none … but the service is exceedingly hard & if the State service be any easier, I would much prefer it on account of my health & reasons of a domestic character."[7]

Many who could no longer take winter quarters simply left. If not quickly apprehended, they had a fair prospect of making their way back to their homes and families, some of which were experiencing even rougher times than the inhabitants of Camp Gregg. Pender could understand the motivation of these men, but he could not condone their behavior. Deserters turned their backs on their comrades as well as on the cause that sustained them in good times and bad. They were more lowly than cowards; they were leeches draining the life's blood of the Southern nation.

Pender did not limit his strictures to those who went over the hill. He saved some of his harshest commentary for those political and legal officials who by word or deed encouraged the practice. His list of "arch traitors" included William W. Holden, editor of the Raleigh *Standard* and instigator of the peace movement in North Carolina, and Chief Justice Richard M. Pearson of the state supreme court, who made a practice of releasing deserters from police or army custody. Pender and other North Carolina officers erroneously believed that Pearson had also decreed the Confederate conscription law of April 1862 unconstitutional. Certainly he did all in his power to limit the scope of that legislation.[8]

In the spring of 1863 Pender informed army headquarters that the influential judge was responsible for desertion having become an intolerable problem in the 10 North Carolina regiments of the Light Division: "In my humble opinion, the whole trouble lies in the fact that when they [deserters] get into North Carolina they will not be molested, and their belief is based upon the dictum of Judge Pearson.... The militia officers ... [say] that they should not arrest any more deserters in the face of Judge Pearson's holding [i. e., ruling] unless protected by the Government, and the boldness of the deserters there proves that they are acting up to their word. Letters are received by the men, urging them to leave; that they will not be troubled when they get home... Unless something is done, and quickly, serious ill be the result. Our regiments will waste away more rapidly than they ever have by battle."[9]

For a time, it appeared that those aching to go home would not have to travel far. In mid-January, in the aftermath of a Union raid along the North Carolina coast, Lee sent a large detachment from his army to garrison the eastern part of the state. Originally, the army leader intended to include Pender's and Lane's brigades in this detachment. An order was drawn up sending both commands to North Carolina via Richmond, but it was rescinded before implemented. This was a great relief to Pender, who believed that if transported to North Carolina, his brigade would experience a tenfold increase in desertions.[10]

The issue of sending at least a part of the brigade to its home state came up again a few weeks later when Colonel McElroy of the 16th North Carolina, apparently without Pender's knowledge, resurrected the idea in a letter to the newly elected governor, Zebulon Baird Vance. McElroy, however, was using the desertion issue as a pretext to visit home, for he admitted that he was "anxious to get back to North Carolina upon any terms." Although Vance shared the hard line Pender took with deserters, he aroused Pender's fears by asking the Confederate War Department to send the 16th home to round up deserters and also to recruit. Fortunately for Pender's peace of mind, General Lee argued against the proposition, and it was dropped.

Ironically, in his letter blasting Judge Pearson, Pender himself called for a regiment to be sent from Virginia into northwestern North Carolina to root out the hundreds of deserters said to be holed up there. It is likely that he expected an outfit from some other brigade—perhaps from another state—would be assigned to the mission. In the end, none of Pender's outfits returned home as a body, forcing any soldier with ideas of leaving to make the long, uncertain journey on his own.[11]

*   *   *

On January 19, 1863, Ambrose Burnside put his army in motion on the Falmouth shore and, to the amazement of his enemy, resumed active operations. His intent was to march to Banks's Ford, about six miles above Fredericksburg, there to cross a large portion of his army on pontoons and strike Lee an unexpected blow. Although the plan seemed to have many of the same flaws as his earlier strategy, this time, at least, he got off to a fast start that appeared to take his opponent by surprise. As one of Pender's officers revealed in a letter written on the 21st, many observers believed Burnside was preparing another crossing opposite Fredericksburg. In that event, his men would "meet with as great [a] defeat as they did in Dec."[12]

What Burnside might have accomplished the second time around would never be known, for one day after his column left Falmouth the weather turned ugly. Over the next 36 hours, freezing rain, sleet, and snow crippled the offensive, turning it into a "Mud March" and forcing his army back to its camps. A few days later Lincoln relieved the luckless Burnside from command and replaced him with one of the general's most vocal critics in the army, "Fighting Joe" Hooker.[13]

Because Fanny was with him during the Mud March, no letters reveal her spouse's attitude toward the operation. In all probability, Pender would have regarded it as doomed from the start. To his mind, no Yankee general—certainly not a plodder such as Burnside—could have outmaneuvered Robert E. Lee. Not enough was known about Burnside's successor to permit an informed decision on Joe Hooker, but Pender would have viewed the man as the latest in a series of pigheaded incompetents.

The Confederacy, he felt, on the other hand, had been blessed with a wealth of talented commanders, especially at the corps and division levels. Yet it could always use one more. Pender had never given up the hope that he would some day be made a major general, perhaps to command the Light Division. He would not have tried to displace A. P. Hill, but by mid-winter rumors of Hill's promotion to corps command and his transfer to the western theater were making the rounds, and Pender took careful note. Then, too, in mid-January, D. H. Hill, who had long been on poor terms with some of his colleagues, was given a command in North Carolina although his division remained in Virginia. Someone would be chosen to hold one or both of these commands—why not William Dorsey Pender, who had demonstrated high ability on so many fields?[14]

In his quest for promotion, he could always count on the support of others. As before, A. P. Hill advanced Pender's claims at division and army headquarters, while Pender's politically influential brother-in-law, Robert Bridgers, did the same at the state level and before the new secretary of war, James A. Seddon. On the brigade level, Pender's subordinate and friend Alfred Scales got up a petition recommending Pender's promotion, signed by the officers of every North Carolina regiment in the army.[15]

Everything came to naught, for two reasons. The rumor mill notwithstanding, A. P. Hill would remain at the head of the Light Division. And Jackson, who had the greatest input on D. H. Hill's successor, claimed not to know enough about Pender as a field leader to consider him for the position. When he learned of Jackson's views, Pender naturally believed he had become a victim of the bad blood that continued to define the Jackson-Hill relationship. Pender, who rarely had a good word to say about Jackson even before the promotion opportunity came up, was decidedly anti-Jackson after Stonewall selected Robert E. Rodes, a Virginian, to replace D. H. Hill.[16]

Some weeks later, Pender found his future claims for advancement badly, perhaps fatally, weakened. Early in March, an officer senior to him, Brigadier General Henry Heth, was assigned permanent command of the brigade once led by Charles Field and, since Field's severe wounding at Cedar Mountain, by Colonel Brockenbrough. Within a few weeks Pender effectively relinquished any lingering hope of promotion. He nevertheless continued to believe that if "claims were considered" in an objective manner, he would soon be a major general.[17]

Pender's longing for, and efforts to win, promotion had many roots. One biographer believes they reflected "an unquenchable desire to excel," while "the need to be a hero in his wife's eyes" was a secondary source of his ambition. But Pender was motivated by more than a desire to improve, to advance, to accomplish; he required tangible recognition of his achievement. Once he attained that recognition, however, he moved on. As soon as he reached a goal, no matter how hard or how long he had striven for it, it seemed to lose importance for him. It was not promotion or advancement that he needed; it was the recognition, the validation of his worth as a soldier, that advancement signified.[18]

*   *   *

Toward the close of February, with the weather temporarily moderating, Pender began to fear that operations would soon heat up. Thus he sent his pregnant wife out of the army and back home. Later he decided, as she did, that her leave-taking had been premature, and they both regretted it. But he had not, as she claimed to believe, packed her off to Good Spring simply because he had the power to do so: "You wrong me in saying that I sent you off to show people or you that I would have my own way. I really think I could rise above such conduct as that."[19]

As on past occasions, he was deeply depressed as the train that took her home pulled out of the station in Richmond. As before, too, he lingered in the capital before returning to camp. He found the city not only lonely but uninteresting: "A duller place I never saw and I am heartily tired of it, and if I can be pardoned for this offense I think I will never come to Richmond again without business."[20]

Once back in camp, he worked hard at finding things to occupy his time and keep his mind off his family. He complained, then and weeks later, that too often he found "time hanging on me as heavy as a millstone." He continued his regular bible readings but now he also read for pleasure, including the works of Dickens. He looked forward to any diversion from daily routine, including court-martial duty, service on an officer examining board, and attendance at the wedding, held at Camp Gregg, of Colonel Scales and his 18-year-old cousin ("poor thing," Pender joked, "she does not know what is in store for her").[21]

As the winter drew to a close, he did not have to go out of his way to keep busy. His expectations of renewed campaigning, once premature, began to take on increasing validity. In mid-March Union cavalry made a surprise attack on Stuart's camps near Kelly's Ford on the upper Rappahannock, not only revealing the growing competence of the enemy but perhaps heralding the spring campaign. Afterward, Pender began to ready his command for renewed operations. When weather permitted, he hauled everyone out to the drill plain and target range. He gave special attention to the many enlistees who had found their way to Fredericksburg over the past three months, as well as to draftees whom Judge Pearson had not been able to keep out of the army. Other newcomers trickled into camp courtesy of the recruiting parties that continued to scour eastern North Carolina and whose activities Pender close-ly monitored.

He took care that his regiments remained well-officered. For this reason he was more than a little upset when Colonel Gray of the 22nd ("a fine sol-dier, and a nice gentleman") succumbed to alcohol poisoning a few days before the coming of spring. Pender regretted his ignorance of Gray's problem and decided that "if his officers had let me know of his condition I could have stopped his drinking in time probably to have saved him." He also selected with care new members of his staff, including Major Joseph A. Englehard, Captain Ashe's successor as brigade adjutant, and Captain L. H. Hunt, the new inspector general of the brigade. Afterward Pender did his best to make the newcomers feel like integral parts of the brigade hierarchy.[22]

By the end of March, Pender's efforts to maintain and increase the strength of his brigade began to pay off. Morning-reports showed some 2,500 effectives, twice as many as on hand after the fight at Fredericksburg. But Pender believed that less than half of the new men—especially the draftees—would render competent service when campaigning resumed. Even so, on the drill field the command gave promise of accomplishing something in active operations. "I am getting a splendid Brigade," he exulted to Fanny. "Good size, fine drill, and discipline." While the rookies gave him cause for concern, veterans continued to predominate, a thought that gave him comfort.[23]

Early April found Pender ready, even eager, for a return to field service, that he might test what was, in some ways, an entirely new command. At first he expected his opportunity would come courtesy of Hooker. He assumed that the new leader would push across the river in or near Lee's front, perhaps a bit more indirectly than his predecessor but hoping, like Burnside, to suc-ceed through brute strength. By mid-month, however, it had become appar-ent that Joseph Hooker was too smart to do his maneuvering within Lee's range of vision.

As the Confederates continued to hug the riverbank, awaiting a blow from the enemy, Pender grew increasingly uneasy and discontented. He hoped that his army would shift from the defensive to the offensive, such as by returning to Maryland or, better still, by marching through the Commonwealth of Pennsylvania. When he mentioned his preferences to his wife, however, Fanny expressed herself as opposed to invasion. She must have recalled how disappointed and upset her husband had been when the foray that ended at Antietam gained no strategic success. Pender tried to refute her objections: "You say you do not want me to go into Md. Honey, I feel nothing [is] left us but to go. If we do not, our Army will be on short rations and discontented, and we accomplish next to nothing. If we go we may do a great deal and I believe we will."[24]

Whereas during the previous invasion Pender had issued strict prohibitions against looting, now he appeared to look forward to giving the enemy a taste of their own bitter medicine. "Our people have suffered from the depredations of the Yankees," he declared, "but if we ever get into their country they will find out what it is to have an invading army amongst them…. They have gone systematically to work to starve us out and destroy all we have, to make the country a desert. I say let us play at the same game if we get the chance…."[25]

Perhaps it was this seeming turnabout in her husband's attitude—his sudden thirst for laying waste to the enemy's homeland—that made Fanny Pender fear his return to the country above the Potomac. Despite what novelists would write of her a century hence, she never suggested that a campaign in the North was doomed to failure or destined to draw the wrath of God. She merely believed that a second invasion, so soon after the failure of the first, invited bad luck, and in this she was correct.[26]

* * *

Fanny Pender need not have worried, for Joe Hooker made sure that his enemy would not be going anywhere for awhile. Through the latter half of April, the Army of the Potomac made obvious preparations to move somewhere. When a small body of Federals crossed the river opposite Port Royal on the 23rd, Lee decided that his enemy was about to resume active operations.

Hooker's intent seemed clear when, early on April 29, he crossed larger numbers of troops on freshly laid pontoons at Deep Run, southeast of Fredericksburg. But when this force failed to make a large demonstration near its bridgehead, Lee began to suspect that "the principal effort of the enemy would be made in some other quarter." That quarter turned out to be well beyond his left flank. Late that day Lee learned that Hooker had stolen a march on him. Thousands of bluecoats had crossed at Kelly's Ford the previous night, heading south in two columns toward the Rapidan. The paths they were taking converged at a crossroads known as Chancellorsville. From Chancellorsville, the reunited force could move against Lee's rear. But to get there they would have to cross the Wilderness, a 10-mile square of scrub oak and second-growth pine.[27]

Of necessity, Lee put his army in motion. He made certain that enough troops were on hand, under Jubal Early, to deal with the units that continued to arrive at the bridgehead. Then, late on the 30th and early on May 1, he dispatched elements of both Longstreet's and Jackson's corps, including the Light Division, to Chancellorsville, where Hooker's people were banging at the Confederate back door.[28]

The hurried movement provided Pender with the activity he craved after weeks of fruitless waiting for something to happen. As he marched toward the threatened sector, he dashed off a letter to Fanny, predicting an easy victory over Hooker. By 8:00 A.M. on May 1 his brigade had hunkered down five miles east of Chancellorsville, to which point Lee's rear guard had been driven.

To secure the perimeter against the advancing enemy, Jackson placed troops on the two main thoroughfares in the Wilderness, the Orange Turnpike and the Orange Plank Road. Via those roads he pressed the enemy, attempting to determine their strength. At first the Yankees gave way and fell back, as if abandoning the forest crossroads. But a deeper probing movement revealed regiments and brigades holding formidable breastworks west of Chancellorsville. Thus far Pender's men had been only lightly engaged, but their commander foresaw a major confrontation in which they and everyone near them would take part.

By early evening the opponents at Chancellorsville seemed to be at a stalemate. The Federals' advance toward Fredericksburg had been halted but they continued to threaten the Army of Northern Virginia's most vulnerable sector. Lee could not permit them to remain there much longer.[29]

Pressed by necessity, he developed a plan. Sometime after 8:00 the next morning Pender's brigade was moving again, as were the rest of the troops under Jackson. With the aid of Stuart's scouts, Lee had discovered that Hooker's right flank, which stretched to a point just beyond Wilderness Church on the Orange Pike, two miles beyond Chancellorsville, was "in the air"—unanchored and vulnerable. At Lee's direction, Jackson was following a local guide on a long winding route to reach the turnpike west of Wilderness Church.

It was perhaps the riskiest maneuver Stonewall ever made, as it took 15 of his brigades—26,000 troops—across the length of Hooker's army, which sprawled less than three miles to the north. So large a force could not hope to achieve complete deception. Hooker's pickets did detect the march, but their commander, who had a capacity for self-delusion rivaling John Pope's, assumed that the movement signaled a full-scale Confederate retreat.[30]

Before 6:00 P.M., Jackson was in position west of Wilderness Church. Just before the sun went down he moved along the turnpike in three carefully arranged lines of attack, Rodes's division in front, the division of Brigadier General Raleigh Colston just behind, and the Light Division in Colston's rear. The brigades of Heth and Pender advanced along the left side of the pike, with Lane's and McGowan's brigades farther to the rear straddling the road. From prisoners taken near Wilderness Church, Pender probably knew that the troops just ahead were members of the Eleventh Army Corps, commanded by his classmate, Major General Oliver Otis Howard. A violent reunion of the West Point Class of 1854 was only minutes away.

When it rolled forward shortly before 6:00, Jackson's attack was a stunning success. Taken wholly unaware, the Eleventh Corps went under almost immediately, its men throwing down their rifles and running for their lives through the forest primeval. After Rodes's division cleared the turnpike of everything but artillery, Colston's line swept forward and Pender moved by his flank to support Colston's left. At first, progress was rapid and smooth, but as it approached Dowdall's Tavern, just off the turnpike east of Wilderness Church, Pender's troops came under an artillery barrage that drove them and supporting units back, permitting most of Howard's fugitives to reach the safety of Hooker's main body farther east.[31]

After Pender pulled his men out of cannon-range, he formed a new line along the pike and prepared to go forward again if ordered. But darkness and unfamiliar terrain prevented him from doing more than advancing a skirmish line toward the presumed location of the enemy. Ignorant of Hooker's dispositions, he feared that his men were in a precarious position, but unless instructed otherwise he would hold on where he was.

Jackson's flanking march and his crushing assault had given the Confederacy one of its greatest battlefield triumphs. The aftermath of victory, however, provided one of the South's greatest tragedies. Seeking an opening

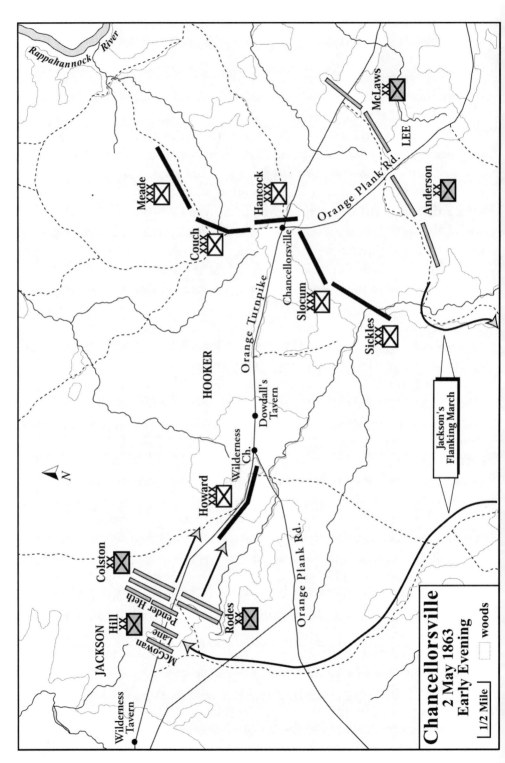

Rappahannock River

McLaws

LEE

Meade
XXX

Hancock
XXX

Anderson
XX

Orange Plank Rd.

Couch
XXX

Chancellorsville

Slocum
XXX

Orange Turnpike

Sickles
XXX

HOOKER

Jackson's
Flanking March

Dowdall's
Tavern

Wilderness
Ch.

N

Howard
XXX

Colston
XX

Orange Plank Rd.

JACKSON

Hill
XX

Pender Heth

Rodes
XX

McGowan
Lane

Wilderness
Tavern

Chancellorsville
2 May 1863
Early Evening

1/2 Mile   woods

for further attacks, Jackson and a small group of officers rode forward in the darkness, only to be fired on by members of Lane's brigade, south of Pender, who mistook the riders for a party of the enemy. Jackson suffered a severe wound in his left arm, complications from which would take his life eight days later. Quickly he was taken up and carried from the field.

En route to the rear, the litter-bearers passed Pender, who, despite his past animosity toward Jackson, offered the suffering man words of sympathy and regret. Then he made the mistake of suggesting that his brigade had been so cut up and lost in the darkness that it might have to withdraw from its position. Jackson seemed to rise up as he rasped: "You must hold your ground, General Pender; you must hold your ground, sir!"[32]

Taken aback, Pender promised to comply with his superior's wishes. Then the litter-bearers carried away an officer whom the Army of Northern Virginia could not afford to lose.

*   *   *

While Jackson's flank attack was in progress, the corps leader had dispatched J. E. B. Stuart, with a small force of cavalry augmented by the 16th North Carolina of Pender's brigade, to block a road the routed enemy might use to reach the Rapidan. In the midst of the mission, Stuart was recalled to the battlefield to take over Jackson's corps. A. P. Hill, the logical choice to replace Stonewall, had been disabled by a wound, and Rodes, who was next in seniority, was too new to divisional command to handle a larger organization on short notice.[33]

Stuart had a reputation for hard-driving offensives, and he applied that style to his temporary command of infantry. On the morning of May 3, he planned to assault every sector of the severely compacted Union line that stretched west, northwest, and southwest of Chancellorsville. After shaking hands with Pender and introducing himself to his classmate's colleagues, Stuart issued instructions to his acquired subordinates. These included General Heth, who, having replaced A. P. Hill, would launch the primary attack along both sides of the Orange Pike. Behind Heth would come the divisions that had borne the brunt of the previous day's fight, Colston's and Rodes's.

It was still dark when the strategy conference broke up, and everyone got moving by daylight. Heth moved out along the turnpike, making dispositions as he went. His right-flank force, Archer's brigade, swung south to challenge the left flank of Major General Daniel E. Sickles's Third Corps, near a clearing called Hazel Grove. In that sector Archer strove to link with part of Longstreet's corps, which was attacking simultaneously from the south and east. Archer's job was made easier when Hooker suddenly withdrew Sickles from Hazel Grove and placed him along the main line at Fairview, a wooded knoll just west of Chancellorsville. Seizing the opportunity, Stuart placed several batteries at Hazel Grove and began to enfilade the Union left.[34]

Meanwhile, fighting raged at white heat along the upper flank. Attacking on the turnpike, Pender's brigade, backed by Lane's, quickly covered the 150 yards that separated the opposing lines on that part of the field. Under their general's relentless prodding, Pender's men made their way against a torrent of musketry to a breastwork of logs and brush which anchored a strategic sector of Hooker's line. There the defenses of Major General Hiram G. Berry's division of the Third Corps ended and those of Brigadier General Amiel W. Whipple's division began. In his battle report Pender noted that getting that far had been the biggest problem; once there, "we carried [the position] without once hesitating."[35]

Pender, not content to have seized one set of defenses, guided his men deep into the woods toward Chancellorsville until he met "obstinate" resistance from a reinforced enemy. The same was true of other elements of the Light Division, most of which had already fallen back. As soon as cannons got his range, Pender calmly led everyone but the 13th North Carolina back to the breastwork they had taken. Meanwhile, his old regiment, whose position protected it from the Union artillery, advanced. It got so close to the main line at Fairview that an officer wounded and captured one of Hooker's brigade commanders, Brigadier General William Hays.[36]

After withdrawing, Pender re-formed his ranks, which were much thinner than they had been only hours earlier. Despite the losses, when Stuart ordered a second wave of attack using Rodes's and Colston's men, Pender joined in. Taking charge of the nearby brigade of Edward Thomas as well as his own men, he advanced in close support of Rodes. As before, he encountered a wall of rifle- and artillery-fire, but he kept moving through the shell-blasted trees. Another line of works loomed up, shielding well-filled rifle pits. Pender formed his enlarged command for a charge, only to see his 22nd North Carolina, which had been cut up badly in the first charge, hang back. Aware that the outfit was virtually leaderless, Pender grabbed the colors from the hands of the regimental flag-bearer and shouted for everyone to follow him.

They did, and Pender, as Robert E. Lee put it, carried the banner "up and over the intrenchments, with the most distinguished gallantry." In minutes, the position was overrun and taken.[37]

After seizing this second trophy, Pender led the men in penetrating a stand of pines which turned out to shelter a large number of Yankees. For a time Pender held his ground, then gingerly withdrew. The maneuver was unavoidable—the right of Pender's brigade had been driven back so far that enemy troops were at least 100 yards in rear of the rest of the command.

During his second withdrawal, Pender discovered that the cartridge boxes of most of his men were empty. Thus he permitted Colston's troops to relieve him. By then, the Union position had been battered so mercilessly that its collapse was a foregone conclusion. By early evening Hooker had been forced to withdraw to a hastily constructed line north of Chancellorsville, leaving Lee in possession of the field. Fighting Joe had no recourse but to return to the east shore of the Rappahannock, ending his well-crafted but poorly executed scheme to strike from Lee's blind side.[38]

No unit in the Army of Northern Virginia had made a greater contribution to this outcome than Pender's brigade, and its commander knew it. In his after-action report he was modest in recording his own accomplishments but generous in citing those of his troops. After detailing many individual heroics, he summed up in one sweeping burst of pride: "I can truly say that my brigade fought May 3 with unsurpassed courage and determination. I never knew them [to] act universally so well. I noticed no skulking, and they never showed any hesitation in following their colors. My list of killed and wounded will show how manfully they fought on that glorious day.... All that I saw behaved as heroes."[39]

Chapter Ten

NO BRIGHTER GLORY

If his past services had not already done so, Pender's heroics at Chancellorsville should have made him a favorite to secure the next promotion Lee was authorized to confer. Not only had he driven large numbers of the enemy from successive positions, he had acquired yet another badge of courage. On Monday, May 4, as Hooker spent his last hours on the south bank of the river, Pender was struck on his right arm near the shoulder by a deflected bullet. He called it "a very slight bruise," although, as he told Fanny, "it killed a fine young officer standing in front of me."[1]

Pender's dramatic, against-all-odds performance on May 3 had been the talk of the division—perhaps of the army—ever since. It had impressed everyone who observed or heard about it, from General Lee down to the corporal from whose grasp Pender had wrestled the colors of the 22nd North Carolina. He believed he knew what his accomplishment would lead to, if no detour appeared in the road: "I won promotion last Sunday and if it can be done I think I shall get it."[2]

Thoughts of advancement were in his head for days after the victory in the forest. Still, it was not an all-consuming preoccupation, for he had to tend to the wants and needs of the soldiers who had followed him from one set of defenses to another. Once again a heavy casualty count—this time more than 750 killed, wounded, and missing—had shriveled the ranks of the brigade. The figure represented almost 30 percent of the loss suffered by the Light Division in the four-day battle. Two of Pender's regiments, the 13th and 22nd, had been nearly emasculated by casualties. Among the fallen were six of the brigade's ten field officers, including Colonel McElroy of the 16th.

The leadership vacuum was a problem Pender had to address sooner rather than later. With Hooker defeated, chances were that Lee might now launch the invasion that Fanny Pender had so strenuously argued against. Even if Lee remained on the Rappahannock, Pender's command had to be made ready and able, as soon as possible, to play any operational role assigned it.[3]

He could see to this work only after the command marched back to Camp Gregg, which it did on May 7. One of his first tasks after returning was to publicly thank his men for the steadfastness they had displayed, against great odds, on the 2nd and 3rd. Calling the thinned-out regiments together on the parade-ground, he made a terse speech in which he announced his pride and gratitude: "I may be exacting and hard to please," he admitted, "but in this instance I am perfectly satisfied. You have pleased me well."[4]

In a more formal proclamation issued on May 13, he expressed his thankfulness in greater detail as well as in plummier prose: "Troops could not have fought better or more gallantly ... [against an enemy] strongly posted and offering stubborn resistance, as evidenced by your loss—greater than of any brigade in the army in proportion to the numbers engaged." Such praise the soldiers accepted in a spirit of quiet pride, as they had an earlier order from General Lee, read to every regiment engaged in the fight, which began: "With heartfelt gratification the general commanding expresses to the army his sense of the heroic conduct displayed by officers and men during the arduous operations in which they have just been engaged...."[5]

Pender had every reason to hope that Lee had a special token of appreciation for him. In the aftermath of Jackson's death, rumor had his senior lieutenant, Dick Ewell, succeeding the fallen hero. Yet other pundits predicted that A. P. Hill, whose command had borne the brunt of the fighting and earned much of the glory from the Peninsula to the Wilderness, would gain the coveted post. Still other prognosticators believed that Stuart, who had stepped into Jackson's shoes so effectively on May 3-4 and who apparently wanted to remain in infantry command, would replace Stonewall. There was even the possibility that should Hill move up, Stuart might take over the Light Division.

Previously, Pender had decried the infighting that too often preceded the filling of command vacancies. This time he took part in it, telling his wife, and perhaps also his associates and subordinates, that Hill had a more legitimate claim to Jackson's command than Ewell, and that Stuart was too much the cavalryman to be entrusted with anything but temporary command of foot soldiers. Stuart had done well enough in an unfamiliar role at Chancellorsville, but his performance had not been flawless. Otherwise, more than two attacks would not have been required to pry the enemy out of their imperfectly constructed works. But however weak Stuart's claims to Hill's or Jackson's positions, Pender was wary of the Virginian's proficiency as a politician, warning Fanny that "he is as scheming [a] fellow as ever you saw." Through influence or guile his classmate might snare a prize that rightfully belonged to an infantry leader.[6]

A decision from Lee would not be long in coming. By mid-May Pender and virtually everyone else in the army realized that with the Federals still quiescent on their side of the river and with activity rippling through the camps on the near shore, "something is brewing—Gen. Lee is not going to wait all the time for them to come to him." In fact, one day earlier Lee had returned from Richmond, where he had attended four days of conferences with President Davis and Secretary of War Seddon. The meetings had produced a consensus that the Army of Northern Virginia would invade the North as a means of relieving war-torn Virginia and to help draw Major General Ulysses S. Grant away from the lower Mississippi Valley. On the 26th, after Grant had begun to besiege the Confederate stronghold at Vicksburg, the army leader returned to Richmond for another conference, with all of Davis's cabinet in attendance. Lee now promoted his invasion plan as a means of lifting Grant's siege, and his civilian superiors, despite expressing some misgivings, yielded to his desires.[7]

Before Lee could march anywhere, he had to reorganize his army and fill its high-level vacancies. As a means of redistributing manpower and resolving some personnel issues, he decided to create a third corps, which he assigned to A. P. Hill. Dick Ewell he elevated to replace Jackson as commander of the Second Corps. In the process, both men were made lieutenant generals.

This much attended to, Lee turned to the issue of division command. He wished to promote Pender as a reward for his many outstanding contributions, but Heth remained senior to him. On May 30, via Special Orders No. 146, he solved the dilemma by promoting both men to major general and assigning each a division under Hill. Pender thus became, at 29, the youngest general of his rank in the army. Hill was also assigned a third division by transferring that of Major General Richard Heron Anderson from Longstreet's corps.

Pender received a truncated version of the Light Division: his own brigade—to be led by Colonel Hoke until Alfred Scales recovered from a wound received on May 3—as well as the brigades of Lane, Thomas, and McGowan (the latter had been commanded by Colonel Abner Perrin of the 14th South Carolina since McGowan's recent wounding). Meanwhile, a new command was created for Heth, who was assigned his old brigade, under Colonel Brockenbrough; Archer's brigade (a move perhaps influenced by its commander's coolness toward Pender); the North Carolina brigade that had been given to General Pettigrew following his release from captivity; and a mostly Mississippi brigade commanded by Jefferson Davis's nephew, Brigadier General Joseph R. Davis. At least at first glance, the reorganization and the assignments stemming from it seemed a masterstroke; everyone promoted as a result seemed content with the force that had been assigned to him.[8]

Lee considered each of these men worthy of the honor bestowed on him, but Pender came especially highly recommended. On May 20 Lee had characterized him to President Davis as "an excellent officer, attentive, industrious, and brave; [he] has been conspicuous in every battle, and, I believe, wounded in almost all of them." Davis, who recalled observing Pender at Mechanicsville and Gaines's Mill, seems to have heartily agreed. Ironically, had Lee acted on a decision he had mulled over about a month earlier, Pender would no longer be a commander of infantry but one of Stuart's cavalry subordinates. It is not known whether Lee broached the idea of a transfer to Pender or rejected it before asking his opinion. Either way, things appeared to have worked out for the best.[9]

But not everyone shared this view. While North Carolinians lauded Pender as "a gallant son of our old State," the South Carolinians in Perrin's brigade professed to have "a perfect horror" of their new division leader, "as being such a strict disciplinarian." In quick time, however, each brigade that Pender inherited came to view him as tough but fair and as an officer who looked after his men, on and off the battlefield.[10]

Given his predilection for losing interest in goals once they had been attained, Pender, when promoted brigadier general, had never mentioned the honor in his letters home; Fanny had learned of it from outside sources. On the present occasion, however, she got the news of his advancement right away, for she had returned to the army, along with both children, some days before the promotion was announced. This was perfect for Pender. It was a time for celebrating, and what better way to celebrate than with one's family.[11]

Unfortunately, Pender's loved ones had arrived too close to the stepping-off point of the invasion. Based on enemy movements, by June 2 Lee was certain that no attack on Richmond was in contemplation; this removed the last stumbling-block to his northern journey. The following day he put his army—elements of Longstreet's and Ewell's corps—in motion toward the fords of the upper Rappahannock near Culpeper Court House. Since the success of the early stages of the campaign hinged on surprising the enemy, Lee ordered Hill's new command to remain on the river, creating the impression that Lee had gone nowhere. Three of Pender's regiments joined one from Heth's division in picketing the shore nearest the enemy.[12]

By June 5, the Third Corps was the only portion of the Army of Northern Virginia still along the Rappahannock. That day a suspicious Hooker threw a new pontoon bridge over the water; the following morning troops crossed to probe for unusual gaps in Hill's defenses. Hill had Pender and Heth make a visible response, Pender moving south to Hamilton's Crossing and advancing a 200-man skirmish line toward the Yankees. Rather than making only a show fight, the skirmishers attacked and routed one of Hooker's regiments, which quickly retreated. The fighting served its purpose. Hooker was duped into believing that the line opposite him continued to be strongly held.

The Union reconnaissance-in-force persuaded Pender that it was time for Fanny and the boys to head for home. This time he could not escort them to the train; the leave-taking took place at soon-to-be-dismantled Camp Gregg. For the last time, he planted kisses on cheeks and lips, waved goodbye, and whispered words of endearment. Perhaps he even shed a tear or two—Fanny, who seems to have sensed a painful finality in their parting, did.[13]

Once again, Fanny feared she had gone off prematurely. In a sense, she was correct. For days after her departure, Pender's command remained in place, searching for nonexistent signs of enemy movements, while miles away most of their comrades continued marching. Pender was still in camp on June 9 when word came that Stuart's horsemen, who had been waiting upriver to join in the invasion, had been caught napping by the upstart Federal cavalry. A day-long series of charges and countercharges near Brandy Station, six miles from Culpeper, left Stuart's legions battered, bruised, and bewildered, but in possession of the field. It is not known whether Pender took satisfaction in his classmate's discomfiture or in the fact that Pender's old dragoon comrade David Gregg, now commanding a Union cavalry division, had been one of Stuart's most vigorous assailants.[14]

By June 15, even Heth's and Anderson's divisions had joined the exodus from the Rappahannock, but the Light Division remained on picket at water's edge. By now, only a skeleton force faced it across the river. Two days before, Hooker had gotten the belated word that most of Lee's army had left his front, heading northwestward. Anxious to protect Washington, Fighting Joe had decamped for Fairfax Station, not far from two battlefields that had witnessed Union defeats and retreats.[15]

That left Pender in an inactive sector, all by himself. He seemed alternately anxious and pleased to be left behind—pleased because he might miss a coming battle and thus be spared to his army and his family ("for once we will be out of the fight"). But he mused in vain, and he must have suspected as much. On the 16th the order came to pack up and depart. By midday he was heading for Culpeper, bring up the rear of Hill's corps. Suddenly he looked forward to returning to Maryland, and possibly ranging beyond. He only hoped that "God in his goodness be more gracious than in our last trial. We certainly may be allowed to hope as our mission is one of peace altho' through blood."[16]

*　　*　　*

This time Lee would invade the North by a more circuitous route than before. From Culpeper, Ewell, followed by Longstreet and, at a distance, by Hill, angled west as well as north. After fording the Rappahannock tributaries, the gray column entered the Valley of Virginia via Chester Gap in the Blue Ridge, and crossed the Shenandoah River near Front Royal. The route ensured that Lee's right flank would be screened by the mountains even as he gained easy access to the Union garrisons at Berryville, Martinsburg, and Winchester, any of which might hamper the invasion.

News of Ewell's approach to the largest of these posts, Winchester, had prompted Hooker to hasten north from the Rappahannock. But although forewarned, the garrison there proved no match for the Second Corps. On June 13-14 while detachments of his command neutralized the smaller outposts, Ewell attacked Winchester from the south and west, routing its defenders and foiling their attempt to escape via Stephenson's Depot, three miles north of the town.

The road north had been cleared of potential obstacles. By the morning of the 15th, Ewell's advance was entering Maryland, and soon afterward Rebel cavalry was trotting through southern Pennsylvania. The main bodies of the First and Second Corps would soon follow.[17]

Pender's men reached Culpeper on the 18th, rested for a time, and three days later returned to the fertile, picturesque country of the Shenandoah Valley. The verdant fields that stretched in all directions raised everyone's spirits, which had been dampened—literally—by recent weather. On June 21, as his troops closed up on Lee's headquarters at Berryville, Pender assured Fanny that "everything thus far has worked admirably." To calm her invasion fears he played up the successes of the operation thus far. Ewell had captured almost 5,000 Federals at Winchester alone; his troops had advanced to the Potomac without interference; and the cavalry assigned to him for the journey "are getting the best of it" while skirmishing near Stuart's erstwhile raiding target, Chambersburg, Pennsylvania.[18]

Pender resumed his progress report two days later, having reached Berryville. He had spoken with Lee himself, whom he had found "in fine spirits." Lee and he had agreed that "our army is in splendid condition and everyone seems hopeful and cheerful. Cheer up my dear little girl and hope for good things ahead." Those good things included not only choice victuals such as "fine mutton, milk, butter, etc.," but also materials for dressmaking: "I have two fine [wagon] trains at my headquarters, and you may rest assured that they will have to haul a goodly quantity of dry goods if we get a chance which I think we shall."[19]

The following day, Pender's division reached the Potomac at Shepherdstown, scene of his post-Sharpsburg exploits. The next morning it crossed the water barrier between North and South, an act, he told Fanny, "I know will cause you grief." He was aware that "we are taking a very important step, but see no reason why we should not be successful."[20]

Once the Third Corps reached dry ground, the march continued through

Boonsboro and Hagerstown. On the 26th another milestone was passed as Hill's command crossed the Pennsylvania line. Suddenly Pender's mood changed from exultant to wary. He became acutely aware that he was acting in the capacity of commander of the rear guard of the entire invasion force. The responsibility began to weigh on him, especially since all that was known of Hooker's whereabouts was that "he is between us and Washington."[21]

The constant need to look out for the enemy complicated Pender's efforts to monitor the conduct of his own troops. He was aware that since entering enemy territory, some of his soldiers had become hard to control. When not closely watched, they indulged a thirst for looting and vandalizing. Like many another Confederate trooping through the Keystone State, Pender sent home pejorative descriptions of the inhabitants: fat, frightened, barely intelligible "Dutch Yankees" and other "miserable people" including "coarse and dirty" women, "dirty looking children," and the like. Many of these wretches nevertheless lived in large, comfortable-looking houses with well-stocked barns and stables attached. Temptation was all around, and difficult to overcome.[22]

It might seem logical had Pender not cared if his men broke ranks to forage off the land—indeed, gathering spoils in Pennsylvania was one of Lee's objectives. But now that he was in the North, his enthusiasm for wreaking vengeance on the Yankees, of which he had written with such feeling while in Virginia, had evaporated. He confessed that although the enemy "have made us suffer all that people can suffer, I cannot get my resentment to that point to make me feel indifferent to what you see here." His high regard for discipline would not permit him to condone, even tacitly, straggling or looting. Were it not for the harm those practices did to military efficiency, however, he might have looked the other way. Had he done so, Pennsylvanians "would feel war in all its horrors."[23]

It was well that Christian forbearance overcame his detestation of the enemy, for Pender was nearing his ultimate fate. When he ended the letter he wrote on June 28 from Fayetteville, on the road from Chambersburg to Cashtown, with "may our Good Father protect us and preserve us to each other to a good old age," he was being unintentionally ironic.[24]

*　　*　　*

J. E. B. Stuart, it was widely believed, was responsible for Lee's ignorance of Hooker's location. On June 22, the cavalryman had secured his commander's permission to gallop around the blue army as he had on the

Chickahominy and when sacking Chambersburg. At the end of his ride, he was to link with the main army somewhere in lower Pennsylvania, thereafter screening its march and keeping tabs on the Yankees in its path. But Hooker's troops were scattered over such a wide area that Stuart had been forced to make a much wider circuit than he had anticipated. Now he was nowhere to be found, thus depriving Lee of the eyes and ears he needed to navigate Pennsylvania. Left in the dark, Lee could only assume that Hooker remained in Virginia, guarding Washington at the expense of the homes and fields farther north.[25]

By the 28th, Lee's army was advancing toward the state capital at Harrisburg with Ewell's corps in the van and Longstreet and Hill providing long-range support at and near Chambersburg. Everyone was enthusiastic at the thought of carrying the war to the Susquehanna River. That evening, however, everything changed.

From a reliable civilian scout, Lee learned some distressing facts. The Army of the Potomac was no longer in Hooker's shaky hands; it was now commanded by George Meade, a resident Pennsylvanian who could be counted on to defend his state. More important, Meade had crossed the Potomac with his entire army and was moving north with a full head of steam. A sobered Lee rushed couriers north to call off Ewell's movement and to order his far-flung detachments to unite with the rest of the army near Cashtown, east of South Mountain. From his maps, Lee knew that many of the roads in that area converged at Gettysburg, the seat of Adams County. That was where he planned to mass in preparation for turning about and facing his pursuers.[26]

The Third Corps marched to Gettysburg via the Chambersburg Pike/Cashtown Road. Heth, in the advance, reached Cashtown on the evening of June 29. The next morning, he dispatched a reconnaissance force from Pettigrew's brigade toward Gettysburg. On the afternoon of the 30th Pender, accompanied by Hill, joined Heth at Cashtown, where they heard Pettigrew report the results of his scout. Just short of noon, Yankee cavalry had advanced from Gettysburg to monitor Pettigrew's movements but had not brought on a fight. Pettigrew lacked the authority to engage, so he had not ascertained the enemy's strength or compositions.

Pender overheard Hill and Heth discuss Pettigrew's findings. They concluded that Heth's entire division should advance to Gettysburg in the morning, scrutinizing the opposing force and sizing up the town as a concentration point. However, Heth, like Pettigrew, was warned not to force a major confrontation. Lee did not want to become involved in a general engagement until most of his army was in hand.[27]

Heth started out, as ordered, at 5:00 A.M. on the sultry morning of July 1. At Hill's orders, Pender left Cashtown for Gettysburg three hours later. Neither division leader was prepared for what happened when Heth, at about 7:00, reached Marsh Creek, some three miles west of the village. On the other side of the stream, a force of Union cavalry, fighting dismounted, fired into the head of the infantry column. Heth abruptly halted, stunned by the volume of fire from the breechloading carbines wielded by members of Brigadier General John Buford's 1st Cavalry Division, Army of the Potomac. After regrouping, Heth's column tried to resume its advance, only to be stopped again when reinforcements strengthened and lengthened the cavalry's picket lines. As Pender drew within a couple of miles of Heth's rear, Heth sent back for his artillery support.

Pender halted his march about three miles from town until the road ahead was cleared. As he waited, Heth's guns pounded away at Buford's troopers, who replied with shells from a battery of shorter-range cannons. When the enemy fire slackened, Heth advanced again—and was again brought to a standstill, this time by several hundred dismounted skirmishers deployed west of high ground known as Herr Ridge. Spluttering with rage, Heth decided to switch from marching formation to line of battle, a process that took an hour or longer. By the time he pressed forward with Davis's brigade north of the road, Archer's south of it, and the rest of the division in Archer's rear, it was past 10:00.[28]

Pender watched intently as Heth's well-formed line drove the dismounted carbineers and their battery for nearly a mile across an open plain, to the top of Herr Ridge. From there Buford's people were slowly forced across Willoughby Run and as far as McPherson's Ridge, about a mile and a half northwest of Gettysburg. But just as Heth's veterans prepared to move in for the kill, they found themselves confronting members of Meade's First Army Corps, including artillerymen, who had rushed up from the town to relieve the troopers.

Some of the war's fiercest close-quarters fighting broke out on the ground in front of the ridge and along both sides of the Cashtown Road, the Yankees gradually getting the upper hand. Finally, Heth withdrew to a point beyond effective artillery range, where he tried to re-form his battered ranks. The process consumed more than an hour, but at the end of that time, although

Heth's men continued to exchange musketry with the enemy, Pender could not say if his colleague could mount an effective counteroffensive.[29]

At about 2:00 P.M., with the sun beating down on the field of battle and more and more Yankees digging in before and atop McPherson's Ridge, Hill ordered Pender to Heth's assistance. The Light Division started at once but had moved only a mile or so closer to the firing-line when General Lee galloped up to confer with Pender's superior. From what Pender had heard of Lee's plans, it seemed obvious that he was reluctant to commit the better part of a division to a fight brought on against his better judgment.

Close to 4:00, however, Pender again got the word to advance. Lee had given his blessing to an engagement that seemed to be going his army's way. The advance of Ewell's corps, en route from Harrisburg and points north, had arrived above the town in perfect position to threaten the upper flank of the Federal line on McPherson's Ridge. Other newly arrived elements of Jackson's old command were taking up a position farther east to oppose the men of the Eleventh Army Corps, which had followed the First Corps from northern Maryland to Gettysburg. As if these movements were not advantageous enough for Lee, another body of Ewell's command had come down the roads northeast of Gettysburg and up against the exposed right flank of the Eleventh Corps. Providence, or good fortune, seemed not only to be favoring the Army of Northern Virginia but charting its strategy.[30]

When Pender advanced to Heth's aid at 4:00 P.M., he moved with only half his command. At Hill's order, he left behind Thomas's brigade to cover the open right flank of the corps. And by the time Pender started forward, Lane's brigade had wandered off to the south where it was being raked by a flank fire from those of Buford's cavalrymen who had refused to retreat to the next stretch of high ground to the east, Seminary Ridge. Thus Pender pushed ahead with his old brigade under Alfred Scales, now a brigadier general and back in command, on the left, most of it south of the road from Cashtown, and McGowan's brigade under Perrin on the right, between the Cashtown and Fairfield Roads.[31]

Ahead of Pender's moving line, Heth's men (without Heth himself, who had been disabled by a head wound, and without Archer, who had been captured) were making ineffective attempts to clear McPherson's Ridge. The effort stalled out as Pender reached the front, and the Light Division passed over and through Heth's broken ranks. Stopping briefly to realign their for-

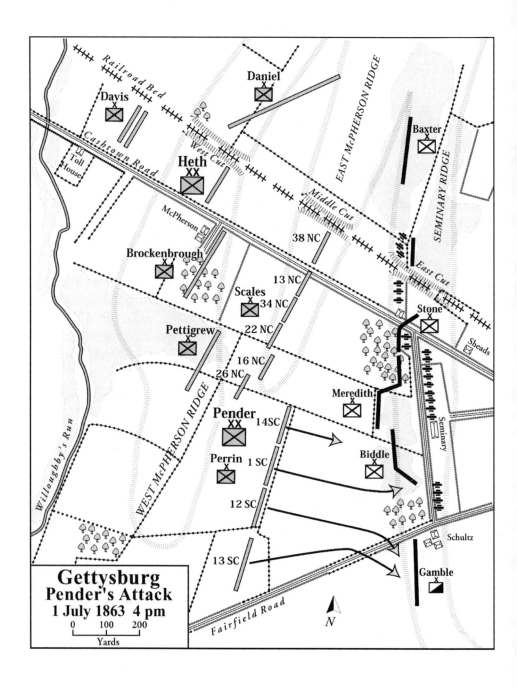

Gettysburg
Pender's Attack
1 July 1863 4 pm

0   100   200
Yards

N

mation, both brigades then drove up the crest of the ridge and, through force of will as much as through numbers, swept the summit free of the enemy.

Without taking time to savor his success, Pender led both brigades eastward to Seminary Ridge, the last natural barrier between them and Gettysburg. As they moved, resistance stiffened. Raked by an enfilading fire from cannons north of the Cashtown Road, Scales's troops stopped at the foot of the ridge, where their leader was severely wounded, but after a time Pender got them moving again.[32]

Meanwhile, Perrin's troops kept pushing into the teeth of what their leader called "the most destructive fire of musketry, grape & canister I have ever been exposed to." Their effort was made the more difficult because Scales's halt had robbed them of support on the left (Perrin would claim that once he forged ahead of Scales's men "I never saw or heard of them until [the] next day"). Neither was Lane's brigade, which supposedly guarded Perrin's right, to be found. Maddened by the galling carbine fire along his own right, Lane had veered south of the Fairfield Road to face his cavalry opponents head-on. There he was of no help to his comrades from South Carolina.[33]

Left to face the fury by itself, Perrin's command went up the slope toward the top under a blizzard of shells and balls, without stopping to return fire. When both of his flanks came under an enfilade, the colonel sent two of his regiments to the right, two to the left. Somehow, both forces broke through to the crest, then swept along it, capturing dozens of the enemy, several cannons, and four battle flags. Their antagonists delivered a final fusillade, then raced toward the town, a mile away. Perrin later claimed that had one or both of his flanks been supported, no Yankee on the ridge would have escaped. Another handicap was the nearly 50 percent casualty rate his brigade had suffered topping the crest.

Having broken the Union's hold west of Gettysburg, Pender was all smiles as he rode among Perrin's men, "telling us we had acted most nobly." A pursuit having already begun, the division leader followed Perrin and detachments of Scales's brigade into the streets of Gettysburg, where they rounded up scores of fugitives, not only members of the First Corps but those of the Eleventh whose line north of town had collapsed a short time before the defenders of Seminary Ridge gave way. Pender also helped Perrin gather up stragglers and looters from his brigade. Then he led everyone back the way they had come.[34]

As the sun began to lower, action shifted to the southern reaches of the field, where the Federals had rallied and were holding on against mounting odds. This, however, was not Pender's fight; at Hill's direction, he placed his brigades into bivouac below the Fairfield Road. Lane's brigade was now on the left, with Perrin's survivors in its rear. Scales's men extended the line farther south, and in early evening Thomas's Georgians came in from their holding position on Herr Ridge to form on Scales's right.

Presumably, once his new position was secure, Pender grabbed some sleep. If so, he slept soundly, the result of long, hard, and successful work. At great cost—more than a thousand men killed, wounded, or captured—and despite being new to divisional command, he had done the job assigned him today, and done it well. Although the overthrow of the Eleventh Corps had preceded the break in the First Corps' sector, smashing the Union left at Gettysburg had been a feat of major proportions.[35]

Not every Confederate commander had done as well on this summer's day in lower Pennsylvania. Neither Lee nor Ewell had exploited opportunities to overwhelm and crush that part of the Army of the Potomac that hung on by its fingertips south of town. Because advantages given them by Pender and other successful subordinates had not been pressed, the Union army, greatly expanded by reinforcements received during the night, continued to hold the high ground south of Gettysburg—Cemetery Hill and Cemetery Ridge—when July 2 dawned.

The thrust of Lee's strategy this day was to outflank the enemy's left by gaining the Emmitsburg Road, south of the point at which Meade had concentrated his troops. Longstreet's corps, whose advance had reached Gettysburg at midnight, was assigned the mission, which Lee wished carried out that morning. But hours of marching and countermarching caused what Longstreet euphemistically called "some delay" in launching the offensive. Not till 4:00 P.M. did it get underway in earnest.[36]

Throughout the morning and most of the afternoon, Pender waited for word to go forward in support of Longstreet's drive. During that time, enemy skirmishers advanced on his position from the vicinity of Cemetery Hill. Crossing the Emmitsburg Road, which ran between the armies, they pushed to within 300 yards of Pender's picket line. Pender responded by ordering General Lane to advance skirmishers of his own. When 75 men of the 37th North Carolina were selected for the mission, Pender called up their ranking officer and asked whether he expected to shove the Yankees back. When the lieutenant hesitated to reply, the temper Pender tried so hard to keep in check caused him to question the man's intestinal fortitude. Pender was delighted, however, when the officer suddenly snapped to attention and promised to clear the road. He was made even happier when the 75 men charged across the field and without firing a shot put the skirmishers to flight.[37]

Pender was still in Lane's sector when a sudden crash of cannonfire off his right flank indicated that Longstreet's attack had finally begun. Seeking an opportunity to join in, the division commander spurred his charger across the front of his line. Reigning in near the division's center, he dismounted and, with his staff trailing behind him, entered a stand of trees that blocked his view of the action to the south.

He was standing at the edge of a wood, probably peering through field-glasses, when the Union guns across the field began to return Longstreet's fire. Solid shot came crashing through the treetops while shrapnel and bursting shell exploded just above ground level. Realizing that his perch had become too precarious, Pender turned to leave, but it was too late. A shell burst in front of him, and he went down with his fifth and final wound of the war. On July 18, 1863, William Dorsey Pender succumbed to that wound.

When considering the possibility of being killed or mortally wounded in battle, Pender had always treated the subject philosophically. "What is the loss of a man's life," he would ask, "compared to the good of the country?" Now the Confederacy would have to answer that question.[38]

*   *   *

When news of Pender's death circulated through the army he had left behind, the universal response was grief tinged with regret. Everyone who knew him, and many of those who only knew of him, realized that the Confederacy had lost one of its ablest and, at the same time, one of its most promising, officers. Pender's achievements were well known; in time they would take on almost legendary proportions. Yet his loss was made more painful by the widespread belief that when he went down, greater things lay in store for him. He had transitioned easily from regimental to brigade to divisional command. There was no doubt in the minds of Lee or any of his senior subordinates that Pender was destined for fame and glory as a corps commander, if not in a higher position.

The eulogies that poured in after his passing praised both his accomplishments and his potential. Colonel (later General) Perrin believed that, although new to the rank, Pender "was the best Major General in the Army.... He was brave, energetic, a thorough disciplinarian & in fact everything that a soldier should be. His place will be hard to fill...." A. P. Hill, whose sense of loss was personal as well as professional, assessed Pender's value with mournful eloquence: "No man fell during this bloody battle of Gettysburg more regretted than he, nor around whose youthful brow were clustered brighter rays of glory."[39]

Pender's importance to his army was such that in postwar years grandiose praise was attributed to his army commander. Brigadier General Gabriel C. Wharton, who never served with the Army of Northern Virginia, declared that sometime in 1864 or early 1865, Lee admitted to having erred in invading Pennsylvania but expressed confidence that "we would have succeeded had Pender lived." And in 1893, Pender's friend William Gaston Lewis quoted Lee to the effect that "General Pender was the only officer in the army that could completely fill the place of 'Stonewall' Jackson."[40]

Wharton's and Lewis's memories may not have been fully accurate, or may have been subject to exaggeration. A more reliable postwar epitaph was rendered by Captain Ashe of Pender's staff, who regretted that his commander's name was not better known. However, had Pender survived Gettysburg, "he, too, would have attained a world-wide fame, and would have taken his place among the great Generals of this age."[41]

Of the scores of tributes paid him in death, it is likely that William Dorsey Pender would have preferred the most succinct. Engraved on his tomb in Calvary Cemetery, Tarboro, North Carolina, are nine words that go far toward summing up his life and career:

"Patriot by Nature, Soldier by Training, Christian by Faith."[42]

NOTES

Abbreviations Used in Notes:

E-, M-, RG-	Entry, Microcopy, Record Group
FSP	Fanny Shepperd Pender
MSS	Correspondence/Papers
NA	National Archives
NCSDA&H	North Carolina State Department of Archives and History
OR	*War of the Rebellion: A Compilation of the Official Records of the Union and Confederate Armies*
SHC	Southern Historical Collection
SHSP	*Southern Historical Society Papers*
TS	Typescript
USMAA	United States Military Academy Archives
WDP	William Dorsey Pender

NOTE: Most, but not all, of the Pender correspondence cited below can be found, arranged chronologically, in *The General to His Lady: The Civil War Letters of William Dorsey Pender to Fanny Pender*, edited by William W. Hassler (Chapel Hill, N. C., 1965). A later edition of the same work is *One of Lee's Best Men: The Civil War Letters of General William Dorsey Pender*, with a new foreword by Brian Wills (Chapel Hill, N. C., 1999).

Unless otherwise noted, cited correspondence is from the Pender Papers in the Southern Historical Collection, Wilson Library, University of North Carolina, Chapel Hill.

Chapter One

1. John D. Imboden, "The Confederate Retreat from Gettysburg," *Battles and Leaders of the Civil War*, 3: 423-24.
2. *Richmond Enquirer*, July 8, 1863.
3. Alfred M. Scales, *The Battle of Fredericksburg: An Address... Before the Association of the Virginia Division of the Army of Northern Virginia...* (Washington, D. C., 1884), 16.
4. Walter A. Montgomery, *Life and Character of Major-General W. D. Pender: Memorial Address, May 10, 1894* (Raleigh, N. C., 1894), 24; *The Southerner* (Tarboro, N. C.), Sept. 19, 1863.
5. Samuel Turner Pender, "General Pender," *The South-Atlantic: A Monthly Magazine of Literature, Science and Art*, 1 (1878): 231.
6. Allen Johnson and Dumas Malone. eds., *Dictionary of American Biography* (20 vols. New York, 1928-36), 14: 416; Kenrick N. Simpson, "Patriot by Nature, Soldier by Training, Christian by Faith: The Life of William Dorsey Pender" (M. A. thesis, East Carolina Univ., 1982), 5-6; Stephen B. Weeks, "William Dorsey Pender," Weeks MSS, NCSDA&H, [1]; R. C. Lawrence, "General William D. Pender," *The State*, 11 (May 1940): 7; D. H. Hill, Jr., *North Carolina*, vol. 4 of *Confederate Military History: A Library of Confederate States History...*, ed. by Clement A. Evans (Atlanta, 1899), 334.
7. WDP, *General to His Lady*, 3; WDP to FSP, Sept. 28, Oct. 19, Nov. 22, 28, 1861, Apr. 23, 1863.
8. WDP to FSP, May 14, June 2, 3, 18, July 9, Aug. 27, Sept. 14, 1861, July 31, Sept. 28, 1862.
9. WDP to FSP, May 18, 1861, Aug. 8, 1862.
10. Pender, "General Pender," 228.
11. [Letter from Pender Brothers, Bryson City, North Carolina], *Confederate Veteran*, 1 (1893): 79; Simpson, "Patriot by Nature," 7-8.
12. *Ibid.*, 8-9; Pender, "General Pender," 228.
13. Montgomery, *Life and Character of Pender*, 7.
14. *Ibid.*; Simpson, "Patriot by Nature," 9; J. R. J. Daniel to G. W. Crawford, Apr. 26, 1850, Cadet Files, USMA Class of 1854, NA; WDP, notice of receipt of USMA appointment, May 6, 1850, *ibid.*
15. WDP, *General to His Lady*, 6; Hill, *North Carolina*, 336.
16. USMA Order No. 36, June 24, 1850, USMAA.
17. WDP, *General to His Lady*, 4; Simpson, "Patriot by Nature," 10.
18. *Ibid.*; Wharton J. Green, *Recollections and Reflections: An Auto[biography] of Half a Century and More* (Raleigh, N. C., 1906), 69-72; Herman Hattaway, *General*

Stephen D. Lee (Jackson, Miss., 1976), 6; Emory M. Thomas, *Bold Dragoon: The Life of J. E. B. Stuart* (New York, 1986), 20-25.

19. Green, *Recollections and Reflections*, 70; Simpson, "Patriot by Nature," 10.

20. WDP to FSP, Sept. 25, 1862.

21. *Ibid.*; WDP to FSP, Mar. 4, 11, 1862, Apr. 26, 1863.

22. *Official Register of the Officers and Cadets of the U. S. Military Academy, West Point, N. Y.: June 1851* (West Point, N. Y., 1851), 13; *Cadets Arranged in Order of Merit in their Respective Classes, as Determined at the General Examination, in June, 1852* (West Point, N. Y., 1852), 11; *Official Register of the Officers and Cadets of the U. S. Military Academy, West Point, N. Y.: June, 1853* (West Point, N. Y., 1853), 9; *Official Register of the Officers and Cadets of the U. S. Military Academy, West Point, N. Y.: June, 1854* (West Point, N. Y., 1854), 7.

23. *Official Register, USMA, June, 1853*, 9; *Official Register, USMA, June, 1854*, 7.

24. *Official Register, USMA, June 1851*, 16-17; *Cadets Arranged in Order of Merit, USMA, June, 1852*, 18; *Official Register, USMA, June, 1853*, 19; *Official Register, USMA, June, 1854*, 18.

25. WDP, USMA Cadet Delinquency Log, USMAA.

26. USMA Special Orders No. 69, June 17, 1851, USMAA; No. 191, Dec. 15, 1851, *ibid.*; No. 84, June 16, 1852, *ibid.*; No. 71, June 17, 1853, *ibid.*; No. 99, Aug. 19, 1853, *ibid.*

27. *Official Register, USMA, June, 1854*, 7-8; Green, *Recollctions and Reflections*, 69-72.

28. USMA Special Order No. 85, June 16, 1852, USMAA; WDP, *General to His Lady*, 4; Simpson, "Patriot by Nature," 11-12.

29. *Ibid.*, 12.

30. *Official Register, USMA, June, 1854*, 7-8; Thomas, *Bold Dragoon*, 31-35.

31. WDP, *General to His Lady*, 4; George W. Cullum, comp., *Biographical Register of the Officers and Graduates of the U. S. Military Academy at West Point, N.Y....* 2 vols. (Boston, 1891), 2: 586; WDP to Samuel Cooper, Aug. 29, 1854, M-567, R-503, NA; WDP to W. G. Freeman, Feb. 13, 1855, M-567, R-524, *ibid.*

32. Theophilus F. Rodenbough and William L. Haskin, eds., *The Army of the United States: Historical Sketches of Staff and Line...* (New York, 1896), 314-15, 318.

33. WDP to J. C. Dobbins, Apr. 14, 1855, M-567, R-524, NA; WDP to Samuel Cooper, May 18, 1855, *ibid.*

34. Rodenbough and Haskin, *Army of the United States*, 155-59, 173-90.

35. Jefferson Davis to WDP, May 25, 1855, Pender MSS, NCSDA&H; WDP, commission as second lieutenant, 1st U. S. Dragoons, July 23, 1856, Pender MSS, Museum of the Confederacy.

36. Cullum, *Biographical Register of USMA*, 2: 586; "General Pender," 229; Simpson, "Patriot by Nature," 12.

37. J. E. B. Stuart to Lizzie Peirce, June 6, 1856, Stuart MSS, Virginia Hist. Soc.; Cullum, *Biographical Register of USMA*, 2: 586; Francis B. Heitman, comp., *Historical Register and Dictionary of the United States Army...* (2 vols. Washington, D. C., 1903), 2: 402; Robert M. Utley, *Frontiersmen in Blue: The United States Army and the Indian, 1858-1865* (New York, 1967), 154; A. L. Diket, *wha hae wi' [Pender]... bled* (New York, 1979), 3.

38. Cullum, *Biographical Register of USMA*, 2: 586; Lawrence Kip, *Army Life on the Pacific* (New York, 1859), 31.

39. WDP to Thomas T. Fauntleroy, Apr. 27, 1857, RG-393, E-3584, Box 12, NA; J. E. B. Stuart to Lizzie Peirce, July 9, 1857, Stuart MSS.

Chapter Two

1. WDP, *General to His Lady*, 4-5; WDP to W. W. Mackall, Sept. 15, 1858, RG-393, E-584, box 14, NA; Special Order No. 158, Dept. of the Pacific, Oct. 2, 1858, M-567, R-586, *ibid.*

2. Cullum, *Biographical Register of USMA*, 2: 586; WDP to W. W. Mackall, Dec. 4, 1857, RG-393, E-3584, box 14, NA.

3. Utley, *Frontiersmen in Blue*, 200.

4. *Ibid.*, 201; Cullum, *Biographical Register of USMA*, 2: 586.

5. Rodenbough and Haskin, *Army of the United States*, 159; Utley, *Frontiersmen in Blue*, 202-03.

6. *Ibid.*, 203-04; Kip, *Army Life on the Pacific*, 39-40; Simpson, "Patriot by Nature," 13-14.

7. Kip, *Army Life on the Pacific*, 52-60, 131-35; Utley, *Frontiersmen in Blue*, 206; *The Southerner* (Tarboro, N. C.), Nov. 6, 1858.

8. Kip, *Army Life on the Pacific*, 63-66, 137-40; Utley, *Frontiersmen in Blue*, 207.

9. Kip, *Army Life on the Pacific*, 66-112; Utley, *Frontiersmen in Blue*, 207-09.

10. Kip, *Army Life on the Pacific*, 133, 139, 142-43; Diket, *wha hae wi' [Pender]... bled*, 4.

11. John B. Floyd to WDP, Sept. 29, 1857, Pender MSS, NCSDA&H.

12. *Raleigh Standard*, Dec. 25, 1858.

13. WDP to W. W. Mackall, Sept. 15, 1858, RG-393, E-3584, box 14, NA; Johnson and Malone, *Dictionary of American Biography*, 14: 416; Pender-Shepperd Family Genealogy, [1], Augustine H. Shepperd MSS, SHC; Pender, "General Pender," 229; WDP, *General to His Lady*, 5; *The Southerner* (Tarboro,

N. C.), Mar. 12, 1859; William G. Lewis to D. W. Gilliam, Oct. 21, 1893, SHC; Lawrence, "General William D. Pender," 7.

14. WDP to Lorenzo Thomas, Mar. 14, 1859, M-567, R-609, NA; Pender, "General Pender," 229.

15. Simpson, "Patriot by Nature," 17-18; WDP to FSP, May 19, 1861; Weeks, "William Dorsey Pender," [5], Weeks MSS.

16. *Ibid.*; Mrs. Elizabeth Pender to the author, Jan. 16, 1996, in author's possession.

17. WDP to FSP, May 13, Aug. 1, 1860, June 6, Sept. 22, Nov. 3, 1861, Mar. 13, 1862, May 14, 1863; "Gen. William Dorsey Pender (1834-1863)," [4], TS in Edgecombe Co. Lib., Tarboro, N. C.

18. Cullum, *Biographical Register of USMA*, 2: 586; WDP to FSP, May 13, 1860, May 19, 1861.

19. WDP to FSP, Aug. 1, 2, 23, 1860, Sept. 19, 1861; Simpson, "Patriot by Nature," 280.

20. James M. McPherson, *Ordeal by Fire: The Civil War and Reconstruction* (New York, 1982), 113-17.

21. WDP to FSP, May 15, 1860; Cullum, *Biographical Register of USMA*, 2: 586; Simpson, "Patriot by Nature," 18.

22. Heitman, *Historical Register and Dictionary*, 2: 405; WDP to FSP, June 26, Aug. 1, 1860.

23. WDP to FSP, May 13, 17, June 26, Aug. 1, 18, 22, 23, 1860.

24. WDP to FSP, June 19, 1860.

25. WDP to FSP, June 19, Aug. 18, 1860.

26. WDP to FSP, Aug. 22, 1860.

27. WDP to FSP, Aug. 22, 23, 1860; Heitman, *Historical Register and Dictionary*, 1: 66; Weeks, "William Dorsey Pender," [1], Weeks MSS; Montgomery, *Life and Character of Pender*, 8.

28. Cullum, *Historical Register of USMA*, 2: 586; E. B. Long and Barbara Long, *The Civil War Day by Day: An Almanac, 1861-1865* (Garden City, N.Y., 1971), 2, 12-13; Weeks, "William Dorsey Pender," [1], Weeks MSS; WDP to Samuel Cooper, Nov. 27, 1860, M-567, R-630, NA; Simpson, "Patriot by Nature," 23.

29. WDP to Lorenzo Thomas, Mar. 9, 1861, M-619, R-45, NA.

30. Long and Long, *Civil War Day by Day*, 31-33, 42; McPherson, *Ordeal by Fire*, 136-38.

31. *Ibid.*, 139-40.

32. WDP to Lorenzo Thomas, Mar. 9, 1861, M-619, R-45, NA.

33. WDP to Simon Cameron, Mar. 9, 1861, M-619, R-45, NA.

34. *Wilmington Daily Journal*, Apr. 16, 1861; WDP to FSP, May 4, 1861.

35. *Ibid.*; Long and Long, *Civil War Day by Day*, 76.

36. Gary W. Gallagher, *The Confederate War* (Cambridge, Mass., 1997), 102; WDP to FSP, Apr. 28, May 4, 18, 1861.

37. WDP to FSP, Mar. 16, 1861.

38. WDP to FSP, May 29, Sept. 25, 1862, Apr. 26, 28, 1863.

Chapter Three

1. WDP to FSP, Mar. 4, 14, 16, 1861; WDP to Leroy P. Walker, Mar. 14, 1861, M-331, R-196, NA; Augustine H. Shepperd to Jefferson Davis, Mar. 4, 1861, *ibid.*; John W. Ellis to Jefferson Davis, Mar. 12, 1861, *ibid.*; John Bragg to Leroy P. Walker, Mar. 14, 1861, *ibid.*

2. WDP to FSP, Mar. 14, 1861; WDP to John W. Ellis, Mar. 17, 1861, Gratz Coll.—Confederate Generals, Hist. Soc. of Pennsylvania, Philadelphia.

3. WDP to FSP, Mar. 14, 1861.

4. WDP to FSP, Mar. 16, 1861.

5. *Ibid.*

6. WDP to FSP, Mar. 16, 1861 ["9P.M."]; WDP to Samuel Cooper, Mar. 18, 1861, Pender MSS, NCSDA&H; WDP personnel return, Mar. 16, 1861, M-331, R-196, NA.

7. Samuel Cooper to WDP, Mar. 21, 1861, Pender MSS, NCSDA&H.

8. *OR*, I, 1: 278-79, 284; Simpson, "Patriot by Nature," 29-30.

9. WDP to FSP, Mar. 26, 1861.

10. WDP, transportation receipt, Mar. 2, 1861, Pender MSS, NCSDA&H; WDP, pay vouchers, Apr. 15, 1861, M-331, R-196, NA; WDP to FSP, Apr. 3, 1861; Simpson, "Patriot by Nature," 31.

11. WDP to FSP, Apr. 11, 1861.

12. WDP to FSP, Apr. 28, 1861; Simpson, "Patriot by Nature," 32.

13. WDP, *General to His Lady*, 15; WDP to FSP, Apr. 26, 1861; *OR*, I, 1: 486; III, 1: 67-68, 72.

14. WDP to FSP, May 8, 1861; Simpson, "Patriot by Nature," 32; *Wilmington Daily Journal*, May 3, 1861.

15. WDP to FSP, Apr. 28, 1861.

16. *Ibid.*; WDP, *General to His Lady*, 19.

17. WDP to FSP, Apr. 28, May 4, 1861.

18. WDP to FSP, May 14, 1861.

19. WDP to FSP, May 14, 18, 1861; Samuel A. Ashe, *History of North Carolina* (2

vols. Raleigh, N. C., 1925), 2: 606; Weeks, "William Dorsey Pender," [2], Weeks MSS.

20. WDP to FSP, May 14, 18, 1861.

21. WDP to FSP, Sept. 28, 1861.

22. WDP to FSP, May 26, 1861.

23. *Ibid.*

24. *Ibid.*; John W. Ellis to WDP, May 27, 1861, Pender MSS, NCSDA&H; John W. Ellis, *The Papers of John Willis Ellis*, ed. by Noble J. Tolbert (2 vols. Raleigh, N. C., 1964), 2: 802; Weeks, "William Dorsey Pender," [2], Weeks MSS; Walter Clark, ed., *Histories of the Several Regiments and Battalions from North Carolina in the Great War, 1861-'65...* (5 vols. Goldsboro and Raleigh, N. C., 1901), 1: 653-54; WDP personnel return, May 27, 1861, M-331, R-196, NA.

25. Simpson, "Patriot by Nature," 38.

26. William J. Hoke to "Commanding Officer 3rd Regt N. C. Vol.," May 28, 1861, Adj. Gen.'s Office, State of North Carolina, Letterbooks, NCSDA&H; WDP to FSP, May 30, 1861; Benjamin F. Huger to John W. Ellis, May 28, 1861, John W. Ellis Letterbooks and Papers, NCSDA&H.

27. Simpson, "Patriot by Nature," 38-39; WDP to FSP, May 30, 1861.

28. WDP to FSP, June 2, 1861.

29. WDP to FSP, June 2, 3, 6, 18, 1861.

30. WDP to FSP, June 15, 1861; R. S. Gannett to WDP, June 3, 1861, Pender MSS, NCSDA&H.

31. WDP to FSP, June 2, 1861.

32. WDP to FSP, May 18, 1861.

33. WDP to FSP, May 14, 30, June 2, 9, 1861.

34. WDP to FSP, June 23, 26, 1861.

35. Simpson, "Patriot by Nature," 39, 314, 316; FSP to WDP, June 30, 1861.

36. *Ibid.*

37. WDP to FSP, July 2, 5, 1861.

38. WDP to FSP, July 5, 11, 1861.

39. Long and Long, *Civil War Day by Day*, 84; WDP to FSP, June 25, 1861.

40. WDP to FSP, June 12, 1861.

41. WDP to FSP, June 12, 18, 28, 1861; WDP, regimental requisition, n.d. [June 1861], M-331, R-196, NA.

42. WDP to FSP, June 12, 1861; *Raleigh Register*, June 18, 1861.

43. WDP to FSP, June 26, 28, 30, 1861.

44. Samuel I. Hunt to T. M. R. Talcott, July 4, 1864, Stuart MSS; Clark, *Regiments and Battalions from North Carolina*, 1: 654; WDP to FSP, July 5, 9, 1861.

45. WDP to FSP, July 9, 1861.

46. WDP to FSP, July 5, 11, 1861.

47. Long and Long, *Civil War Day by Day*, 93-94; WDP to FSP, July 11, 20, 1861.

48. WDP to FSP, July 11, 1861.

49. WDP to FSP, July 17, 18, 20, 1861; Simpson, "Patriot by Nature," 44.

50. Mark Mayo Boatner III, *The Civil War Dictionary* (New York, 1959), 99-101.

51. William C. Davis, *Battle at Bull Run: A History of the First Major Campaign of the Civil War* (Garden City, N. Y., 1977), 201, 207, 222, 246; WDP to FSP, Aug. 27, 1861; Officers of the 6th N. C. State Troops to Henry T. Clark, Aug. 17, 1861, Henry T. Clark Letterbooks and Papers, NCSDA&H; Richard W. Iobst, *The Bloody Sixth: The Sixth North Carolina Regiment, Confederate States of America* (Raleigh, N. C., 1965), 28; James C. Birdsong, *Brief Sketches of the North Carolina State Troops in the War between the States....* (Raleigh, N. C., 1894), 17.

52. WDP to FSP, Aug. 16, 1861.

53. WDP, commission as colonel, 6th N. C. State Troops, Aug. 17, 1861, Pender MSS, NCSDA&H; WDP to FSP, Aug. 13, 16, 27, 1861; WDP, personnel return, n.d., M-331, R-196, NA.

Chapter Four

1. WDP to FSP, Aug. 27, Sept. 5, 1861.

2. Benjamin F. White diary, Oct. 31, 1861, SHC.

3. WDP to FSP, Sept. 22, 1861.

4. WDP to FSP, Sept. 5, 14, 1861.

5. WDP to FSP, Sept. 14, 1861; Iobst, *Bloody Sixth*, 60; Bartlett Y. Malone, *Whipt 'em Everytime: The Diary of Bartlett Yancey Malone, Co. H 6th N. C. Regiment*, ed. by William Whatley Pierson, Jr. (Jackson, Tenn., 1960), 47.

6. WDP to FSP, Sept. 14, 1861; WDP to Henry T. Clark, Aug. 27, 1861, Clark Letterbooks and Papers.

7. *Ibid.*; WDP to FSP, Sept. 5, 1861; Simpson, "Patriot by Nature," 48.

8. WDP to FSP, Sept. 1, 5, 1861.

9. Benjamin F. White diary, Sept. 24, 29, 1861.

10. WDP to FSP, Aug. 27, 1861.

11. WDP to FSP, Sept. 19, Oct. 17, 1861; Benjamin F. White diary, Sept. 20, 1861; Iobst, *Bloody Sixth*, 37.

12. WDP to FSP, Oct. 17, 1861; WDP, *General to His Lady*, 262.

13. Iobst, *Bloody Sixth*, 37-38; WDP to FSP, Sept. 14, 1861; Peter W. Hairston to Fanny Hairston, Oct. 11, 1861, Hairston MSS, SHC.

14. WDP to FSP, Sept. 22, 1861; Iobst, *Bloody Sixth*, 38.

15. *Ibid.*, 38-39; WDP to FSP, Sept. 26, 28, 30, Oct. 1, Nov. 3, 1861.

16. WDP to FSP, Sept. 8, 11, 19, 22, 26, 28, Oct. 26, 29, Nov. 3, 1861.

17. WDP to FSP, Sept. 30, 1861.

18. WDP to FSP, Sept. 11, 30, Oct. 17, 1861.

19. WDP to FSP, Oct. 7, 14, 1861; Simpson, "Patriot by Nature," 286-87; Benjamin F. White diary, Oct. 6, 1861; J. William Jones, *Christ in the Camp; or, Religion in Lee's Army* (Atlanta, 1904), 42; Anthony T. Porter, *Led On! Step by Step, Scenes from Clerical, Military, Educational, and Plantation Life in the South, 1828-1898: An Autobiography* (New York, 1898), 133; Hattaway, *General Stephen D. Lee*, 35.

20. WDP to FSP, Oct. 14, Nov. 3, 22, 1861.

21. WDP to FSP, Mar. 4, 1862; Edward G. Longacre, ed., "A 'Christian Warrior' in Winter Quarters," *Manuscripts*, 33 (1981): 242.

22. WDP to FSP, Oct. 17, Dec. 7, 1861.

23. WDP to FSP, Aug. 14, 1862.

24. WDP to FSP, Mar. 4, May 25, 1862; Pender, "General Pender," 234; Kensey J. Stewart to J. B. Cheshire, Sept. 16, 1894, Joseph Blount Cheshire MSS, NCSDA&H.

25. WDP to FSP, Nov. 18, Dec. 4, 1861.

26. WDP to Henry T. Clark, Aug. 27, 1861, Clark Letterbooks and Papers; Iobst, *Bloody Sixth*, 59-60; WDP to FSP, Nov. 21, 1861.

27. WDP to FSP, Oct. 21, 1861.

28. WDP to FSP, Nov. 24, 1861.

29. *Ibid.*

30. Iobst, *Bloody Sixth*, 46; WDP to FSP, Oct. 26, Nov. 3, 18, 21, 24, 28, 1861.

31. WDP to FSP, Oct. 19, 21, Nov. 3, 1861; Simpson, "Patriot by Nature," 55-56; Iobst, *Bloody Sixth*, 53-54.

32. WDP to FSP, Nov. 12, 21, 1861.

33. Iobst, *Bloody Sixth*, 51-52; J. G. Martin to WDP, Dec. 19, 1861, Jan. 14, 1862, Adj. Gen.'s Office Letterbooks, NCSDA&H.

34. WDP to FSP, Nov. 4, Dec. 4, 11, 1861; Iobst, *Bloody Sixth*, 48; James G. Martin to WDP, Jan. 28, Feb. 3, Mar. 31, Apr. 10, 1862, Adj. Gen.'s Office Letterbooks.

35. WDP to FSP, Mar. 23, 27, 1862.

36. WDP, *General to His Lady*, 113; WDP to FSP, Feb. 21, 1862; Diket, *wha hae wi' [Pender]... bled*, 23; Malone, *Whipt 'em Everytime*, 31.

37. WDP to FSP, Mar. 6, 1862.

38. WDP to FSP, Mar. 6, 15, 1862.

39. WDP to FSP, Sept. 11, 1861.

40. WDP to FSP, Feb. 21, 1862.

41. Joseph E. Johnston, *Narrative of Military Operations* (Bloomington, Ind., 1959), 97; Douglas Southall Freeman, *Lee's Lieutenants: A Study in Command* (3 vols. New York, 1942-44), 1: 136; Stephen W. Sears, *To the Gates of Richmond: The Peninsula Campaign* (New York, 1992), 13.

42. WDP to FSP, Feb. 21, 1862.

43. Freeman, *Lee's Lieutenants*, 1: 139-40; Iobst, *Bloody Sixth*, 56-57; WDP, *General to His Lady*, 120-21; Clark, *Regiments and Battalions from North Carolina*, 1: 300.

44. WDP to FSP, Mar. 11, 1862.

45. Clark, *Regiments and Battalions from North Carolina*, 1: 349.

46. WDP to FSP, Mar. 15, 18, 1862; Iobst, *Bloody Sixth*, 61.

47. WDP to FSP, Mar. 20, 1862.

Chapter Five

1. Sears, *To the Gates of Richmond*, 23-27, 45-46.

2. WDP to FSP, Mar. 25, 1862.

3. WDP to FSP, Apr. 3, 1862.

4. WDP to FSP, Mar. 30, 1862.

5. WDP to FSP, Apr. 7, 1862.

6. WDP to FSP, Apr. 8, 10, 11, 1862; Iobst, *Bloody Sixth*, 62; Malone, *Whipt 'em Everytime*, 49.

7. *Ibid.*, 49-50.

8. Clark, *Regiments and Battalions from North Carolina*, 1: 300; Benjamin F. White to James J. Phillips, Apr. 26, 1862, Phillips MSS, NCSDA&H.

9. WDP to FSP, Apr. 14, 19, 1862.

10. WDP to FSP, Apr. 19, 1862.

11. Sears, *To the Gates of Richmond*, 40-48.

12. WDP to FSP, Apr. 25, 26, 1862.

13. WDP to FSP, Apr. 22, 1862.

14. WDP to FSP, Apr. 25, 1862; Iobst, *Bloody Sixth*, 65.

15. Sears, *To the Gates of Richmond*, 47-48, 59-61; WDP to FSP, May 8, 1862; Kensey J. Stewart to Joseph B. Cheshire, Sept. 16, 1864, Cheshire MSS.

16. *Ibid.*

17. Clark, *Regiments and Battalions from North Carolina*, 1: 301.

18. WDP to FSP, May 8, 1862; Sears, *To the Gates of Richmond*, 68-70; OR, I, 11, pt. 1: 629.

19. Dwight E. Stinson, Jr., "Eltham's Landing—the End Run that Failed," *Civil War Times Illustrated*, 1 (Feb. 1963): 38-41; Clark, *Regiments and Battalions from North Carolina*, 1: 301.

20. WDP to FSP, May 8, 1862; Diket, *wha hae wi' [Pender]... bled*, 30; Malone, *Whipt 'em Everytime*, 53-54.

21. *Ibid.*; WDP to FSP, May 8, 1862; Simpson, "Patriot by Nature," 73.

22. Freeman, *Lee's Lieutenants*, 1: 199.

23. WDP to FSP, May 11, 1862.

24. *Ibid.*

25. WDP to FSP, May 17, 1862.

26. WDP to FSP, Apr. 22, 1862.

27. WDP to FSP, May 14, 1862.

28. Sears, *To the Gates of Richmond*, 117-18.

29. *Ibid.*, 118; *OR*, I, 11, pt. 1: 933.

30. *Ibid.*, 933-34; Sears, *To the Gates of Richmond*, 118-20.

31. *Ibid.*, 121-24; Iobst, *Bloody Sixth*, 69; Malone, *Whipt 'em Everytime*, 55.

32. *OR*, I, 11, pt. 1: 934; Janet Hewett et al, eds., *Supplement to the Official Records of the Union and Confederate Armies* (3 pts., 95 vols to date. Wilmington, N. C., 1994-), 2: 372; WDP to FSP, June [1], 1862; Clark, *Regiments and Battalions from North Carolina*, 1: 302, 351; Iobst, *Bloody Sixth*, 69; Malone, *Whipt 'em Everytime*, 55; Simpson, "Patriot by Nature," 80-82.

33. *OR*, I, 11, pt. 1: 991-92; Hewett et al, *Supplement to the Official Records*, 2: 372-73, 385; Clark, *Regiments and Battalions from North Carolina*, 1: 351-52; Benjamin F.White to James J. Phillips, June 6, 1862, Phillips MSS; Iobst, *Bloody Sixth*, 69; Simpson, "Patriot by Nature," 82-83.

34. Hewett et al, *Supplement to the Official Records*, 2: 373; Simpson, "Patriot by Nature," 83; C. B. Denson, "William Henry Chase Whiting, Major-General C. S. Army," *SHSP*, 26 (1898): 142-43.

35. Samuel A. Ashe, Memoir of General William Dorsey Pender, 1, Civil War MSS, NCSDA&H; WDP to FSP, June [1], 1862; Montgomery, *Life and Character of Pender*, 13; Iobst, *Bloody Sixth*, 70; Clark, *Regiments and Battalions from North Carolina*, 1: 352.

Chapter Six

1. Sears, *To the Gates of Richmond*, 140-47; *OR*, I, 11, pt. 1: 992-94.

2. Freman, *Lee's Lieutenants*, 1: 262-63, 271.

3. *OR*, I, 11, pt. 3: 569; 51, pt. 2: 566; Louis G. Young, "Reminiscences of Maj. Genl. William Dorsey Pender," 1, Civil War MSS, NCSDA&H; WDP, person-

nel return, June 3, 1862, M-331, R-196, NA; Weeks, "William Dorsey Pender," [2], Weeks MSS; Henry T. Clark to WDP, June 3 [1862], Clark Letterbooks and Papers.

4. John W. Hinsdale memoirs, 11-12, Special Colls., Duke Univ., Durham, N. C.

5. *Ibid.*, 22, 68-69, 72.

6. Young, "Reminiscences of Pender," 1; George H. Mills, *History of the 16th North Carolina Regiment...* (Rutherfordton, N. C., 1901), 16.

7. WDP to FSP, June 13, 1862; Hinsdale memoirs, 15; Simpson, "Patriot by Nature," 87-88; Burwell T. Cotton and George J. Huntley, *The Cry Is War, War, War: The Civil War Correspondence of Lts. Burwell Thomas Cotton and George Job Huntley, 34th Regiment North Carolina Troops*, ed. by Michael W. Taylor (Dayton, Ohio, 1994), 16-17; George W. Flowers, "The Thirty-eighth N. C. Regiment: Its History in the Civil War," *SHSP,* 25 (1897): 249; *OR,* I, 11, pt. 2: 487.

8. WDP to FSP, June 22, 1862.

9. WDP to FSP, June 14, 1862; Simpson, "Patriot by Nature," 88.

10. Ashe memoir, 2.

11. *OR,* I, 11, pt. 3: 589, 591-92; Hinsdale memoirs, 17; James I. Robertson, Jr., *General A. P. Hill: The Story of a Confederate Warrior* (New York, 1987), 63.

12. *Ibid.*, 326; Ezra J. Warner, *Generals in Gray: Lives of the Confederate Commanders* (Baton Rouge, La., 1959), 134-35.

13. WDP to FSP, June 6, 1862.

14. Hinsdale memoirs, 21-22.

15. WDP to FSP, June 22, 1862.

16. Sears, *To the Gates of Richmond,* 167-74; Thomas, *Bold Dragoon,* 108-31; *OR,* I, 11, pt. 2: 489-90.

17. *Ibid.*; Sears, *To the Gates of Richmond,* 174-76.

18. WDP to FSP, June 25, 1862.

19. *Ibid.*

20. William J. Hoke, "Organization and Movements of the Thirty-eighth Regiment North Carolina Troops, January 17, 1862-June 25, 1864," 15, Hoke Family MSS, SHC.

21. *OR,* I, 11, pt. 2: 834-35, 898-99; Simpson, "Patriot by Nature," 92-93; Young, "Reminiscences of Pender," 2; Hinsdale memoirs, 27-29.

22. *OR,* I, 11, pt. 2: 835, 899; Simpson, "Patriot by Nature," 94-95; K. C. McNeely memoirs, [4], Civil War MSS, NCSDA&H; Hoke, "Thirty-eighth North Carolina,"28; Young, "Reminiscences of Pender," 2-3; Hinsdale memoirs, 30-31; D. H. Hill, Jr., *Bethel to Sharpsburg* (2 vols. Raleigh, N. C., 1926), 2: 152-53; Flowers, "Thirty-eighth N. C. Regiment," 249-50; Sears, *To the*

Gates of Richmond, 206; Robertson, *A. P. Hill*, 74; Joseph P. Cullen, *The Peninsula Campaign, 1862: McClellan & Lee Struggle for Richmond* (Harrisburg, Pa., 1973), 93.

23. *OR*, I, 11, pt. 2: 899; Simpson, "Patriot by Nature," 95-96.

24. *OR*, I, 11, pt. 2: 491, 623, 647-48, 782, 899; Roswell S. Ripley to J. W. Ratchford, July 11, 1862, Ripley MSS, East Carolina Univ., Greenville, N. C.; Simpson, "Patriot by Nature," 96-98; Diket, *wha hae wi' [Pender]... bled*, 43; Young, "Reminiscences of Pender," 3; Montgomery, *Life and Character of Pender*, 15; Daniel H. Hill, "Lee's Attacks North of the Chickahominy," *Battles and Leaders of the Civil War*, 3: 361; A. C. Avery, "Memorial Address on the Life and Character of Lieut.-General D. H. Hill," *SHSP*, 21 (1893): 125; Freeman, *Lee's Lieutenants*, 1: 514-15; Sears, *To the Gates of Richmond*, 206-07; Hinsdale memoirs, 32; Cullen, *Peninsula Campaign*, 94-95.

25. Douglas Southall Freeman, *R. E. Lee: A Biography* (4 vols. New York, 1934-35), 2: 134-35; Hill, "Lee's Attacks," 361.

26. Sears, *To the Gates of Richmond*, 208-11.

27. *OR*, I, 11, pt. 2: 504, 900-01.

28. Young, "Reminiscences of Pender," 2.

29. *Ibid.*; *OR*, I, 11, pt. 2: 902; Hinsdale memoirs, 51-52.

30. Young, "Reminiscences of Pender," 4-5.

31. *Ibid.*, 3-4.

32. *OR*, I, 11, pt. 2: 899-900; Clark, *Regiments and Battalions from North Carolina*, 1: 756-57; Young, "Reminiscences of Pender," 5.

33. *OR*, I, 11, pt. 2: 836, 900; Simpson, "Patriot by Nature," 104; Ashe, *History of North Carolina*, 2: 729; Hinsdale memoirs, 33.

34. *OR*, I, 11, pt. 2: 836-37, 900; Simpson, "Patriot by Nature," 105, 108; Hinsdale memoirs, 34-37; Sears, *To the Gates of Richmond*, 231.

35. *OR*, I, 11, pt. 2: 837, 900; John Brevard Alexander, *Reminiscences of the Past Sixty Years* (Charlotte, N. C., 1908), 72.

36. WDP to FSP, June 29, 1862; *OR*, I, 11, pt. 2: 900; Young, "Reminiscences of Pender," 5; Hinsdale memoirs, 41; Simpson, "Patriot by Nature," 105; Sears, *To the Gates of Richmond*, 226.

37. *OR*, I, 11, pt. 2: 493, 570, 757-58, 837.

38. *Ibid.*, 493-94, 901; Simpson, "Patriot by Nature," 109-10; Hinsdale memoirs, 53.

39. *Ibid.*, 55; A. J. Dula memoirs, 4, Gettysburg Natl. Mil. Park Lib., Gettysburg, Pa.

40. *OR*, I, 11, pt. 2: 901; Simpson, "Patriot by Nature," 110.

41. *OR*, I, 11, pt. 2: 901; Hinsdale memoirs, 54-58; Robertson, *A. P. Hill*, 89-91.

42. *OR*, I, 1, pt. 2: 838, 889, 901; WDP to FSP, July 1, 1862; Young, "Reminiscences of Pender," 6; Simpson, "Patriot by Nature," 110-11; McNeely memoirs, [5]; Hinsdale memoirs, 57-59; Sears, *To the Gates of Richmond*, 305.

43. Hinsdale memoirs, 56.

44. *OR*, I, 11, pt. 2: 901; Simpson, "Patriot by Nature," 111-12; Hinsdale memoirs, 59-61; Young, "Reminiscences of Pender," 6; Alexander, *Reminiscences*, 72-73.

45. Sears, *To the Gates of Richmond*, 308-36; *OR*, I, 11, pt. 2: 495-97, 627-29, 670-72, 790.

46. Hinsdale memoirs, 71-72; Pender, "General Pender," 231.

Chapter Seven

1. *OR*, I, 11, pt. 2: 504, 983; Hinsdale memoirs, 42, 53, 65.

2. Pender, "General Pender," 231; WDP to FSP, July 29, 1862.

3. Peter Cozzens, *General John Pope: A Life for the Nation* (Urbana, Ill., 2000), 74-82.

4. WDP to FSP, July 29, 1862; *OR*, I, 12, pt. 2: 176; Robertson, *A. P. Hill*, 95-100.

5. WDP to FSP, July 31, Aug. 6, 24, 1862.

6. WDP to FSP, July 31, Aug. 6, Sept. 8, 22, 1862.

7. Simpson, "Patriot by Nature," 114; *State Journal* (Raleigh, N. C.), Oct. 1, 1862; WDP to FSP, Apr. 21, 1863; *OR*, I, 25, pt. 2: 746-47.

8. WDP to FSP, Aug. 4, 6, 1862; Simpson, "Patriot by Nature," 115.

9. Young, "Reminiscences of Pender," 6.

10. WDP to FSP, Aug. 4, 6, 1862.

11. Cozzens, *General John Pope*, 90-92.

12. Ashe memoir, 5.

13. *Ibid.*

14. WDP to FSP, Aug. 14, 1862.

15. *OR*, I, 12, pt. 2: 225; Ashe memoir, 5; Diket, *wha hae wi' [Pender]... bled*, 59; Mills, *16th North Carolina*, 20; Simpson, "Patriot by Nature," 122; Freeman, *Lee's Lieutenants*, 2: 31, 40-41; Dula memoirs, 4.

16. Robertson, *A. P. Hill*, 107; *OR*, I, 12, pt. 2: 225.

17. *Ibid.*; WDP to FSP, Aug. 14, 1862.

18. Cozzens, *General John Pope*, 83-84, 98.

19. *OR*, I, 12, pt. 2: 551-52; WDP to FSP, Aug. 14, 1862.

20. Cozzens, *General John Pope*, 98-100; *OR*, I, 12, pt. 2: 552, 641-42.

21. WDP to FSP, Aug. 24, 1862.

22. Ashe memoir, 3-4.

23. *Ibid.*, 4.

24. *OR*, I, 12, pt. 2: 553-64, 564, 644-45.

25. *Ibid.*, 643, 739; Hill, *Bethel to Sharpsburg*, 2: 224.

26. *OR*, I, 12, pt. 2: 643, 645, 739; Diket, *wha hae wi' [Pender]... bled*, 62.

27. *OR*, I, 12, pt. 2: 697, 739.

28. *Ibid.*, 643-44, 670; Hewett et al, *Supplement to the Official Records*, 2: 777.

29. Ashe memoir, 6-7; *OR*, I, 12, pt. 2: 739.

30. Cozzens, *General John Pope*, 121-23.

31. *OR*, I, 12, pt. 2: 644, 670.

32. *Ibid.*, 645, 697.

33. *Ibid.*, 645-46, 703; Edward McCrady, Jr., "Gregg's Brigade of South Carolinians in the Second Battle of Manassas," *SHSP,* 13 (1885): 33-34; Robertson, *A. P. Hill*, 120.

34. *OR*, I, 12, pt. 2: 646, 697-98, 703; Hewett et al, *Supplement to the Official Records*, 2: 778; McCrady, "Gregg's Brigade in Second Battle of Manassas," 34-35; Flowers, "Thirty-eighth N. C. Regiment," 252; Robertson, *General A. P. Hill*, 121.

35. *OR*, I, 12, pt. 2: 556, 698, 711-12; WDP, *General to His Lady*, 169n.; Ashe memoir, 7-8; John J. Hennessy, *Return to Bull Run: The Campaign and Battle of Second Manassas* (New York, 1993), 254-58.

36. WDP to FSP, Sept. 2, 1862.

37. Cozzens, *General John Pope*, 149-56; Hennessy, *Return to Bull Run*, 309-13.

38. WDP to FSP, Aug. 31, Sept. 2, 1862; *OR*, I, 12, pt. 2: 557, 646-47, 698; Ashe memoir, 8; Hennessy, *Return to Bull Run*, 361-73; Hill, *Bethel to Sharpsburg*, 2: 286-99.

39. *OR*, I, 12, pt. 2: 657, 698, 701, 703; Hewett et al, *Supplement to the Official Records*, 2: 778; Freeman, *Lee's Lieutenants*, 2: 124.

40. WDP to FSP, Sept. 2, 1862.

Chapter Eight

1. WDP to FSP, Sept. 7, 1862.

2. WDP to FSP, Sept. 2, 1862; *OR*, I, 12, pt. 2: 647, 672.

3. Stephen W. Sears, *Landscape Turned Red: The Battle of Antietam* (New Haven, Conn., 1983), 63-69.

4. *Ibid.*, 69-71.

5. *Ibid.*, 77-82; John F. Shaffner to "My Dear Friend," Sept. 7, 1862, Shaffner MSS, NCSDA&H.

6. WDP to FSP, Sept. 7, 1862.

7. Robertson, *A. P. Hill*, 131-33.

8. Mills, *16th North Carolina*, 24; WDP to FSP, ca. Sept. 19, 1862.

9. WDP to FSP, Sept. 8, 1862.

10. Sears, *Landscape Turned Red*, 90-92, 112-13.

11. *Ibid.*, 143-49.

12. *OR*, I, 19, pt. 1: 952-53; Robertson, *A. P. Hill*, 134-35.

13. *OR*, I, 19, pt. 1: 953, 980, 1004.

14. *Ibid.*, 853-54, 863, 913; James V. Murfin, *The Gleam of Bayonets: The Battle of Antietam and the Maryland Campaign of 1862* (New York, 1965), 155-58.

15. *OR*, I, 19, pt. 1: 980.

16. *Ibid.*, 147, 586, 954, 980, 1000, 1004, 1006; Mills, *16th North Carolina*, 24; Robertson, *A. P. Hill*, 136.

17. Freeman, *Lee's Lieutenants*, 2: 196; Sears, *Landscape Turned Red*, 124-28.

18. *OR*, I, 19, pt.1: 148, 539-40, 955; Freeman, *Lee's Lieutenants*, 2: 197; Murfin, *Gleam of Bayonets*, 201-02; Robertson, *A. P. Hill*, 138-39; Paul R. Teetor, *A Matter of Hours: Treason at Harper's Ferry* (Rutherford, N. J., 1982), 185-207, 229-30.

19. WDP to FSP, ca. Sept. 19, 1862.

20. Robertson, *A. P. Hill*, 138-39.

21. *OR*, I, 19, pt. 1: 146-50; Sears, *Landscape Turned Red*, 276-85; Murfin, *Gleam of Bayonets*, 267-82; Phillip Thomas Tucker, *Burnside's Bridge: The Climactic Struggle of the 2nd and 20th Georgia at Antietam Creek* (Mechanicsburg, Pa., 2000), 83-142.

22. *OR*, I, 19, pt. 1: 150, 981, 985-86, 988, 1000-01, 1004.

23. *Ibid.*, 151; Sears, *Landscape Turned Red*, 293-97, 303-07.

24. WDP to FSP, Sept. 22, 28, 1862.

25. *OR*, I, 19, pt. 1: 982; Robertson, *A. P. Hill*, 148-49.

26. *OR*, I, 19, pt. 1: 152, 986, 1001-02, 1004, 1006; WDP to FSP, Sept. 22, 1862; Freeman, *Lee's Lieutenants*, 2: 233; Flowers, "Thirty-eighth N. C. Regiment," 254; Dula memoirs, 5.

27. *OR*, I, 19, pt. 1: 982.

28. WDP to FSP, Sept. 22, 1862.

29. *OR*, I, 19, pt. 1: 152.

30. WDP to FSP, Sept. 25, 1862.

31. WDP to FSP, Sept. 28, 1862.

32. *Ibid.*

33. *OR*, I, 19, pt. 1: 152.
34. WDP to FSP, Oct. 21, 1862.
35. WDP to FSP, Oct. 21, 24, 1862; Long and Long, *Civil War Day by Day*, 270.
36. WDP to FSP, Sept. 28, Oct. 21, 1862.
37. WDP to FSP, Oct. 21, 1862.
38. *Ibid.*; *OR*, I, 19, pt. 2: 683-84.
39. A. P. Hill to George W. Randolph, Oct. 30, 1862, M-331, R-196, NA; WDP to FSP, Sept. 25, 1862; *OR*, I, 19, pt. 2: 698-99.
40. WDP to FSP, Oct. 29, 1862; Alfred M. Scales to "My Dear Cousin Kate," Nov. 15, 1862, Scales MSS, NCSDA&H.
41. *OR*, I, 19, pt. 1: 152, 983; Scales, *Battle of Fredericksburg*, 5; History of the Eighteenth North Carolina Infantry, 33, William B. McLaurin MSS, SHC; Sears, *Landscape Turned Red*, 338-45.
42. *OR*, I, 19, pt. 2: 552-54; 21: 83-85, 103-04, 759-60, 765-66, 776.
43. WDP to FSP, Nov. 22, Dec. 3, 1862; Clark, *Regiments and Battalions from North Carolina*, 1: 664; 2: 170; J. R. Cole, "Sketches of the 22d Regiment of North Carolina State Troops: First Two Years of the War," *Our Living and Our Dead*, 1 (1874): 305; W. W. Scott, *Annals of Caldwell County* (Lenoir, N. C., ca. 1930), 147.
44. *OR*, I, 21: 545-47, 552; WDP to FSP, Dec. 11, 1862.
45. WDP to FSP, Dec. 3, 1862.
46. *OR*, I, 21: 547, 553-54, 623-24, 630-31, 645-46, 649, 661-62, 668; Alfred M. Scales to "My Own Dear Kate," Dec. 22, 1862, Scales MSS; Scales, *Battle of Fredericksburg*, 12-15; Cole, "22d North Carolina," 310-11; Birdsong, *North Carolina State Troops*, 56-57.
47. *OR*, I, 21: 554, 632-34, 646-47, 662; WDP to FSP, Dec. 31, 1862; History of the Eighteenth North Carolina, 34, McLaurin MSS; Scales, *Battle of Fredericksburg*, 16-18; Robertson, *A. P. Hill*, 160-67; John F. Shaffner to "My Dearest Friend," Dec. 15, 1862, Shaffner MSS.
48. *OR*, I, 21: 647-48; WDP, *General to His Lady*, 194; Charles W. Turner, ed., "Captain Greenlee Davidson: Letters of a Virginia Soldier," *Civil War History*, 17 (1971): 218; Robert K. Krick, "William Dorsey Pender," in William C. Davis, ed., *The Confederate General* (5 vols. to date. Harrisburg, Pa., 1991-), 5: 11.

Chapter Nine

1. *OR*, I, 21: 560.

2. *Ibid.*, 547-48, 555, 1067-68; Freeman, *Lee's Lieutenants,* 2: 429; William G. Lewis to D. W. Gilliam, Oct. 21, 1893, SHC.

3. WDP to FSP, Dec. 5, 31, 1862.

4. Simpson, "Patriot by Nature," 186; Diket, *wha hae wi' [Pender]… bled,* 108; John F. Shaffner to "My Dearest Friend," Dec. 26, 1862, Shaffner MSS.

5. Scott, *Annals of Caldwell County,* 147; Cotton and Huntley, *The Cry is War, War, War,* 131.

6. McNeely memoirs, [6].

7. J. F. Miller to Zebulon B. Vance, Dec. 20, 1862, Vance Letterbooks and Papers, NCSDA&H.

8. WDP, *General to His Lady,* 212n., 227n.; WDP to FSP, Mar. 26, Apr. 21, 1863.

9. *OR,* I, 25, pt. 2: 746-47.

10. *Ibid.,* 18: 782-83; 21: 1095; J. Kelly Turner and John L. Bridgers, Jr., *History of Edgecombe County, North Carolina* (Raleigh, N. C., 1920), 208; Simpson, "Patriot by Nature," 185-86.

11. John S. McElroy to Zebulon B. Vance, Jan. 23, 1863 [with Vance's endorsement], Vance Letterbooks and Papers; James A. Seddon to Zebulon B. Vance, Feb. 9, 1863, *ibid.*; *OR,* I, 18: 856.

12. Cotton and Huntley, *The Cry is War, War, War,* 130.

13. *OR,* I, 21: 945, 976-79, 984-86, 990-91, 994-95, 1004-05; 25, pt. 2: 4.

14. WDP to FSP, Feb. 21, Mar. 15, 1863; Freeman, *Lee's Lieutenants,* 2: 510.

15. A. P. Hill to Robert E. Lee, Jan. 31, 1863, M-331, R-196, NA; Simpson, "Patriot by Nature," 193-94.

16. WDP to FSP, Feb. 25, 1863; Warner, *Generals in Gray,* 263.

17. *Ibid.,* 133; *OR,* I, 25, pt. 2: 654; WDP to FSP, Mar. 28, 1863.

18. Simpson, "Patriot by Nature," 196.

19. WDP to FSP, Feb. 28, Mar. 10, 1863.

20. WDP to FSP, Feb. 25, 1863.

21. WDP to FSP, Mar. 13, 19, 21, 28, 1863.

22. WDP to FSP, Dec. 31, 1862, Feb. 28, Mar. 19, 21, 26, Apr. 8, 1863.

23. WDP to FSP, Mar. 28, Apr. 1, 11, 1863.

24. WDP to FSP, Apr. 8, 17, 1863.

25. WDP to FSP, Apr. 19, 1862.

26. In his influential novel, *The Killer Angels,* Michael Shaara exaggerates Fanny Pender's invasion fears. The exaggeration is repeated in the film version of the novel *Gettysburg.*

27. *OR,* I, 25, pt. 1: 796.

28. *Ibid.,* 796-97; Stephen W. Sears, *Chancellorsville* (Boston, 1996), 187-89.

29. *Ibid.,* 189-213; WDP to FSP, Apr. 30, 1863; Cotton and Huntley, *The Cry is*

War, War, War, 103; Oliver C. Hamilton to his father, May 17, 1863, Eli Spinks Hamilton MSS, SHC; History of the Eighteenth North Carolina, 35-36, McLaurin MSS; Dula memoirs, 6, 9.

30. *OR,* I, 25, pt. 1: 798; Sears, *Chancellorsville,* 264-72.

31. *OR,* I, 25, pt. 1: 798, 935; Sears, *Chancellorsville,* 272-78; Cotton and Huntley, *The Cry is War, War, War,* 105; Freeman, *Lee's Lieutenants,* 2: 557-58.

32. John Esten Cooke, *Wearing of the Gray: Being Personal Portraits, Scenes and Adventures of the War* (Baton Rouge, La., 1997), 295; Hunter McGuire, "Death of Stonewall Jackson," *SHSP,* 14 (1886): 155; John Purifoy, "Jackson's Last Battle," *Confederate Veteran,* 28 (1920): 96; Freeman, *Lee's Lieutenants,* 2: 574-75.

33. *OR,* I, 25, pt. 1: 885-87, 889; Mills, *16th North Carolina,* 32.

34. *OR,* I, 25, pt. 2: 887-88, 892; Sears, *Chancellorsville,* 302-03, 312-18.

35. *OR,* I, 25, pt. 1: 888, 891, 935; Oliver C. Hamilton to his father, May 17, 1863, Hamilton MSS; Freeman, *Lee's Lieutenants,* 2: 587.

36. *OR,* I, 25, pt. 1: 886, 891, 935; WDP to Zebulon B. Vance, May 12, 1863, Vance Letterbooks and Papers; Freeman, *Lee's Lieutenants,* 2: 588.

37. *OR,* I, 25, pt. 1: 803, 887, 892, 913, 935; Pender, "General Pender," 232; WDP, *General to His Lady,* 234; Oliver C. Hamilton to his father, May 17, 1863, Hamilton MSS.

38. *OR,* I, 25, pt. 1: 888, 935; Cotton and Huntley, *The Cry is War, War, War,* 106; History of the Eighteenth North Carolina, 41-42, McLaurin MSS.

39. *OR,* I, 25, pt. 1: 936.

Chapter Ten

1. WDP to FSP, May 5, 7, 1863; John F. Shaffner to "My Dearest Friend," May 5, 1863, Shaffner MSS.

2. WDP to FSP, May 7, 1863.

3. *Ibid.*; *OR,* I, 25, pt. 1: 937; *The Southerner* (Tarboro, N. C.), May 23, 1863.

4. Mills, *16th North Carolina,* 33.

5. Birdsong, *North Carolina State Troops,* 140-41; Flowers, "Thirty-eighth N. C. Regiment," 258; *OR,* I, 25, pt. 1: 805.

6. WDP to FSP, May 14, 22, 1863; Freeman, *Lee's Lieutenants,* 2: 690-91, 694-95; Simpson, "Patriot by Nature," 229.

7. WDP to FSP, May 18, 1863; Edwin B. Coddington, *The Gettysburg Campaign: A Study in Command* (New York, 1968), 5-7.

8. *Ibid.,* 11-13; Freeman, *R. E. Lee,* 3: 12-15; *OR,* I, 25, pt. 2: 827, 840.

9. *Ibid.*, 752-53, 811, 827; Freeman, *R. E. Lee*, 3: 13; WDP, *General to His Lady*, 241.

10. *The Southerner* (Tarboro, N. C.), June 13, 1863; J. R. Boyles, *Reminiscences of the Civil War...* (Columbia, S. C., 1890), 38-39.

11. WDP, *General to His Lady*, 151; WDP to FSP, June 14, 1863; Simpson, "Patriot by Nature," 234-36.

12. *OR*, I, 27, pt. 2: 293, 305, 313; 51, pt. 2: 720; Coddington, *Gettysburg Campaign*, 51-53.

13. Hoke, "Thirty-eighth North Carolina," 66; Simpson, "Patriot by Nature," 237-38; James Sidney Harris, *Historical Sketches of the Seventh Regiment North Carolina Troops...* (Mooresville, N. C., 1893), 32-33; James F. J. Caldwell, *The History of a Brigade of South Carolinians, Known First as "Gregg's," and Subsequently as "McGowan's Brigade"* (Philadelphia, 1866), 90-91; Thomas A. Martin memoirs, 6, Fredericksburg-Spotsylvania Natl. Mil. Park Lib., Fredericksburg, Va.

14. WDP to FSP, June 12, 1863; Coddington, *Gettysburg Campaign*, 54-66.

15. *Ibid.*, 70-74; WDP to FSP, June 12, 15, 1863; James J. Pettigrew to anon., June 13, 1863, Pettigrew Family MSS, NCSDA&H.

16. WDP to FSP, June 10, 15, 1863.

17. WDP to FSP, June 17, 1863; Coddington, *Gettysburg Campaign*, 80-81, 86-91.

18. WDP to FSP, June 17, 21, 1863; Spencer Glasgow Welch, *A Confederate Surgeon's Letters to His Wife...* (New York, 1911), 55; Draughton Stith Haynes, *The Field Diary of a Confederate Soldier While Serving with the Army of NorthernVirginia, C. S. A.* (Darien, Ga., 1963), 30; Harris, *Seventh North Carolina*, 33; Caldwell, *Brigade of South Carolinians*, 92; Thomas M. Littlejohn memoirs, 2, Gettysburg Natl. Mil. Park Lib.

19. WDP to FSP, June 23, 1863.

20. WDP to FSP, June 24, 1863.

21. *Ibid.*

22. WDP to FSP, June 28, 1863.

23. *Ibid.*

24. *Ibid.*

25. Coddington, *Gettysburg Campaign*, 198-208.

26. *Ibid.*, 196-97; WDP to FSP, June 28, 1863; Freeman, *R. E. Lee*, 3: 61-62.

27. *OR*, I, 27, pt. 2: 607, 637; David G. Martin, *Gettysburg, July 1* (Conshohocken, Pa., 1995), 22-23; Hoke, "Thirty-eighth North Carolina," 68; Welch, *Confederate Surgeon's Letters*, 61-62; Boyles, *Reminiscences*, 39-40; Simpson, "Patriot by Nature," 252.

28. *Ibid.*; *OR*, I, 27, pt. 2: 607, 637; Martin, *Gettysburg, July 1*, 59-82.

29. *Ibid.*, 83-165; *OR*, I, 27 pt. 2: 637-38.

30. *Ibid.*, 656-57; Freeman, *R. E. Lee*, 3: 68-72; Martin, *Gettysburg, July 1*, 338-41; Simpson, "Patriot by Nature," 253-54.

31. *OR*, I, 27, pt. 2: 657, 661, 665, 668-70; Milledge L. Bonham, Jr., ed., "A Little More Light on Gettysburg," *Mississippi Valley Historical Review*, 24 (1937-38): 521.

32. *OR.*, I, 27, pt. 2: 657-58, 661, 670; Martin, *Gettysburg, July 1*, 426-28; Flowers, "Thirty-eighth N. C. Regiment," 259; Bonham, "More Light on Gettysburg," 521-22.

33. *OR.*, I, 27, pt. 2: 662-63; 665; Bonham, "More Light on Gettysburg," 522; Martin, *Gettysburg, July 1*, 401-14; Harris, *Seventh North Carolina*, 34; Martin memoirs, 6-7; Welch, *Confederate Surgeon's Letters*, 65-66; Daniel A. Tompkins, *Company K, Fourteenth South Carolina Volunteers* (Charlotte, N. C., 1897), 20; Caldwell, *Brigade of South Carolinians*, 97; Berry Benson, *Berry Benson's Civil War Book: Memoirs of a Confederate Scout and Sharpshooter*, ed. by Susan Williams Benson (Athens, Ga., 1992), 45-46; John A. Leach to John B. Bachelder, Sept. 12, 1882, Bachelder MSS, New Hampshire Hist. Soc., Concord; Littlejohn memoirs, 6.

34. Bonham, "More Light on Gettysburg," 522-23; *OR*, I, 27, pt. 2: 607, 662-63; Martin, *Gettysburg, July 1*, 415-47; Varina D. Brown, *A Colonel at Gettysburg and Spotsylvania...* (Columbia, S. C., 1931), 80-82; Caldwell, *Brigade of South Carolinians*, 97-99; Littlejohn memoirs, 6-7; Martin memoirs, 7.

35. *OR*, I, 27, pt. 2: 344-45, 658, 663, 665, 668, 671.

36. *Ibid.*, 318, 358, 445; Coddington, *Gettysburg Campaign*, 315-21.

37. *OR*, I, 27, pt. 2: 665; W. H. Lucas to J. B. Neathery, Dec. 9, 1887, Neathery MSS, NCSDA&H; Pender, "General Pender," 233; Dula memoirs, 10.

38. *OR*, I, 27, pt. 2: 658-59, 675; WDP, *General to His Lady*, 259-60; William G. Lewis to D. W. Gilliam, Oct. 21, 1893, SHC; Montgomery, *Life and Character of Pender*, 23; Diket, *wha hae wi' [Pender]... bled*, 156-57; Brown, *Colonel at Gettysburg*, 121; James H. Lane, "Leading Confederates on the Battle of Gettysburg: Letter from General James H. Lane," *SHSP*, 5 (1877): 38; Pender, "General Pender," 232-33.

39. Bonham, "More Light on Gettysburg," 523; *OR*, I, 27, pt. 2: 608.

40. Montgomery, *Life and Character of Pender*, 25-26; William G. Lewis to D. W. Gilliam, Oct. 21, 1893, SHC.

41. Ashe memoir, 10.

42. Steve Davis, "'Killed July 3' but Died July 18... and Buried Where?" *Grave Matters* 7 (Summer 1991): 3-4. Pender's grave erroneously carries July 3, 1863, as his date of death.

Upon receiving word of her husband's passing, Fanny Pender locked herself in her bedroom in Good Spring; by the time she reemerged her hair had turned white. That fall she gave birth to her third son, Stephen Lee Pender, named for her husband's friend and classmate.

Fanny never remarried. In postwar life she supported herself and her family by operating a boarding-school until 1885, when she was appointed post-mistress of Tarboro, North Carolina. She died of acute colitis and "general debility" on July 3, 1922, at age 82. By then she had seen Pender County, North Carolina, named in honor of the man whom she had loved so much and whom Robert E. Lee had described in these words: "The confidence and admiration inspired by his courage and capacity as an officer were only equaled by the esteem and respect entertained by all with whom he was associated...."

General William Dorsey Pender's trousers, sash and sword. (*The Museum of the Confederacy, Richmond Virginia. Photograph by Katherine Wetzel.*)

BIBLIOGRAPHY

Manuscripts and Unpublished Records:

Adjutant General's Office, State of North Carolina. Letterbooks, 1861-63. North Carolina State Department of Archives and History, Raleigh.

Ashe, Samuel A. Memoir of General William Dorsey Pender. Civil War Collection, North Carolina State Department of Archives and History.

Branch, Lawrence O'Bryan. Letter of October 2, 1861. Stephen B. Weeks Papers, North Carolina State Department of Archives and History.

Choate, J. W. Correspondence. Newman Library, Virginia Polytechnic Institute and State University, Blacksburg, Va.

Clark, Henry T. Letterbooks and Papers, 1861-62. North Carolina State Department of Archives and History.

Daniel, John W. Papers. Special Collections Library, Duke University, Durham, N.C.

Dula, A. J. Memoirs. Gettysburg National Military Park Library, Gettysburg, Pa.

Ellis, John W. Letterbooks and Papers, 1861. North Carolina State Department of Archives and History.

"Gen. William Dorsey Pender (1834-1863)." TS in Edgecombe County Library, Tarboro, N. C.

Gillespie, Jasper A. Papers. Georgia Department of Archives and History, Atlanta.

Gray, R. H. Papers. North Carolina State Department of Archives and History.

Hairston, Peter W. Correspondence. Southern Historical Collection, Wilson Library, University of North Carolina, Chapel Hill.

Hamilton, C. G. and Oliver C. Correspondence. Eli Spinks Hamilton Papers, Southern Historical Collection, Wilson Library, University of North Carolina.

Hill, Ambrose P. Papers. North Carolina State Department of Archives and History.

Hill, Charles. Papers. Museum of the Confederacy, Richmond, Va.

Hinsdale, John W. Memoirs. Special Collections Library, Duke University.

History of the Eighteenth North Carolina Infantry. William B. McLaurin Papers, Southern Historical Collection, Wilson Library, University of North Carolina.

Hoke, William J. "Organization and Movements of the Thirty-eighth Regiment North Carolina Troops, January 17, 1862-June 25, 1864." Hoke Family Papers, Southern Historical Collection, Wilson Library, University of North Carolina.

Lane, James H. Papers. Ralph Brown Draughon Library, Auburn University, Auburn, Ala.

Lanier, A. S. "Speech… in Receiving the Portraits of Governor Zebulon Vance; General William D. Pender; Colonel Charles F. Fisher; and Captain Frank Shepperd, on Behalf of the Lady Managers of the North Carolina Room of the Confederacy Museum," n.d. Museum of the Confederacy.

Leach, John A. Correspondence. John B. Bachelder Papers, New Hampshire Historical Society, Concord.

Lewis, William G. Letter of October 21, 1893. Southern Historical Collection, Wilson Library, University of North Carolina.

Littlejohn, Thomas M. Memoirs. Gettysburg National Military Park Library.

Lucas, W. H. Letter of December 9, 1887. J. B. Neathery Papers, North Carolina State Department of Archives and History.

McMillan, Alexander. Papers. Special Collections Library, Duke University.

McNeely, K. C. Memoirs. Civil War Collection, North Carolina State Department of Archives and History.

Martin, Thomas A. Memoirs. Fredericksburg-Spotsylvania National Military Park Library, Fredericksburg, Va.

Morrison, James Lunsford, Jr. "The United States Military Academy, 1833-1866: Years of Progress and Turmoil." Ph.D. dissertation, Columbia University, 1970.

Patterson, Josiah B. Papers. Georgia Department of Archives and History, Atlanta, Ga.

Pender, Mrs. William C. Letter of January 16, 1996. In possession of the author, Newport News, Va.

Pender, William Dorsey. Cadet Application Files, United States Military Academy, Class of 1854. National Archives, Washington, D. C.

———. Cadet Delinquency Log. Special Collections, United States Military Academy Archives, West Point, N. Y.

———. Compiled Service Records, 1861-63. National Archives.

———. Correspondence, Reports, etc. General and Staff Officers, C.S.A., File (Microcopy 331), National Archives.

———. Correspondence, Reports, etc. Letters Received, Department of the Pacific, 1854-1858 (Record Group 393, Entry 3584, Box 12), National Archives.

———. Correspondence, Reports, etc. Letters Received, Headquarters Troops in Florida and Department of Florida, 1850-1858 (Microcopy 1084), National Archives.

———. Correspondence. Letters Received, Office of the Adjutant General, 1822-1860 (Microcopy 567), National Archives.

_____. Correspondence. Letters Received, Office of the Adjutant General, 1861-1870 (Microcopy 619), National Archives.

_____. Correspondence, Reports, etc. Confederate Military Leaders Collections, Museum of the Confederacy.

_____. Correspondence, Reports, etc. Letters Sent by the Ninth Military Department, Department of New Mexico, and District of New Mexico, 1849-1890 (Microcopy 1072), National Archives.

_____. Letter of March 17, 1861. Gratz Collection—Confederate Generals, Historical Society of Pennsylvania, Philadelphia.

_____. "Orders Relating to William D. Pender, While a Cadet at the United States Military Academy, from 1 July 1850 to 1 July 1854." United States Military Academy Archives.

_____. Papers. Museum of the Confederacy.

_____. Papers. North Carolina State Department of Archives and History.

_____. Papers. Robert W. Woodruff Library, Emory University, Atlanta, Ga.

_____. Papers. Southern Historical Collection, Wilson Library, University of North Carolina.

Pender-Shepperd Family Genealogy. Augustine H. Shepperd Papers, Southern Historical Collection, Wilson Library, University of North Carolina.

Pettigrew, James J. Letter of June 13, 1863. Pettigrew Family Papers, North Carolina State Department of Archives and History.

Proffit, A. J. Correspondence. Proffit Family Papers, Southern Historical Collection, Wilson Library, University of North Carolina.

Ramseur, Stephen Dodson. Papers. Southern Historical Collection, Wilson Library, University of North Carolina.

Ripley, Roswell S. Papers. Joyner Library, East Carolina University, Greenville, N.C.

Scales, Alfred M. Letter of June 17, 1862. Simon Gratz Collection—Confederate Generals, Historical Society of Pennsylvania.

_____. Memoir of Pickett's Charge at Gettysburg. Gettysburg National Military Park Library.

_____. Papers. North Carolina State Department of Archives and History.

Settle, Thomas L. Papers. Special Collections Library, Duke University.

Shaffner, John F. Papers. North Carolina State Department of Archives and History.

Shooter, Washington P. Correspondence. Gettysburg National Military Park Library.

Simpson, Kenrick N. "Patriot by Nature, Soldier by Training, Christian by Faith:

The Life of William Dorsey Pender." M.A. thesis, East Carolina University, 1982.

Stewart, Kensey J. Letter of September 16, 1894. Joseph Blount Cheshire Papers, North Carolina State Department of Archives and History.

Stuart, J. E. B. Papers. Virginia Historical Society, Richmond, Va.

Van Noppen, Charles L. Papers. Special Collections Library, Duke University.

Vance, Zebulon B. Letterbooks and Papers, 1862-63. North Carolina State Department of Archives and History.

Weeks, Stephen B. "William Dorsey Pender." Weeks Papers, North Carolina State Department of Archives and History.

Welch, Spencer G. Correspondence. Joyner Library, East Carolina University.

White, Benjamin F. Correspondence. James J. Phillips Papers, North Carolina State Department of Archives and History.

_____. Diary, 1861. Southern Historical Collection, Wilson Library, University of North Carolina.

Willis, John J. and Marcus M. Correspondence. Gettysburg National Military Park Library.

Young, Louis G. "Reminiscences of Maj. Genl. William Dorsey Pender." Civil War Collection, North Carolina State Department of Archives and History.

Newspapers

Daily Richmond Enquirer, 1861-63.

New York Times, 1861-63.

Raleigh News-Observer-Chronicle, 1894.

Raleigh Standard, 1858-63.

Richmond Daily Whig, 1861-63.

Richmond Examiner, 1861-63.

State Journal (Raleigh, N. C.), 1862.

Tarboro Mercury, 1861.

The Southerner (Tarboro, N. C.), 1861-65.

Wilmington Daily Journal, 1861-63.

Articles and Essays

"Alfred and Susan Jane (DeBose) Gurganious Letters." *Lower Cape Fear Historical Society, Inc. Bulletin*, 16 (May 1973): 1-6.

Avery, A. C. "Memorial Address on the Life and Character of Lieut.-General D. H. Hill." *Southern Historical Society Papers* , 21 (1893): 110-50.

Bolton, Channing M. "With General Lee's Engineers." *Confederate Veteran,* 30 (1922): 298-302.

Bonham, Milledge L. Jr., ed. "A Little More Light on Gettysburg." *Mississippi Valley Historical Review,* 24 (1937-38): 521-23.

"Brig. Gen. James T. [sic] Archer." *Confederate Veteran,* 8 (1900): 65-67.

Brown, B. F. "A. P. Hill's Light Division." *Confederate Veteran,* 30 (1922): 246-47.

Childs, H. T. "Cedar Run Battle as I Saw It." *Confederate Veteran,* 28 (1920): 24.

Cole, J. R. "Sketches of the 22d Regiment of North Carolina State Troops: First Two Years of the War." *Our Living and Our Dead,* 1 (1874): 305-13.

Daves, Graham. "Twenty-second North Carolina Infantry: Its History" *Southern Historical Society Papers,* 24 (1896): 256-67.

Davis, Steve. "Killed July 3' but Died July 18… and Buried Where?" *Grave Matters* 7 (Summer 1991): 3-4.

Denson, C. B. "William Henry Chase Whiting, Major-General C. S. Army." *Southern Historical Society Papers,* 26 (1898): 129-81.

Englehard, Joseph A. "Gettysburg: Report of Pender's Division." *Southern Historical Society Papers,* 8 (1880): 515-21.

Flowers, George W. "The Thirty-eighth N. C. Regiment: Its History in the Civil War." *Southern Historical Society Papers,* 25 (1897): 245-63.

Garnett, James M. "Battle of Second Manassas, Including Ox Hill." *Southern Historical Society Papers,* 40 (1915): 224-29.

Hassler, William W. "Dorsey Pender." *Civil War Times Illustrated,* 1 (October 1962): 18-22.

Hill, Daniel H. "Lee's Attacks North of the Chickahominy." *Battles and Leaders of the Civil War,* 2: 347-62.

Hoke, W. J. "Sketch of the 38th Regiment N. C. Troops." *Our Living and Our Dead,* 1 (1874): 545-51.

Hunt, Henry J. "The First Day at Gettysburg." *Battles and Leaders of the Civil War,* 3: 255-84.

Imboden, John D. "The Confederate Retreat from Gettysburg." *Battles and Leaders of the Civil War,* 3: 420-29.

Krick, Robert K. "William Dorsey Pender." In William C. Davis, ed., *The Confederate General.* (5 vols. to date. Harrisburg, Pa.: National Historical Society, 1991-), 5: 10-11.

Lane, James H. "Leading Confederates on the Battle of Gettysburg: Letter from General James H. Lane." *Southern Historical Society Papers,* 5 (1877): 38-40.

Lawrence, R. C. "General William D. Pender." *The State,* 11 (May 1940): 7, 28.

Leigh, Benjamin W. "The Wounding of Stonewall Jackson—Extracts from a Letter of Major Benjamin Watkins Leigh." *Southern Historical Society Papers,* 6 (1878): 230-34.

[Letter from Pender Brothers, Bryson City, North Carolina.] *Confederate Veteran,* 1(1893): 79.

Longacre, Edward G., ed. "A 'Christian Warrior' in Winter Quarters." *Manuscripts,* 33 (1981): 241-44.

Longstreet, James. "The Battle of Fredericksburg." *Battles and Leaders of the Civil War,* 3: 70-94.

McCrady, Edward Jr. "Gregg's Brigade of South Carolinians in the Second Battle of Manassas." *Southern Historical Society Papers,* 13 (1885): 1-40.

McGuire, Hunter. "Death of Stonewall Jackson." *Southern Historical Society Papers,* 14 (1886): 154-63.

McIntosh, David Gregg. "The Campaign of Chancellorsville." *Southern Historical Society Papers,* 40 (1915): 44-100.

Meredith, Jaquelin Marshall. "The First Day at Gettysburg… A Description by an Eye Witness." *Southern Historical Society Papers,* 24 (1896): 182-87.

Mockbee, R. T. "Heroes in Last Charge of Lee's Army." *Confederate Veteran,* 6 (1898): 311.

Pender, Samuel Turner. "General Pender." *The South-Atlantic: A Monthly Magazine of Literature, Science and Art,* 1 (1877): 228-35.

Peters, Winfield. "A Maryland Warrior and Hero." *Southern Historical Society Papers,* 29 (1901): 243-50.

Pope, John. "The Second Battle of Bull Run." *Battles and Leaders of the Civil War,* 2: 449-94.

Porter, Fitz John. "Hanover Court House and Gaines's Mill." *Battles and Leaders of the Civil War,* 2: 319-43.

Purifoy, John. "The Battle of Gettysburg, July 1, 1863." *Confederate Veteran,* 31 (1923): 22-25.

_____. "Jackson's Last Battle." *Confederate Veteran,* 28 (1920): 93-96.

_____. "The Myth of the Confederate Hollow Squares at Gettysburg." *Confederate Veteran,* 33 (1925): 53-55.

_____. "A Night of Horror." *Confederate Veteran,* 33 (1925): 95-97.

_____. "Robert E. Lee, the Peerless Soldier—III." *Confederate Veteran,* 34 (1926): 420-22.

Scales, Alfred M. "Battle of Fredericksburg." *Southern Historical Society Papers,* 40 (1915): 195-223.

Shepherd, Henry E. "Gallant Sons of North Carolina." *Confederate Veteran,* 27 (1919): 413-14.

Smith, Gustavus W. "Two Days of Battle at Seven Pines (Fair Oaks)." *Battles and Leaders of the Civil War,* 2: 220-63.

Smith, James Power. "Stonewall Jackson's Last Battle." *Battles and Leaders of the Civil War,* 3: 203-14.

Stinson, Dwight E. Jr. "Eltham's Landing—the End Run that Failed." *Civil War Times Illustrated,* 1 (February 1963): 38-41.

Turner, Charles W., ed. "Captain Greenlee Davidson: Letters of a Virginia Soldier." *Civil War History,* 17 (1971): 197-221.

"U. D. C. Notes." *Confederate Veteran,* 31 (1923): 230-32.

Books and Pamphlets

Alexander, John Brevard. *Reminiscences of the Past Sixty Years.* Charlotte, N. C.: Ray Printing Co., 1908.

Allen, T. Harrell. *Lee's Last Major General: Bryan Grimes of North Carolina.* Mason City, Ia.: Savas Publishing Co., 1999.

Ashe, Samuel A. *History of North Carolina.* 2 vols. Raleigh, N. C.: Edwards & Broughton, 1925.

Bartholomees, J. Boone, Jr. *Buff Facings and Gilt Buttons: Staff and Headquarters Operations in the Army of Northern Virginia, 1861-1865.* Columbia: University of South Carolina Press, 1998.

Battle, Laura E. *Forget-Me-Nots of the Civil War: A Romance Containing Reminiscences and Original Letters of Two Confederate Soldiers.* St. Louis: Fleming Printing Co., 1909.

Bennett, William W. *A Narrative of the Great Revival Which Prevailed in the Confederate Armies...* Harrisonburg, Va.: Sprinkle Publications, 1976.

Benson, Berry. *Berry Benson's Civil War Book: Memoirs of a Confederate Scout and Sharpshooter.* Edited by Susan Williams Benson. Athens: University of Georgia Press, 1992.

Biographical Directory of the American Congress, 1774-1961. Washington, D.C.: Government Printing Office, 1961.

Birdsong, James C. *Brief Sketches of the North Carolina State Troops in the War between the States...* Raleigh, N. C.: State Printer, 1894.

Blackford, Charles M., and Susan Leigh Blackford. *Letters from Lee's Army...* Edited by Charles Minor Blackford III. New York: Charles Scribner's Sons, 1947.

Boatner, Mark Mayo, III. *The Civil War Dictionary.* New York: David McKay Co., Inc., 1959.

Boyles, J. R. *Reminiscences of the Civil War.* Columbia, S. C.: privately issued, 1890.

Brown, Varina D. *A Colonel at Gettysburg and Spotsylvania....* Columbia, S. C.: State Co., 1931.

Cadets Arranged in Order of Merit in their Respective Classes, as Determined at the General Examination, in June, 1852. West Point, N. Y.: privately issued, 1852.

Caldwell, James F. J. *The History of a Brigade of South Carolinians, Known First as "Gregg's," and Subsequently as "McGowan's Brigade".* Philadelphia: King & Baird, 1866.

Carter, Sidney. *"Dear Bet": The Carter Letters, 1861-1863.* Edited by Bessie Mell Lane. Greenville, S. C.: Keys Printing Co., 1978.

Cheshire, Joseph Blount. *The Church in the Confederate States: A History of the Protestant Episcopal Church...* London: Longmans, Green, & Co., 1912.

Clark, Walter, ed. *Histories of the Several Regiments and Battalions from North Carolina in the Great War, 1861-'65...* 5 vols. Goldsboro, N. C.: Nash Brothers; Raleigh, N. C.: E. M. Uzzell, 1901.

Coddington, Edwin B. *The Gettysburg Campaign: A Study in Command.* New York: Charles Scribner's Sons, 1968.

Cooke, John Esten. *Wearing of the Gray: Being Personal Portraits, Scenes and Adventures of the War.* Baton Rouge: Louisiana State University Press, 1997.

Cotton, Burwell T., and George J. Huntley. *The Cry Is War, War, War: The Civil War Correspondence of Lts. Burwell Thomas Cotton and George Job Huntley, 34th Regiment North Carolina Troops.* Edited by Michael W. Taylor. Dayton, Ohio: Morningside, 1994.

Cozzens, Peter. *General John Pope: A Life for the Nation.* Urbana: University of Illinois Press, 2000.

Cullen, Joseph P. *The Peninsula Campaign, 1862: McClellan & Lee Struggle for Richmond.* Harrisburg, Pa.: Stackpole Books, 1973.

Cullum, George W., comp. *Biographical Register of the Officers and Graduates of the U.S. Military Academy at West Point, N.Y.* 2 vols. Boston: Houghton, Mifflin & Co., 1891.

Current, Richard N., ed. *Encyclopedia of the Confederacy.* 4 vols. New York: Simon & Schuster, 1993.

Davidson, Greenlee. *Captain Greenlee Davidson, C. S. A.: Diary and Letters, 1851-1863.* Edited by Charles W. Turner. Vienna, Va.: McClure Press, 1975.

Davis, William C. *Battle at Bull Run: A History of the First Major Campaign of the Civil War.* Garden City, N. Y.: Doubleday & Co., Inc., 1977.

Diket, A. L. *wha hae wi' [Pender]... bled.* New York: Vantage Press, 1979.

Doubleday, Abner. *Chancellorsville and Gettysburg.* New York: Charles Scribner's Sons, 1882.

Ellis, John W. *The Papers of John Willis Ellis.* Edited by Noble J. Tolbert. 2 vols. Raleigh: North Carolina State Department of Archives and History, 1964.

Faust, Patricia L., ed. *The Historical Times Illustrated Encyclopedia of the Civil War.* New York: Harper & Row, 1986.

Fitzpatrick, Marion H. *Letters to Amanda from Sergeant Major Marion Hill Fitzpatrick, Company K, 45th Georgia Regiment...* Culloden, Ga.: Mansel Hammock, 1976.

Frazer, Robert W. *Forts of the West: Military Forts and Presidios and Posts Commonly Called Forts, West of the Mississippi River to 1898.* Norman: University of Oklahoma Press, 1965.

Freeman, Douglas Southall. *Lee's Lieutenants: A Study in Command.* 3 vols. New York: Charles Scribner's Sons, 1942-44.

_____. *R. E. Lee: A Biography.* 4 vols. New York: Charles Scribner's Sons, 1934-35.

Gallagher, Gary A. *The Confederate War.* Cambridge, Mass.: Harvard University Press, 1997.

Green, Wharton J. *Recollections and Reflections: An Auto[biography] of Half a Century and More.* Raleigh, N. C.: Edwards and Broughton, 1906.

Harris, James Sidney. *Historical Sketches of the Seventh Regiment North Carolina Troops.* Mooresville, N. C.: Mooresville Printing Co., 1893.

Harsh, Joseph L. *Taken at the Flood: Robert E. Lee and Confederate Strategy in the Maryland Campaign of 1862.* Kent, Ohio: Kent State University Press, 1999.

Hattaway, Herman. *General Stephen D. Lee.* Jackson: University Press of Mississippi, 1976.

Haynes, Draughton Stith. *The Field Diary of a Confederate Soldier While Serving with the Army of Northern Virginia, C. S. A.* Darien, Ga.: Ashantilly Press, 1963.

Heitman, Francis B., comp. *Historical Register and Dictionary of the United States Army...* 2 vols. Washington, D. C.: Government Printing Office, 1903.

Hennessy, John J. *Return to Bull Run: The Campaign and Battle of Second Manassas.* New York: Simon & Schuster, 1993.

Hewett, Janet, et al, eds. *Supplement to the Official Records of the Union and Confederate Armies.* 3 pts., 95 vols. to date. Wilmington, N. C.: Broadfoot Publishing Company, 1994- .

Hill, D. H. Jr. *Bethel to Sharpsburg.* 2 vols. Raleigh, N. C.: Edwards & Broughton, 1926.

_____. *North Carolina.* Volume 4 of *Confederate Military History: A Library of Confederate States History.* Edited by Clement A. Evans. Atlanta: Confederate Publishing Co., 1899.

Horn, Stanley F., ed. *The Robert E. Lee Reader.* Indianapolis: Bobbs-Merrill Co., Inc., 1949.

Iobst, Richard W. *The Bloody Sixth: The Sixth North Carolina Regiment, Confederate*

States of America. Raleigh: North Carolina Confederate Centennial Commission, 1965.

Johnson, Allen, and Dumas Malone, eds. *Dictionary of American Biography*. 20 vols. New York: Charles Scribner's Sons, 1928-36.

Johnston, Joseph E. *Narrative of Military Operations*. Bloomington: Indiana University Press, 1959.

Jones, J. William. *Christ in the Camp; or, Religion in Lee's Army*. Atlanta: Martin & Hoyt Co., 1904.

Kip, Lawrence. *Army Life on the Pacific*. New York: Redfield, 1859.

Krick, Robert K. *Lee's Colonels: A Biographical Register of the Field Officers of the Army of Northern Virginia*. Dayton, Ohio: Press of Morningside Bookshop, 1979.

_____. *Stonewall Jackson at Cedar Mountain*. Chapel Hill: University of North Carolina Press, 1990.

Long, E. B., and Barbara Long. *The Civil War Day by Day: An Almanac, 1861-1865*. Garden City, N. Y.: Doubleday & Co., Inc., 1971.

Longacre, Edward G. *The Man Behind the Guns: A Biography of General Henry Jackson Hunt, Chief of Artillery, Army of the Potomac*. South Brunswick, N. J.: A. S. Barnes & Co., Inc., 1977.

McPherson, James M. *Ordeal by Fire: The Civil War and Reconstruction*. New York: Alfred A. Knopf, 1982.

Malone, Bartlett Y. *Whipt 'em Everytime: The Diary of Bartlett Yancey Malone, Co. H 6th N. C. Regiment*. Edited by William Whatley Pierson Jr. Jackson, Tenn.: McCowat-Mercer Press, Inc., 1960.

Martin, David G. *Gettysburg, July 1*. Conshohocken, Pa.: Combined Books, 1995.

Mills, George H. *History of the 16th North Carolina Regiment*. Rutherfordton, N. C.: privately issued, 1901.

Montgomery, Walter A. *Life and Character of Major-General W. D. Pender: Memorial Address, May 10, 1894*. Raleigh: Edwards & Broughton, 1894.

Murfin, James V. *The Gleam of Bayonets: The Battle of Antietam and the Maryland Campaign of 1862*. New York: A. S. Barnes & Co., Inc., 1965.

Official Register of the Officers and Cadets of the U.S. Military Academy, West Point, N.Y.: June 1851. West Point, N. Y.: privately issued, 1851.

Official Register of the Officers and Cadets of the U.S. Military Academy, West Point, New York: June, 1853. West Point, N. Y.: privately issued, 1853.

Official Register of the Officers and Cadets of the U.S. Military Academy, West Point, New York: June, 1854. West Point, N. Y.: privately issued, 1854.

Palfrey, Francis Winthrop. *The Antietam and Fredericksburg*. New York: Charles Scribner's Sons, 1882.

Pender, William Dorsey. *The General to His Lady: The Civil War Letters of William Dorsey Pender to Fanny Pender.* Edited by William W. Hassler. Chapel Hill: University of North Carolina Press, 1965.

_____. *One of Lee's Best Men: The Civil War Letters of General William Dorsey Pender*, with a New Foreword by Brian Wills. Edited by William W. Hassler. Chapel Hill: University of North Carolina Press, 1999.

Pitts, Charles F. *Chaplains in Gray.* Nashville, Tenn.: Broadman Press, 1957.

Porter, Anthony T. *Led On! Step by Step, Scenes from Clerical, Military, Educational, and Plantation Life in the South, 1828-1898: An Autobiography.* New York: G. P. Putnam's Sons, 1898.

Powell, William S., ed. *Dictionary of North Carolina Biography.* Chapel Hill: University of North Carolina Press, 1979.

Regulations for the U.S. Military Academy, at West Point, New-York. New York: John F. Trow, 1853.

Robertson, James I. Jr. *General A. P. Hill: The Story of a Confederate Warrior.* New York: Random House, 1987.

_____. *Stonewall Jackson: The Man, the Soldier, the Legend.* New York: Macmillan Publishing USA, 1997.

Rodenbough, Theophilus F., and William L. Haskin, eds. *The Army of the United States: Historical Sketches of Staff and Line.* New York: Merrill & Co., 1896.

Scales, Alfred M. *The Battle of Fredericksburg: An Address... Before the Association of the Virginia Division of the Army of Northern Virginia.* Washington, D. C.: R. O. Polkinhorn & Son, 1884.

Scott, W. W. *Annals of Caldwell County.* Lenoir, N. C.: *News-Topic* Print., ca. 1930.

Sears, Stephen W. *Chancellorsville.* Boston: Houghton Mifflin Co., 1996.

_____. *Landscape Turned Red: The Battle of Antietam.* New Haven, Conn.: Ticknor & Fields, 1983.

_____. *To the Gates of Richmond: The Peninsula Campaign.* New York: Ticknor & Fields, 1992.

Silver, James W. *Confederate Morale and Church Propaganda.* Tuscaloosa, Ala.: Confederate Publishing Co., Inc., 1957.

Sitterson, Joseph Carlyle. *The Secession Movement in North Carolina.* Chapel Hill: University of North Carolina Press, 1939.

Sloan, John A. *North Carolina in the War Between the States.* Washington, D. C.: Rufus H. Darby, 1883.

Tanner, William R. *Reminiscences of the War Between the States.* Cowpens, S. C.: privately issued, 1931.

Teetor, Paul R. *A Matter of Hours: Treason at Harper's Ferry.* Rutherford, N. J.: Fairleigh Dickinson University Press, 1982.

Thomas, Emory M. *Bold Dragoon: The Life of J. E. B. Stuart.* New York: Harper & Row, 1986.

Thomas, John P. *Career and Character of General Micah Jenkins, C. S. A.* Columbia, S. C.: State Co., 1903.

Tompkins, Daniel A. *Company K, Fourteenth South Carolina Volunteers.* Charlotte, N. C.: *Observer* Printing & Publishing House, 1897.

Tucker, Glenn. *Zeb Vance, Champion of Personal Freedom.* Indianapolis: Bobbs-Merrill Co., Inc., 1965.

Turner, J. Kelly, and John L. Bridgers Jr. *History of Edgecombe County, North Carolina.* Raleigh, N. C.: Edwards & Broughton, 1920.

Utley, Robert M. *Frontiersmen in Blue: The United States Army and the Indian, 1848-1865.* New York: Macmillan Co., 1967.

Vance, Zebulon B. *The Papers of Zebulon Baird Vance.* Edited by Frontis W. Johnston. 2 vols. Raleigh: North Carolina State Department of Archives and History, 1963.

Warner, Ezra J. *Generals in Blue: Lives of the Union Commanders.* Baton Rouge: Louisiana State University Press, 1964.

_____. *Generals in Gray: Lives of the Confederate Commanders.* Baton Rouge: Louisiana State University Press, 1959.

War of the Rebellion: A Compilation of the Official Records of the Union and Confederate Armies. 4 series, 70 vols. in 128. Washington, D. C.: Government Printing Office, 1880-1901.

Welch, Spencer Glasgow. *A Confederate Surgeon's Letters to His Wife...* New York: Neale Publishing Co., 1911.

Welsh, Jack D. *Medical Histories of Confederate Generals.* Kent, Ohio: Kent State University Press, 1995.

Wright, Marcus J. *General Officers of the Confederate Army.* New York: Neale Publishing Co., 1911.

INDEX